D0600154

Gunkholing*
in the
San Juans

*'Gunkholing', the boatman's term for cruising in sheltered waters and anchoring every night, may have originated among the shallow estuaries of Chesapeake Bay, where the anchor usually sinks into soft mud, or 'gunk'—thus gunkholing for those who engage in this low key, relaxed sort of cruising.

Gunkholing in the San Juans

by
Al Cummings and Jo Bailey-Cummings

Photos by the authors
Illustrations by Edward D. Leche III

Cover photo by Louise Kincaid

Published by Nor'westing, Inc.
Edmonds, Washington

Fourth Printing 1986
Third Printing 1986
Second Printing 1985
First Printing 1984

ISBN 0-931923-00-X

DEDICATION

This book is dedicated to the memory of four islanders who were our friends: Gladys Prince, Littlewolf, John 'Doc' Bell, and North Burn. To the degree that books survive longer than their readers or writers, we wish to help keep alive the reminiscence of these people who have become little legends in this waterlocked world of ours.

"No man is an island, intire of it selfe;
every man is a peece of the Continent,
a part of the maine ..."

—John Donne: Devotions

A TABLE OF CONTENTS

Preface/Acknowledgements (For those who read such things).

Bibliography: Books we stole from and *you* should own.

The Geographical Index: Nearly 400 charted and uncharted features of the San Juan Archipelago.

The General Index: The people, the legends and sundry local knowledge.

PREFACE

We can't believe it! *You're actually reading a preface?* We never do, none of our friends do, either. You must be an intellectual!

Well, since we never touch them, we asked around among our literary friends, what do prefaces do? They said, prefaces sort of tell something about the book, like what it has to offer, or how come you wrote it in the first place. We were told that all worthwhile books have prefaces—some of them a hundred pages long. So we thought we'd give it a try. So here goes ...

First of all, thanks for buying this book. (If you borrowed it from somebody, how about going out and buying a copy for yourself?) The way we have it figured, if enough of you folks were to buy these books, we could become thousandaires, maybe even make the last payment on the electric toaster!

Why did we write this book? Well, aside from the super-valid reason mentioned in the previous paragraph, we thought somebody ought to turn out a tome that talked about *all* of the spots in the San Juans—even the crummy little ones that you wouldn't be found dead on. So, we started at Cattle Pass and did round robins of the major islands and clusters. We took about a million pictures that looked great when we were standing on the bow of a boat, but are just blobs of beach and water in a photograph. But, every once in a while we would come up with one that showed something that a boater might find worthwhile.

As we cruised around, we located every little bight and bay and rock that had a name and made an effort to say *something* about it. We found ourselves describing rocks that even the gulls didn't favor. But we hung in there. As a result, there is more information about more totally blah hunks of water and real estate than your patience will be able to bear. After we wrote it all up, we went over it again and again and again—and we kept finding things we had overlooked. The publisher finally howled, "Never mind if it isn't gospel! Get the darned thing finished! If we print a second edition, we will make corrections."

So here it is. If you find any boo-boos, come and tell us about it. Help us escape our paranoia!

A friend looked at our manuscript and said, "That's fine for skippers and navigators. But how about just ordinary boat passengers and lowly crew people? They might like to read something that had a little *flavor* in it—the atmosphere of the San Juan Islands. You must have some stories about the various places. Throw in a little history for the browsers, and maybe an anecdote or two."

Well, looking at the hundreds of pages of typewritten manuscript, we got worried about another thing: it might get boiled down in printing to where it would be only a few dozen pages long. Nobody wants to buy a skinny book. So we started mixing in little stories we had heard, and some of the ones we tell our cruising friends: you know, like adding 'hamburger helper' to the meat loaf. We also scrounged up all of the books we could find on the San Juans. We stole liberally from all of them. We did, however, give credit to all of the authors from bygone years, you'll find the list under 'Bibliography' at the end of the book.

We also got help from dozens of islanders and visiting skippers. We'll list them at the end of this preface. We intend to sell them a copy of the book at cost (we're all heart).

So that's how come, 'Gunkholing In The San Juans'.

Who are we?

Jo Bailey-Cummings, called 'Zozo', is an ex-school teacher and sailboat junkie. She came to the San Juan Islands to find her fortune in 1978. (She's still looking.)

Al Cummings is a fugitive from a life of obloquy and radio broadcasting in the Puget Sound area. He fled to the San Juans to escape creditors in 1979.

We pooled our resources in 1979. Zozo contributed a 29-foot Monk sloop called *Sea Witch*, a functioning automobile, a portable electric typewriter, two cameras, and a number of pots and pans. Al Cummings offered a 50-foot cruiser named *Roanoake*, a standard IBM electric, standing headroom and a shower—and a number of inadequately-washed dishes. All in all, a fairly symbiotic pair, you must admit.

Both of us are freelance writers. The term 'freelance' means, as we're sure you know, 'sworn to a life of near poverty'. We write for several newspapers and magazines. One of the periodicals we supply is *Nor'westing,* a boating magazine published in Edmonds, Washington. It is this publisher who, in an addled moment, volunteered to publish the book you have just purchased (or borrowed—shame!)

Only one thing remains to be included as biographical material in this preface: what made us think we were qualified to write about the San Juan area? All we can claim is that television reception in Friday Harbor, where we live, is lousy, so we cruise a lot.

Add to this the fact that both of us poked around in the archipelago for a number of years before emigrating there. We added up the total the other day. We debated including the shocking figure in this report. We decided that even if it means we starve for lack of sales, we are never, never going to tell!

Now for the last item in this preface. We *know* you are not going to read the following lines. We also know that if we didn't include a list of all of the folks we have browbeaten into contributing time and energy, we would have to sneak out of port in the dead of night!

So here goes:

A lot of people helped us with this book, including our families, some of whom got to see too much of us when they put us up away from home. And others who claimed they didn't see us often enough because we were working on this tome.

So many thanks to Dean and Linda, Jim and Irene, Dad, (Millard) Carol, Megan and Elan on the Cummings side of the family, and Megan, Robin, Debi, John, Bill and Mom (Claribel Imeson) on the Bailey-Cummings side.

Also thanks to those who helped with information, questions and bits of prodding: Jim and Ruth Byers, Lee and Marilyn Campbell, Tom Chamberlain, Ray Chesnut, Jack and Nan Culver, Dave Duggins, John and Louise Dustrude, Etta Egeland, Cy Finley, Jack Giard, Hildegarde Goss, Mac and Lee Greely, Frank Hastings, Greg Hertel, Fred and Peg Hoeppner, Jan and Lulu Johnson, Fred Krabbe, Carl Lange, Ted Leche, Ken Lloyd, Wil Lorenz, Pete and Jean McCorison, Mary Morgan, Mary Mulvey, Charles Nash, Doug Pesznecker, Robert Reese, Marshall Sanborn, Ray Sheffer, Craig Staude, Tom Talman, Neil Tarte, Mike Valiga, Sunny Vynne, Peg Warrack, Bill and Doree Webb, Don Wegars, Zan and Harold Whitaker and Dennis Willows.

Special thanks to Lynne Taylor and Lynn Hernandez of Nor'westing Magazine, who spent many extra hours without complaint; Lynne doing all the design, make-up, etc., and Lynn with all the typesetting.

And, of course, thanks to Tom and Louise Kincaid and Ole Hansen, of Nor'westing, who helped on the book and are our publishers.

Happy reading while you cruise our San Juan Islands.

Love,
Al and Jo

INTRODUCTION

Before we all (figuratively) ship out together on our cruise of the San Juan Islands, a cluster of populated and barren rocks in the Northwest corner of the United States, we might just study a chart of the area. #18421, which covers the area from the Strait of Juan de Fuca up to the Georgia Strait, gives us a good look at the whole archipelago, with some chunks of the Lower Gulf Islands of Canada, and parts of Island and Whatcom County.

As you stare at the complex which is called 'The San Juan Islands', you wonder if, in the dim centuries of the world's settling-in process, this whole area might not have been one land mass which sort of hunkered down until sea water separated the higher elevations.

We keep promising ourselves that some day we will get a book on the subject like McLellan's *Geology of the San Juan Islands* and study up on it. But we have a suspicion that it might get a skoshie too technical and we'd either learn nothing at all or more than we wanted to know.

We also have trouble dealing with phrases like the 'Pleistocene Epoch', and the 'Jurassic Era'. What we want to know (and we suspect you do, too) is: did all this happen before or after 'The Flintstones'?

About this time, we happened upon a paragraph or two in one of our favorite books, *100 Days in the San Juan Islands*, by June Burn. It is a recent printing, so you can find a copy of it in one of the local bookstores—and you ought to have one.

She and her husband, Farrar, were glorious ragamuffins in the early 40s. They explored the islands in a cockleshell of a boat; and June wrote a journal, pages of which were printed in the *Seattle Post-Intelligencer*.

She does a beautiful job of thumbnail geology:

> *"It was back in one of those mysterious ages that a mountain range, northwest of what is now Seattle, went down like a vast ship, bits of it left sticking up. It sank so far that the valleys between the peaks fell below sea level, whereupon the sea stepped in ...*
>
> *"During the Ice Age, glaciers gouged the valleys deeper. At one time, they completely covered the islands even to the highest peak in the submerged range. Geologists say that the top of Mt. Constitution is 'deeply striated and polished by glacial action'. At the heads of certain beaches there are glacial moraines still to be seen.*
>
> *"Later on—'recently'—the geologist says, meaning only a few tens of thousands of years ago—the same mountain range rose again so that you can row along below the sheer bluffs and see, 20 feet above the high tide line, a wave-cut bench where the water line used to be ..."*

(June doesn't say so, but we guess that the last paragraph refers to a time just before Fred Flintstone—possibly the epoch of 'Alley Oop'.)

So, dear shipmate, when we get to exploring Sucia and the rugged south coast of Lopez Island, we suggest you begin to think in terms of the deep breaths that Mother Nature must have taken during those restless sleeps.

Well, so much for garden variety poetics and bluegrass philosophy! What are we waiting for? Let's throw off the lines and get this old slab of yours out to sea!

The renowned and beautiful

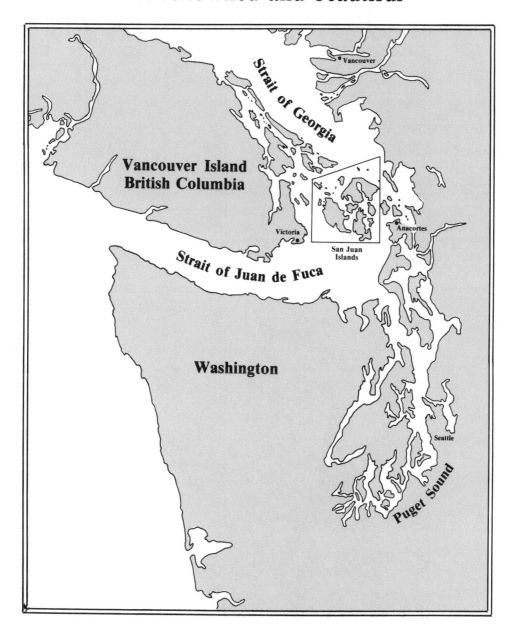

San Juan archipelago

LOPEZ STORE
LOPEZ IS., WASHINGTON

LOPEZ ISLAND

The Lopez Island Loop

We'd like to come aboard on your next San Juan Islands cruise as amateur pilots, tour guides and good shipmates.

With that in mind, let's make our first trip around the first island you will meet on your way across the Strait and into **Cattle Pass**. It's **Lopez**. It's probably the most varied and picturesque of them all. It has a wealth of little known places to visit.

For the Lopez Island Loop you will need two charts, #18434 entitled 'San Juan Channel', and #18429, 'Rosario Strait'.

Let's start with the San Juan Channel chart and note that the first features you come across are:

Whale Rocks and Mummy Rocks

First, let's take a look at **Whale Rocks**. And while they may look something like a whale—post-impressionist sculpture, you understand—**Mummy Rocks** do not look like bandaged old Egyptian Pharaohs. It beats us how they ever got their names. They are, as a matter of fact, some of the most uninspiring bits of rockery to be found anywhere. Stay clear—they would not be good to be washed up on.

Cattle Pass

Let's take an anatomical look at **Cattle Pass**. Off to the left (west) as you approach is **Goose Island.** It's an interesting place with an interesting history which we've written in a special section. There is a passage between Goose Island and San Juan, and we'll devote some paragraphs to that tricky but useful entrance.

But as you near Cattle Pass, you should have gotten some clue as to the current situation. The chart shows 'tide rips and eddies' in the pass—that is a vast understatement.

1

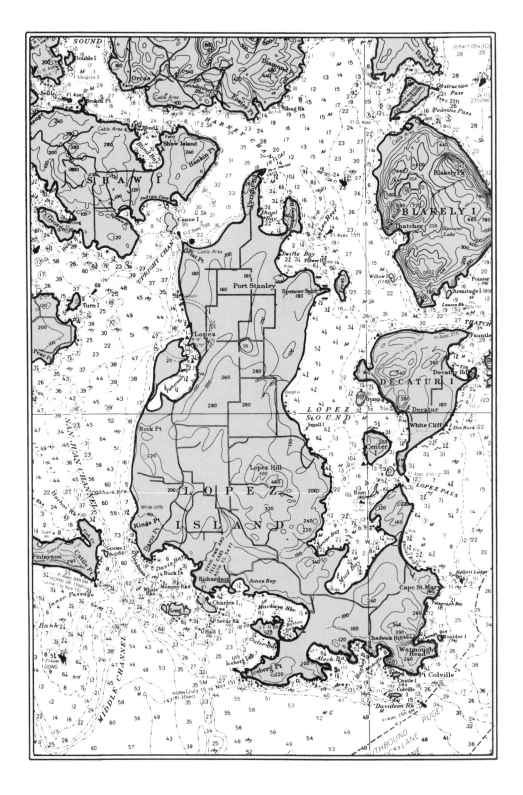

If you are in one of those 20-knot planing boats, you are not going to worry about a few knots of adverse current or the rips and eddies. But if you are in a six to 10-knot vessel, the makeup of the current and any winds can be important. There are three possible situations:

1. The wind and current may be with you. In this case, you will schuss through with only some minor bounces from tide rips and whirlpools.

2. The wind and current against you will put you on the world's slowest roller coaster. Your forward speed may be only one knot, but your speed up and down may be denture-loosening! This usually convinces you to study current charts in the future, once you dig them out of the debris on the cabin sole.

3. With the wind and the current heading in different directions—now, there's a situation! You will get the sensation you might have on one of those mechanical bucking broncos they have in Western bars.

Goose Island Passage

A quick look at the chart will show you there is no navigable passage between **Goose** and **San Juan Islands**. Indeed, the Coast Pilot advises against it. You may, therefore, be surprised to see a number of boats thread their way through this saltwater back alley. These are skippers with local knowledge. One thing they know is that there is a useful back current in this passage.

If the current is setting against you in Cattle Pass, it will be going your way in

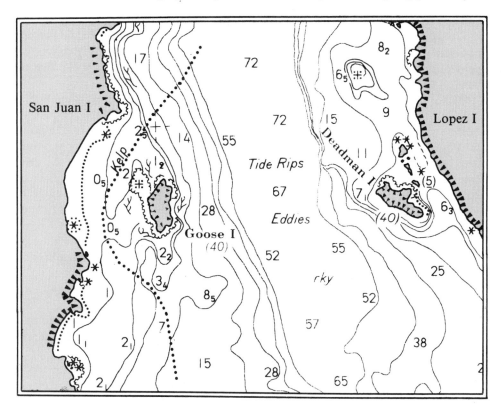

Cattle Point Lighthouse - a welcome sight

Goose Island Passage. It's a tricky trip, though. You'd be well-advised to follow a boat with a San Juan port registry on its transom on your first trip through. Local fishing boats use it all the time, just like suburban folks use short-cut paths across vacant lots. We've been through it a couple of times, once aboard a local gillnetter, and the second time in our own boat with a fisherman guiding us.

We'll tell you what the local fishermen say about the path, but understand, we are not responsible for your safety if you try it, because there are no markers or guideposts and what looks like 100 yards to a fisherman may not look like that to you.

"Take the distance between Goose Island and the San Juan Island shoreline," says our mentor. "Now visually divide it in thirds. The safe channel is in the portion nearest the San Juan shoreline—keep about one-third of the way offshore. *Go slowly! Watch your depth sounder!* If you get in about the correct area and get nervous, take 'er out of gear and pretend you're a log. The current is the strongest in the clear channel. It makes a slight dogleg following the San Juan shoreline. You may have to go through kelp, but don't let that spook you. (See section: Kelp, the Skipper's Friend.) During the fishing season, the gillnetters and purse seiners will chomp away the kelp and give you a clearly marked channel."

Incidentally, don't try this if your boat draws more than eight feet. At low tides, it can get shallow in this passage. It's not a bad idea to put somebody up in the bow to keep a sharp lookout.

Deadman Island and Shark Reef Park

Just opposite Goose Island on the Lopez side of San Juan Channel is **Deadman Island**. The current rushes rapidly through the narrow slot between Deadman and Lopez and it's treacherous except for small, fast boats.

But on the Lopez shore above Deadman Island there is a well-kept secret—**Shark Reef Park**, owned by the Department of Natural Resources (DNR). This is a

'Lopezoids'—No!

Ah, the people of Lopez! How to describe them? Well, your composite Lopez Islander is white, black, Indian and a little Oriental. He is rich, grubs for a living at minimum wage, is on welfare, fishes, builds houses or boats, writes best-selling novels, makes medieval musical instruments, appears on concert stages, is a jet-set consultant, digs sewer drainfields, throws pots, collects six-figure retirement checks from large corporations, grows a little cannabis in his backyard ... we could go on, but you get the idea.

There is a great slogan on the island: "Wave—you're on Lopez." Now you're going to say that's some sort of Chamber of Commerce hype, but that's dead wrong. Everybody waving at everybody is a way of life on Lopez Island. We know hundreds of Lopez Islanders and it's true. Incidentally, they do not much like being called 'Lopezians.' One lady on the island, who is a wag, calls them 'Lopezoids'. Don't you do it!

Yes, we know hundreds of folks on that island and they all wave—except one guy who makes it a matter of pride that he doesn't wave—not even to friends.

Now by 'wave' we don't mean big Homecoming Queen gestures. We mean, usually, finger waves. Two cars approach each other on the county road. As they draw near, both drivers lift a few fingers from the wheel and salute each other. They have made an art of the type of waves they do—one, two or three finger waves. Exuberant drivers may even remove one hand from the wheel to wave.

If you go ashore at Lopez and stroll along the roads, be sure to wave back, or nod your head or smile. If your salutation is not returned, it means you have just encountered a tourist who doesn't know the custom—or you've met our one non-waving friend.

Lopez Island folks may squabble with their neighbors, but they are exceedingly protective of each other with outsiders. We have met right-wing Lopez Islanders and left-wing Lopez Islanders. We have even met a few whom we suspect of being middle-of-the-road, but we wouldn't dare spread that.

How does all of this affect you? If a generality can be permitted, it might be this: they usually like tourists and newcomers. They don't waste much time and energy grousing about 'off-islanders' and 'furriners'. Their spirit of acceptance is rather unique in the San Juan Islands.

Some anecdotes might focus this statement.

During the 'off-season', the local folks inhabit the Islander Lopez resort and the Galley Restaurant, both on Fisherman Bay Road, a short distance apart. In the tourist season, more of the locals gravitate to the Galley, where all the faces are pretty familiar.

There is a wonderful sign on the entrance to the Galley: "Shirt and shoes required to eat at the Galley. (Socks may eat wherever they wish.)"

Across the road from the Galley, by the dock, is a covered bin that is dedicated to the thousands of bike riders who visit the island each year. Called the 'Bikers' Information Box', it is filled with neatly stacked brochures, maps, notices on camping information. Just please close the lid so the printed material won't blow away or get wet from early morning dew.

On one of Lopez Island's side roads, fresh eggs are for sale. There is a little open box with an A-frame shake roof covering the full cartons of eggs. A printed sign says simply, "EGGS—leave empty carton—$1.00."

That's Lopez Island.

The White House - a local landmark

beautiful spot, a fragile and gentle 40 acres which is enjoyed by those who appreciate the wilderness and want to keep it that way. There is no moorage nearby, but if you tour Lopez you might want to stop there. There are no amenities, just a trail in from the road, which is the way Lopez Islanders want to keep it. The park on the rocks overlooking San Juan Channel will not endure heavy traffic because of the delicate nature of the forest floor. Lopez Islanders have fought with the DNR to maintain the park as it is during the recent years when the state wanted to log trees in the area. 'White Cliffs', which are in reality light-colored sandy bluffs, are shown on the chart between Kings Point and **Shark Reef**.

Shark Reef

Shark Reef Park is not at Shark Reef, however. It is just south of **Kings Point**. **Shark Reef** itself is a wildlife preserve offshore about one-half mile north of Kings Point. It is comprised of three large rocks in a row which jut out into San Juan Channel. The rocks show at most tides and are jagged and forbidding with a big kelp bed surrounding. It is a mean and dangerous set of snags—you wouldn't want to go ashore anyhow. The wildlife is welcome to it! Avoid it like a fat lip—it wasn't named ''Shark'' reef for nothing.

Kelp, The Sailor's Friend

Commercial fishermen, especially the gillnetters, learn to 'read' kelp beds almost like a chart. While most pleasure boaters go to great pains to avoid fields of kelp, fishermen will often plow right through it. When there are large patches of the growth, as in Goose Island Passage at Cattle Pass, the steady stream of fishboats will cut a clear path through it. And usually it's pretty safe to follow them if you stay close.

There are some things to remember about kelp. First of all, it almost always indicates a rocky bottom — so, of course, it favors reefs and shoals. It always indicates that the surrounding water is at least five feet deep at low tides and you will seldom see it in water over 50 feet in depth. That five-foot minimum refers, and this is important, to the sea bed at any place. There can be, and often are, rocks that extend up to near the surface. The thing to remember is that the Coast and Geodetic Survey people examine depths in and around kelp beds. If there is a rock hidden under the foliage, it will appear on the chart — and you should avoid it just like you would in apparently open water.

The charts do a good job of indicating major kelp beds. These growths can be used in navigation, if you're careful. The thing to know is that kelp is migratory at times. Individual plants will decide to move to new neighborhoods and they will hoist their little root anchors and get carried by the tide to the next moorage. As they float around free, they often get tangled up with other itinerant kelps and can create large free rafts. So, you can see patches of kelp in very deep water. The trick is to recognize the uprooted plants.

The next time you go beachcombing, take a look at some of the specimens that wash up on the beach. Notice that the 'bulb' is not a tuber; it is not part of the root system. It's a buoy that holds the plant up so the long tendrils can get sunlight.

So, if you see the little branching creepers that are the 'hold-fasts' — the root-grabbers — in the floating kelp, you will know it's cruising just like you are and isn't giving you any message about the sea-bed underneath.

As long as we've got you interested in the subject, we might as well pass along some interesting trivia.

It can grow at the rate of two inches per day.

It can reach 100 feet in length.

Indians made rope out of it by curing it and knotting lengths together. They also used the hollow bulbs to store liquids.

You can make pickles out of chunks of kelp, but we haven't done it — the directions say it takes six days to prepare.

Rock Point

This is only shown on the newest charts and was obviously named for the **Big Rock** marked on the chart—it is a whopper, clearly visible from a long way off, which makes it a useful navigation aid.

The White House

Presidents don't live there, and as far as we know, no president has ever visited it. It's a nice, white, well-kept private home. It is noted here because the local

About Charts

You will want to supply yourself with several charts for the San Juan Cruise. There is one large-scale chart and a number of small scale ones.

First of all, let's review what 'large' and 'small' scale means.

Take the recommended 'Small Scale' chart, #18421 entitled 'Strait of Juan de Fuca to Strait of Georgia'. It covers all of the San Juan Islands and the approaches. It extends from Smith Island in the Strait of Juan de Fuca to Point Roberts, the farthest northwest point in the continental U.S. From the east, it covers the Swinomish Slough and Guemes Channel — one of the favorite approaches to the San Juans for small boats that don't want to risk the currents of Deception Pass or the possible high seas of the Strait of Juan de Fuca. The Deception Pass area is also included in this chart. On the western edge of the chart, you will see Victoria, B.C. You may be surprised to see that the capitol city is a bit south of the lower end of Lopez Island. Also along the western edge of the chart, you will see the coastline of Vancouver Island. It extends up beyond Sidney, B.C. — where the international ferry lands — up to the entrance to the Gulf Islands of Canada.

It's a honey of a chart. It could suffice, if you didn't have the more detailed charts we recommend. Almost all of the navigation information you need is included — but in small detail.

Which brings us to the definition of 'Small' and 'Large' scale charts. It turns out that the term 'small' or 'large' doesn't refer to the scale at all! It refers to the size of the detail shown on the chart. Take, for instance, good old #18421. It is drawn to a ratio of 1:80,000. Don't bother to figure it out — we'll tell you — it's about one and

1/10th nautical miles per inch. That means it covers a large area and the detail is quite small. So, it's a 'small-scale' chart.

If you are confused, don't be embarrassed. When we started writing this book, we discovered that for at least two decades we had been mixed up on this terminology. To make it even more shameful — we took a Power Squadron piloting course, memorized it properly for the test — and then promptly went back to the old error of our ways! .

Now, to further complicate matters: charts are divided into degrees and minutes. There are 60 minutes to a degree of longitude or latitude just like divisions of an hour on the clock. But the minutes are divided into tenths, not seconds. So you can have something at 20° 15.5 minutes of latitude North. To make it more maddening, the Coast Guard will tell you something has been located at 20° 15 minutes and 30 seconds latitude North.

So, after you've made the trip to the medicine chest for aspirin, we'll continue about charts for the San Juans.

Before heading up to this area go to a big nautical supply company in one of the larger cities. Don't depend on buying charts up in the San Juans. There are a number of places that sell them, but they always seem to be out of the ones you want — especially after the beginning of the tourist season.

So march in and tell the clerk you want the following charts, all in a large scale of 1:25,000 — 1 inch = 1/3 of a nautical mile:

#18425, "San Juan Channel — Friday and Roche Harbors".

#18429, "Rosario Strait — Southern Part".

#18430, "Rosario Strait — Northern

Part".

#18431, "Rosario Strait to Cherry Point".

#18432, "Boundary Pass".

#18433, "Middle Bank to Stuart Island".

#18434, "San Juan Channel".

#18465, "Strait of Juan de Fuca" — Eastern End.

The San Juan Channel one is great — the detail is even better than the others — 1:20,000 to an inch — a **must** to have.

The Strait of Juan de Fuca Chart is also a must if you plan to cross the Strait from Port Townsend. It will help you find your way across that body of water without bumping into Partridge Bank, Smith or Minor Islands.

These seven charts overlap somewhat, but they will give you a complete picture of the whole archipelago. Furthermore, they are large-scale charts — you won't need a magnifying glass.

At this point, we're going to preach a little marine heresy. There's nothing wrong with using books of cruising charts. If they are complete enough and recent enough, they'll work all right. They might be somewhat inconvenient to use parallel rules on to find courses, though.

There's a commonly accepted sneer about folks using table placemats for navigation. You know the kind, the ones that are plastic-covered pictures of charts. They say on them in large print "Not to be used for navigation". The fact is that you could probably do all right using them if you didn't want to go gunkholing, just pass through an area. We certainly don't recommend it, though.

You cannot use a Texaco road map, and expect to avoid ending up on a reef or a rock!

Another thing we'd like to recommend: make notes on your charts. Pencil things in. Charts are not sacred. If you want to make a little memo saying "Funny-looking house, X", go ahead. As a matter of fact, the U.S. Power Squadrons have been working with NOAA for some time, feeding them little bits of valuable local information for the new charts. Notice, for instance, that on Chart #18434 on the western shoreline of Lopez Island, you will see a notation 'big rock' at Rock Point. That is not on the small scale chart #18421. It's part of the updating and improving processing that the Power Squadrons Cooperative Charting Activity is engaged in.

So, feel free to make notes on your charts of items we include in this book. Check them out for accuracy and then pencil them in. If we have made boo-boos, let us know and we'll correct them in forthcoming editions of this book.

Incidentally, while you're in the nautical suppliers' store, pick up a copy of Charts #1 & #2. Number 1 gives you the latest set of symbols and abbreviations. Number 2 is a chart of charts that are available for various areas.

Two books you might find useful are 'The Coast·Pilot' and 'Light Lists', especially the latter. With an up-to-date light list book you can correct an old chart and use it. After all, the land masses don't change over the years and rocks don't suddenly appear out of nowhere.

An absolute must are tide and current books. Our currents in the islands can be horrendous and you need all the help you can get to have them help you instead of fight you.

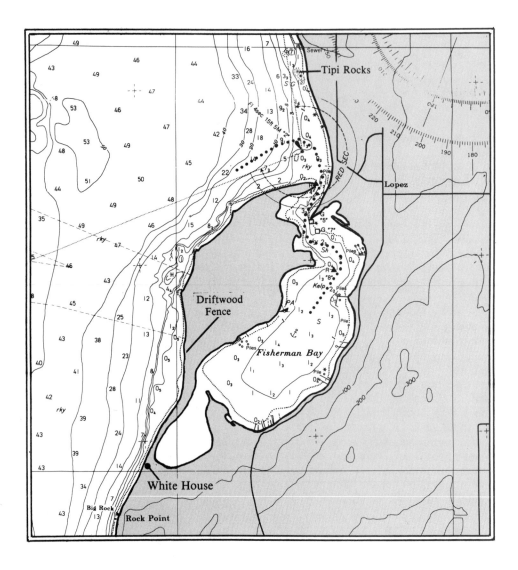

fishermen use it as a navigational mark. About one and a half miles north of Shark Reef, you can't mistake the semi-Victorian home with its porches, gables and red roof just above the beach. There is a large shade elm or maple tree partially in front, and a tall rangy evergreen tree about 50 feet away.

In a pea soup fog it is often the only thing you can see on shore. It shows up pretty well at night, too. Local folks figure distances from it. "I was just off the White House when …," "Once you see the White House, be sure to bear west to avoid Shark Reef—if you're heading south," "There is a reefnet rig about one and a half miles north of the White House …" and so on. We once helped rescue several young Indian fishermen who were aboard a sinking gillnetter just a half-mile off the White House.

Docking Tip

Before you pull into an open slip at a marina, it is wise to get some idea of what the current and wind will do to your boat. Strong currents flowing around floats may make no discernible patterns but they still can cause your boat to be carried away before you can get a line on the dock.

Here's how to save yourself some embarrassment: as you approach the open slip, look at the boats in the surrounding slips. It is seldom that boats are strapped in tight to the dock. There is usually some slack in their mooring lines. Look to see which boats are pressed against the dock and which are pulled out to the scope of their mooring lines. That will tell you what you will encounter when you ease into the slip.

It wouldn't hurt to note it in passing and make a small mark on your chart.

Driftwood Fence

On the northeasterly curving shoreline of this part of Lopez Island, about halfway between the White House and the entrance to Fisherman Bay, get your binoculars out and look for the beautiful driftwood fence on shore. There are plenty of driftwood fences in the San Juans, but this is the most spectacular one we know of.

Entrance to Fisherman Bay

Now repeat after us: **Fisher*man* Bay!** Not—no, never—Fisher*men's*. There is no apostrophe s. Get it right or get agonized looks from Lopez Islanders! If you want to be very hip, you can abbreviate that to 'Fish Bay' as in "... so we decided to go into Fish Bay, etc. ..."

We are about to pilot you through the entrance to Fisherman Bay. In this area, you have your choice of two small scale charts and two large scale charts. On 18430, called 'Rosario Strait, Northern Part', Fisherman Bay is in the lower lefthand corner. The outside of the entrance shows up in detail in the Friday and Roche Harbor Chart, 18425, but that won't get you through.

Best chart for Fisherman Bay is 18434, published in March 1983, a welcome addition for mariners.

By studying this chart and with a little help right now, we'll get you through the slot. The legend at the entrance light, just a couple of yards north of the actual entrance, reads 'F14 sec 15 ft 5 M '2' '. Note also the dotted line called 'red sector'—that means if you can see the red light at night you are some place you shouldn't be—namely in the shallows that surround the entrance. (If you're confused by all this, see a book on navigational aids.)

Notice also the little dotted pale green oval on the chart just due south of the light. It is telling you that at an average low tide the water is only two feet deep. You will see that over near the Lopez shoreline to the east, it is also shallow. What it doesn't show you is that there is a dredged channel that runs just east of that light in a straight line down to the middle of the entrance. The marker on the west side of that entrance is a red light which gives the warning at night called the 'red sector' mentioned above.

Here is something to remember: that channel is narrow. Hug the Number 2 light and make a straight-arrow run into the channel from there. Stay fairly close to the marker at the outer end of the sandspit. A couple of dozen feet to either side of the center line can get you into not hot, but very shallow water. We have touched bottom a couple of times at low tide with no serious side effects, but we've seen accidentally beached boats often enough to be very careful.

Dean Jacobsen, owner of the Islander Lopez and a sailor with lots of local knowledge, says that if the tide is at zero there is about four-and-a-half to five feet of water above the muddy bottom of the center of the channel.

To be on the safe side, if you think it's touch-and-go as far as depth for your boat, make the entrance on an incoming tide. Then if you get stuck (and dozens of boats

Driftwood fence - one of the most elaborate in the islands

do every year—even some local boats) all you have to do is sit tight until the sea rushes back in and floats you off.

We have also tacked back and forth through the channel at a reasonable tide with our four-and-a-half-foot draft sailboat (when the engine wasn't working) and managed beautifully, so be of stout heart.

Once past that little sandy finger with the red light at the entrance, you are pretty safe. All you have to do is follow the markers into the bay. When the current is running in this narrow channel it can get speedy, so keep power on for steerage, and remember the old adage—'red right returning'—watch the markers.

This sandy point we were discussing on the way into the bay has a couple of remarkable-looking boats on the beach near the end of the spit. If you hadn't already guessed, these are reefnet boats. There is quite a variation in the quality of maintenance of these boats. Some will never float again, others are painted up and Bristol-fashion. We've seen some of them looking like the Indians of bygone years had just abandoned them there.

Those stilt-like observation platforms are for the watchers who stand atop them in fishing season and study the water below, waiting patiently for a school of salmon to enter the net. Once the fish have entered, the signal is given and the lookouts scamper down the ladders to help the rest of the crew with the winches that reel in the net with its captured fish. Reefnetting is one of the most primitive fishing methods around. Those who reefnet are a closeknit group, fiercely loyal to their fishing method and each other.

Medical Emergencies

Each of the three major islands, San Juan, Orcas and Lopez, has a team of no-nonsense, gung-ho, highly-trained emergency medical personnel which are part of the local fire departments. When they are called, they ACT FAST and PROFESSIONALLY!

If someone aboard your boat—or perhaps a scuba diver—has a serious medical problem, try to get to a dock or on shore and get someone to call the County Sheriff's office.

If you are at sea, call on the VHF Channel 16 for aid, or call on CB Channel 9 for the local Radio Watch team which handles emergencies. Fishermen normally monitor CB Channels 11 or 14. There is help all around.

A few minutes later you will find yourself in a whirlwind of fast, expert help. If the problem can't be treated at the medical centers on one of the islands by the local doctors, the patient will be whisked to an airport where a med-evac plane will be warming up. A trained EMT will accompany the patient to a mainland hospital only minutes away. Once on the ground at Anacortes, Mount Vernon, Bellingham or Seattle, you will find an ambulance waiting with doors open. Big city folks have marveled at the fact that a patient can be stabilized and transported to a full-service hospital in the same length of time it would take an ambulance in your metropolis to fight the freeways and side streets.

Folks in the San Juan Islands are very serious about their medical teams.

People Trees

There is some uncertainty about the correct pronunciation of this species, some folks who are of a scientific turn of mind call it 'Mah-drone'. Most San Juan folks call it 'Mah-dron-a'. There is something spooky about this tree—it's smooth surface looks a lot like tanned human skin. If people were turned into trees by some evil spell, they might very well look like madronas.

Fisherman Bay

Once you are out of the narrow channel and into Fisherman Bay, you will see several docks. First is 'Ron Meng's place', known officially as Islands Marine Center, run by Ron and his wife, Jennifer. They repair boats, mostly outboards and outdrives, sell all manner of needed parts, and Ron is even Lopez Island's fire chief.

The Mengs have just completed a new 56-slip marina for permanent and transient moorage. They have haulout capability for boats up to 45 feet and 15 tons. They permit do-it-yourself work; they have a launch ramp and most amenities as well as a chandlery.

The next dock is that of the Islander Lopez Resort. This is the 'compleat' resort on Lopez. There is moorage for 50 boats, gas, a dock store, restaurant and lounge, motel, swimming pool, jacuzzi, laundromat, meeting rooms, bike and boat rentals, gift shop and other amenities, but no propane. The Islander is the hub of activities for Lopez Islanders.

About a quarter-mile south of the Islander dock you will find a pier belonging to the Galley Restaurant. There is a sign welcoming visitors to tie up while they are at the Galley. Small kicker boats and tenders from anchored craft come in there and tie up sometimes while folks go to 'town'—Lopez Village. The owners of the Galley naturally want space left for their patrons but they're not sticky about it.

Immediately south of this dock is a private marina for folks living onshore and it is locked and inaccessible.

Now, about anchorage in Fisherman Bay. There is little variation in the depths as you can see from the chart, with about eight feet of water at the average lowest tide, in most of the bay.

The holding quality is quite good and there is a lot of eel grass, which means if you are anchored there through low tides, check your sea water strainer for bits of grass. There are crabs too, and that could mean cracked crab for dinner if you are lucky when you set your pot.

Don't You Believe It!

You can't have a thick fog and high winds at the same time — right? The wind would blow the fog away, wouldn't it?

No — wrong — wrong — wrong! You can have fog thick enough to float croutons and a wind that is strong enough to blow you to Helengone.

We don't know why this is true — ask some meteorologist — but we know it *is* true, nonetheless! We've been in it.

There is a narrow sandspit at the southwestern side of Fisherman Bay, separating the bay from San Juan Channel. When there is a storm, the wind whistles over the spit and rattles your rigging, but usually doesn't kick up too much of a chop in the bay itself.

This makes the bay a great place for the kids to practice sailing the dinghy, rowing around in protected waters, or sailing a windsurfer. The water is a little less cold for swimming in Fisherman Bay than out in the channel.

Once you've got the hook down, you may decide to walk into Lopez Village. It's a nice walk, about a mile or so from the Galley or Islander docks. You'll pass the fire station, the recycling station, the library, a beautiful little church on the way, and maybe pick some succulent blackberries at the side of the road if you're there during July and August.

Lopez Village store is a modern supermarket, scaled down a tad, and across from it is Holli B's Bakery, an outstanding spot for hot fresh homebaked goodies. There are a number of other small shops in the Village including a needlecraft and fabric shop, book and clothing stores, a restaurant, bank, post office, medical center, beauty parlor, real estate office, thrift shop, library and museum—in short, just about everything you need.

And while you're in the Village, you ought to visit the museum. The Lopez folks are proud of their museum for good reason: it is light and airy—unlike other San Juan area museums—and you can see and touch the exhibits. Our favorite items are the cherry pitter, the old switchboards and a wonderful turn-of-the-century teaching chart. Just recently the Historical Society added an outdoor annex with old farm machinery on display.

Nearby is the Thrift Shop in a red, old remodeled fire station. This is the place to pick up the items you forgot to bring along and benefit the clinic at the same time.

O.K., back aboard. Let's go cruising from Fisherman Bay, heading north out of the channel, avoiding Tipi Rocks, of course.

Tipi Rocks

Let's practice running a fathom-line. Once you leave the light at the entrance to Fisherman Bay, pick up the 15-fathom line which you will find about 400 yards offshore. When you are in that contour, your depth sounder will read about 90 feet (give or take 10 feet for tide conditions). If you were in a deep fog and wanted to find the marker at Flat Point, the 90-foot line would be safe and easy to follow. Since the 15-fathom contour is relatively straight and narrow here, try steering by depth—keeping the fathometer on one reading as much as possible. You'll also avoid **Tipi Rocks**.

They aren't labeled that way on the chart. As a matter of fact, that is not a common name for them, but they deserve their own moniker, and that's what we call them since there is no other name on the chart.

Tipi Rocks are just offshore about three-fourths of a mile north, more or less, of the entrance light to Fish Bay.

On the 100-foot high bluff above the rocks is a sparkling white Indian-style tepee. You can locate the rocks on the chart by the asterisk(*) with dots around it and the number 7, which means that the rocks become invisible when the tide reaches seven feet. So, as you approach, look for the tepee on the bluff and the long

A white tepee on the bluff can clue you in to Tipi Rocks.

stairway leading from it to the beach. Nearly straight out from it you will find the rocks. There are other rocks along that shore, but they are all pretty close into the beach and you're not likely to be in there cruising around. Incidentally, we understand the cod fishing is supposed to be pretty good around the rocks.

Flat Point

It's just a bit over one-and-a-half nautical miles from the entrance marker to Fisherman Bay to the light at **Flat Point**. If your boat travels at six knots, it makes one mile every ten minutes, therefore the run to Flat Point would take 15 minutes, right?

If you have an eight-knot boat, you make a mile every seven and a half minutes, roughly, so you'll be abeam the light in about 11 minutes.

If you have visitors on board and don't want them to know you're practicing navigation, just keep an eye on the depth sounder dial and the ship's clock and don't mention what you're doing. A little practice in good weather can save your skin—and your boat—in bad weather.

Flat Point is a fairly long sandspit extending into **Upright Channel.** There are typical summer homes and a smattering of trees. Just before you reach the point, you may notice more reefnet gears stationed to the south. Keep clear during fishing season.

Upright Channel has an enormous number of drift logs floating about, possibly because the Friday Harbor-bound large ferries use the channel and the wash from them carries driftwood off the beaches. There are cable crossings on either side of Flat Point which won't be any problem as long as you're not anchoring. There is a daybeacon off the end of Flat Point with a flashing white light every 2.5 seconds.

Odlin Park

About one-and-a-quarter miles northeast of Flat Point is **Odlin County Park,** a favorite with Lopez Islanders and visitors alike. This 80-acre park includes a campground, concrete launching ramp and a small dock. It is the most convenient launch-

---

CB Stations in the San Juans

Unless you are an avid CB'er, you might have become turned off by the welter of strange voices that clamor stridently on the channels. Sometimes it seems that everybody on CB sounds like Huckleberry Hound!

Up in the San Juans, however, citizen band radio is a very organized means of communication from island to island. Folks who live on Waldron and Stuart, for instance, depend upon channels for information. The local fishermen, both commercial and sport, seem to prefer this radio to the VHF. They monitor several frequencies rather regularly.

There is also a network of security stations in the island similar to REACT. They stay on channel 9 to listen for emergencies. If you get in trouble and don't have a VHF, you will very likely be able to raise one of them in your locality.

Here's a list of the **Radio Watch** stations:

UNIT 1 is located at Cape San Juan, near Cattle Point—San Juan.

UNIT 14 is at Eagle Cove—San Juan.

UNIT 9 is on Limestone Point—San Juan.

UNIT 12 is in Hannah Heights—on the western shore of San Juan.

UNIT 8 is in Deer Harbor—Orcas.

UNIT 5 is at Spencer Spit—Lopez.

The San Juan County Sheriff's office watches on channel 9.

There are also REACT monitor stations in Bellingham.

A number of non-affiliated CB'ers are scattered throughout the islands. Here's a list of them and the channels they use.

Most stations on San Juan Island use Channel 11.

Crane Island—14.

Orcas—14.

Decatur—11.

Cypress—3 & 4.

Center—14 & 1.

Henry—4 & 14.

Stuart—14 & 11.

Waldron—10.

Pearl—14.

Lopez—7 & 14.

Blakely—4 & 20.

The Coast Guard in Port Angeles guards Channel 9 intermittently and networks with both REACT and Radio Watch Stations.

Famous Odlin Park cannon

ing spot in the islands. It is only about a mile from Lopez Ferry Landing, which is the first stop for the ferries. It is in the middle of all of the cruising grounds. It is also close to some good fishing grounds. It's a great starting-out point for trailered boaters.

The park has some drawbacks as far as an anchorage, however. The water is quite deep to within 100 feet or so of the sandy shelf beach, and the ferries create quite a wake; they run fairly frequently during the summer— the last one passing about midnight. There is also a strong current running up or down Upright Channel most of the time.

The dock is used by small boats as an unloading and loading spot before and after launching.

One of the favorite features of the park is an old cannon of World War II vintage which fascinates kids. This is a great spot for people trailering small boats to use as a base for exploring the islands. Families love it because of the wide, shallow, sandy, beach, softball field, an old beached boat for kids to play pirate in, trails, picnic tables and lots of room for kids to play.

Odlin Park has water, pit toilets, a group camp, fireplaces, and plenty of beach to comb.

Upright Head
Upright Head is about a mile north of Odlin Park and is the location of the Lopez

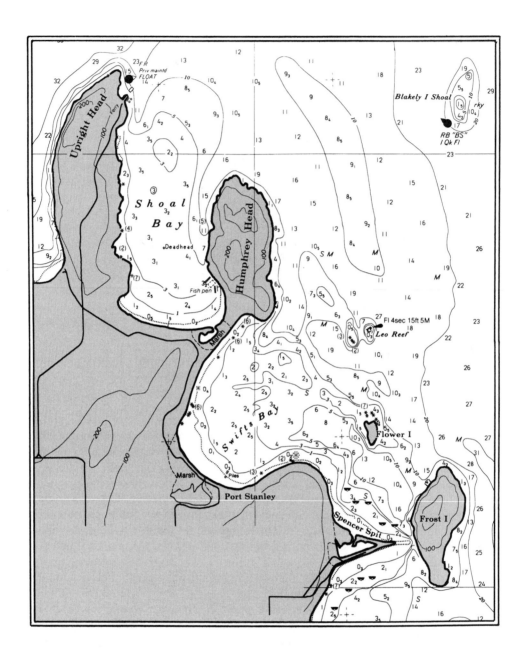

Ferry Landing. Between the park and the head the shoreline is high and forested and there are several resident eagle families that fish from lofty perches. Keep an eye out for these majestic birds as they patiently await their dinner from on high.

The ferry dock at Lopez is of no practical value to the cruising boater. As a matter of fact, there is no way to get from a boat to the ferry dock except to anchor out in deep water and dinghy to shore. So if you plan to pick up passengers who have come to the islands by ferry, it's far easier to meet them at Shaw, Orcas or Friday Harbor ferry landings where there are docking facilities nearby.

Shoal Bay

Shoal Bay, just east of Upright Head, has no public facilities but is a good anchorage in a south wind. The controlling depth is about 25 feet and is good holding ground. The shores of Shoal Bay are pretty heavily populated—for the islands—and there are a considerable number of private mooring buoys and crab pots along the shores which can make entering after dark rather tricky. There are some interesting sights in the little bay, however. There is a big private marina at the southeasterly end of the bay. The big boathouse that you can see next to the marina belongs to famous Seattle boatbuilder, Anchor Jensen.

Just north of the marina is an elaborate sytem of fish pens which are no longer in use. At one time Aquasea Farms experimented with raising salmon trout to sell to Pacific Northwest restaurants. The costs of production and labor, and the fluctuating price of the fish apparently doomed the fledgling enterprise.

There is another smaller aquaculture venture that seems to be succeeding in Shoal Bay—it is growing mussels and oysters in Japanese lantern-shaped nets suspended from a network of barrels and rafts.

An abandoned quarry along the eastern shore of Shoal Bay has dramatic towering rock cliffs, often featuring perched eagles always awaiting a meal.

As we round Humphrey Head, it is time to bring out our second chart of the Lopez area—#18429, 'Rosario Strait'. This will give us a good big-scale representation of the eastern shore of Lopez, all the way around to Iceberg Point on the south end of the island.

Humphrey Head

Humphrey Head is a hilly peninsula between **Shoal** and **Swifts Bay** connected to Lopez by a marshy isthmus. The first settler in the north end of Lopez was William Humphrey who arrived in the area in the late 1870s. He had a tidy little place of 166 acres, raised wheat, hay and chickens, with a 500-tree orchard of apples and plums.

Now it is a mostly residential area with homes and Grace Episcopal Church tucked among the trees.

Swifts Bay

As you head south and east along the peninsula, the land becomes low and there are beaches and waterfront homes in **Swifts Bay**. This large, almost semi-circular bay offers excellent anchorage, but look out for crab pots and private mooring buoys near the shores.

Port Stanley

Port Stanley was once a community just sort of waiting to be—and it never really fulfilled its expectations, from all we can gather. The Port Stanley Townsite Development Company started in June 1892 with the beginnings of a Christian community. Frank Baum, an idealistic, opportunistic, moralistic attorney who had tried to start a newspaper in Friday Harbor with less than successful results, named Port

Stanley after the African explorer and got himself appointed postmaster of the community. He built a combined post office, store, residence and newspaper office, but the development was barely underway when economic conditions abruptly put the new company out of business.

The San Juan Islander newspaper gave Port Stanley rave reviews in 1901, but blamed the lack of growth on the "good roads leading to Lopez and other parts of the island."

"Surrounding Port Stanley is a fine grazing and fruit-raising country, which only awaits the proper people to make it as prosperous and thrifty as any place in this part of the state. A community of most excellent houses and thriving and hardy orchards and of prolific trees already exists here, but a wharf is needed and a trading post is desired in order to facilitate the development of natural resources which are so very abundant here ... The bay and harbor here is an excellent one and the water advantages superior to other places which have more improvements. The steamer *Buckeye* touches here every day."

Leo Reef

Leo Reef, off the northeast shore of Lopez between Humphrey Head and **Spencer Spit**, is an ugly collection of rocks that seem to crop up in open water out of nowhere. Passing ferries give it a wide berth. A number of careless private skippers wish they had too. They have run up on the rocks by trying to go too close behind the rock, which has the navigation sign. Leo Reef also has a Flashing 4-second light. The charts show several rocks that can be hidden at high tides.

The Obligatory Sea Story

I'll never forget the time when, about a dozen years ago, I was on wheel watch when the 70-foot charter boat 'Pagan' approached Cattle Pass headed south. It was about midnght and I was alone in the wheel house. I knew we had about two knots of current going with us. What I didn't know was that the wind had wakened up out yonder and all the air in the world wanted to stampede its way up the channel. Long before I could pick up the backflash of the lighthouse and we were still a quarter mile away from Goose Island, the stem of the 'Pagan' began to play porpoise.

The skipper was asleep in his cabin below. He had had a hard day and I didn't want to bother him. So I stood there sawing the wheel back and forth, trying to figure where-in-hell the next wave might be coming from. Pretty soon I decided I wanted some help. The trouble was that the intercom was on the after bulkhead and I couldn't let go the helm long enough to reach for it.

As we got abeam Goose Island, he appeared in the passageway at the head of the ladder. He was wearing his bathrobe, holding onto the rungs, blinking his eyes trying to focus on what was happening in the inky pilothouse. When the boat calmed for a second, he let go of the handhold and started to come toward me. At that point we took a whitecap and the next thing I knew we were holding onto each other like a couple of dance-marathon

The sign on the reef reads:

> submerged
> DANGER
> rocks

A sign frequently seen throughout the islands—often in what seems unlikely places—but it is always posted for good reason.

Flower Island

As you head southeasterly from Swifts Bay, notice little **Flower Island**, one of the many owned by the U.S. Fish and Wildlife Service. There is one small tree and a few shrubs on the north end of the four-and-a-half acre island. There were no flowers that we could see on Flower Island. Signs are posted to dissuade visitors—although it's hard to believe anybody would be much interested in visiting it. There are rocks, which are a danger, off the north and east sides of Flower.

Spencer Spit

Spencer Spit is a long, curving finger of beach that almost seems to touch Frost Island. This 129-acre park is one of the most popular of the state marine parks in the islands. It's not as far out in open water as the Sucia group, closer to amenities than Stuart, and quite protected. There's a nice sandy beach for kids to play on, lots of driftwood logs above normal high tideline, and the sun always seems to shine there. There are even a few clams around waiting to be dug and fishing is good nearby.

---

contestants. When we separated, he did a tour jete across the deck that Nureyev would have envied. Then he bounced off the starboard wall and caromed into the pilot's chair which was behind me. He hit it with enough force to break its shackle and the high swivel chair began to walk drunkenly from one side of the house to the other. When it danced by like the Sorcerer's Apprentice we would try to grab it and it would playfully elude us.

I remembered the Victor Hugo story of the loose cannon on the deck of the man-of-war. I said small prayers that it would not crash into the switch panel on the back wall and knock out the electrical circuits.

On one of its passes, Captain Biles tackled the chair and wrestled it to the floor and secured it with a piece of line. For the next 15 minutes we didn't speak much to each other; nothing coherent, that is. I recall that we did from time to time shout phrases that would seriously prejudice our chances of entering the Pearly Gates—a consideration that seemed rather close at hand.

Eventually a large wave burped the 'Pagan' out of the bottleneck. The waves then began to take on some semblance of order. The skipper finally went below. I noted the time—0110. I still had more than an hour of watch ahead of me.

I suppose the fact that in these situations a person is not in much real danger is some consolation; nonetheless, it is still a chastening experience.

Normally, there are 12 buoys available for moorage, eight on the north side and four on the south side of the spit. State parks has plans for four more on the south side. When you dinghy ashore, you'll find car and bike campers on the upper park grounds, but motor vehicles are no longer allowed at the beach campsites.

Spencer Spit Park has been improved recently and there are new restrooms, a trail for the handicapped, forest trails, limited fresh water, fire rings, in addition to the campgrounds and beachcombing.

At the end of the nearly mile-long spit is a restored 16- by 20-foot log picnic shelter. The original log cabin was built on the land owned by the Spencer and Troxell families many years ago, and eventually fell into decay. When the state bought the land, the old logs were preserved and used as part of the present picnic shelter.

The Spencers moved to Lopez in 1886 and homesteaded 160 acres on the eastern side of the island, including the sandspit which bears their name.

Before the Spencer and Troxell families were in the area, there were two sandspits reaching out from the shore. Eventually they blended together and a small shallow lagoon was formed between them. The Indians used the area as a campsite for centuries.

The University of Washington Archaeology Department has found some ancient fire pits, tools and middens. Occasionally beachcombers still come up with spear points and hide scrapers made of bones. Such finds must be reported to the park ranger.

It may be easier to find clams than Indian artifacts at low tide at Spencer Spit. Be sure to check for red tide alerts before eating any shellfish in the San Juans. Often the edible critters are cleaned out early in the season by hungry visitors.

Frost Island

When you go through the passage at the end of Spencer Spit favor the **Frost Island** side for the deepest water. You can see the light green water at the end of the spit which is a good giveaway that there are shallows. The passage is navigable even at lowest tides for most recreational boats. Ferries have even been known to go through the pass, but it is not advisable.

Frost Island is privately owned. The only visible house is on the far southern tip, but a couple of tepees appear on the western slopes. Around the point, on the east side, there is a little cove with a boat ramp for the owners.

Blakely Island

Before we explore the delights of Lopez Sound, we ought to discuss seldom-mentioned **Blakely Island** just north of Decatur Island.

Blakely isn't talked about much, mainly because it is basically a privately-owned island. There are no county roads or county docks, although there is a large private marina. Blakely was settled by early homesteaders as were most of the islands, and had its share of farmers, cattle, sheep, loggers and fishermen. There is an old, no longer used, one-room schoolhouse inland. The few kids who live on Blakely now attend school on Orcas.

Starting at the south end and heading northeasterly on a quick trip around, there is an attractive wood home just above the beach in a bight less than a half-mile from

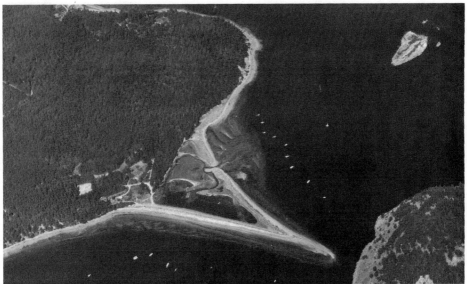

The long finger at Spencer Spit seems to almost touch Frost Island. (Photo courtesy Doug Pesznecker, state parks ranger.)

the **Thatcher Pass** light. The decks and overhanging roof lines of this large home inspire admiring remarks from passengers on nearby ferries.

Willow Island, off the southwestern shore, is a wildlife refuge, so don't go ashore.

There is a large bay on the west shore at **Thatcher,** although there is no town. The bay was, and is still, sometimes used for tying up logs. A stream from Spencer Lake enters the bay by means of a waterfall which has recently been fitted with a generator to help get power on the island. Spencer Lake is also the location of the large Blakely Island Campus of Seattle Pacific University. The college has summer programs for youngsters as well as serving as a research outpost for upperclassmen and graduates.

Proceeding north past **Bald Bluff,** keep well offshore—it is shallow and foul along here and you will see no homes. The westerly unnamed point on Blakely, just across the water from **Blakely Island Shoal** (a frequent mark for local sailboat races) is the beginning of the settlement on Blakely. In a nearly northerly direction from here there is a paved airstrip for residents (also served by San Juan Airlines) which can even handle small jets. Homes ranging from small cabins to luxury villas line the strip and continue south to the point, although there are only a handful of permanent residents on the island. (Blakely is often referred to by other San Juan Islanders as the 'rich man's ghetto'.)

The marina in the tiny cove on the northwest corner of the island, just off Peavine Pass, has private moorage, gas and groceries. Heading north and east through Peavine Pass, you can go between Blakely and **Spindle Rock,** but keep well off Blakely's shores, as there are all kinds of rocks and shoals. The farther south around the island, the fairer the shore and you can hug it pretty close. Blakely has a 1,042-foot peak which dominates the northeastern skyline.

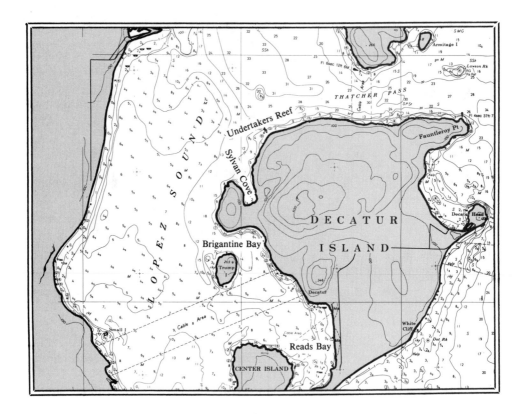

Well-marked **Black Rock** is off the southeastern shore about a half-mile, with **Pointer Island** about a mile south of that. **Armitage Island** provides protection for moorage in a private anchorage in the southeastern tip, but you can anchor in there, although the buoys are private.

Lawson Rock, at the eastern end in Thatcher Pass—again a well-marked pile of rocks.

And now, back to the Lopez area.

Lopez Sound

Once past Spencer Spit, you are in delightful **Lopez Sound**—a little known, little cruised area. This is not a favorite area for transient cruising, possibly because visitors to the San Juans simply bypass the Sound after crossing Rosario Strait. Perhaps they are anxious to check in at Friday Harbor for supplies and be on their way north. Or maybe they are heading for the marine parks. At any rate, it makes Lopez Sound a good area for cruisers who don't mind anchoring instead of tying to a mooring buoy or docking in a marina.

Since Lopez Sound is almost completely landlocked on three sides by Lopez and Decatur Islands to the west, south and east, it offers protection from southerly winds. Blakely and Decatur to the north and east—both of which are hilly, tend to cut down the fetch of northeasterly winds also.

Since Lopez Sound is one of those beautiful cruising areas of the Islands that are bypassed by many northbound boaters and San Juan visitors, we'll devote some time to its exploration.

We'll begin by drifting down along the western shore of **Decatur Island**, snoop into the lower bays and return northward along the western shores of the Sound.

Let's head for **Sylvan Cove.**

Sylvan Cove

Sylvan Cove, in Decatur's northwest profile, is a convenient first anchorage for boaters who have just cleared **Thatcher Pass** and want to explore Lopez Sound.

Or for those who have entered the Sound by way of Spencer Spit Marine Park.

'Sylvan' is defined as "relating to, or characteristic of the woods or forest, or formed of woods or trees, or abounding in woods or trees." This Sylvan Cove fits the definition perfectly.

Sylvan Cove is lovely with woods and trees along both shores of the sides of the bay and a stately home at the end of the cove surrounded by grassy fields. It is a private shore, of course, but there is good anchorage for a half-dozen boats in 12 to 30 feet, in a beautifully 'sylvan' setting.

Brigantine Bay

The protrusion of land on Decatur that makes the hook for Sylvan Cove has another good moorage on its south side, **Brigantine Bay**—obviously named for some Brigantine-rigged ship which anchored there once upon a time.

This bay has some very inviting, but unfortunately private, beaches. Good anchorage for several boats can be found in the relatively shallow water at the north end of the bay.

Trump Island

This 200-foot high island forms the south and west boundaries of Brigantine Bay. Although it offers some shelter from westerlies, the water is a bit deep for anchorage just offshore. If you decide to anchor here, stay close to Decatur inside the six-fathom line.

Reads Bay

Just south of Trump and Brigantine is Decatur Shores, a large real estate development. There is a big, private dock signed 'Decatur Shores Members Only'. There is good anchorage in the northeast corner of **Reads Bay** in about 25 feet at low water.

Decatur Island itself is one of those non-ferry-served islands which are being developed privately. Back in the homesteading days near the turn of the century, there were a fair number of residents who farmed and ran sheep and cattle. There were also fishermen, boatbuilders and loggers on the island.

As the years passed, population dwindled, but a recent upsurge in real estate development and sales has sent would-be part-time residents back to Decatur and the island is once again experiencing growth. There is a grassy airfield for easy access, and for the small but growing number of permanent families, there is a new

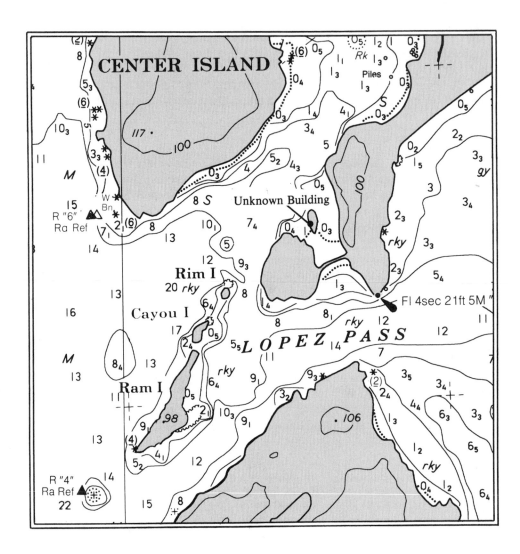

modern one-room school, built and administered by the Lopez Island School District.

There are no shopping facilities on Decatur.

Center Island

Just west of the southern portion of Decatur—across Reads Bay—is **Center Island**. Watch out for the rock that bares at a five-foot tide. In fact, the whole passage between Center and Decatur is relatively shallow.

Center has a fairly substantial number of summer homes. Residents reach the little island by airplane, landing on the grassy strip, or by boat. A local mail plane recently set a Guinness Book of Records entry by having the shortest flight between two mail stops—44 seconds—from Center Island to Decatur Island. Center is posted

What is this structure?

with private signs, but there is some DNR land on the western shore which is seldom used.

At the southern end of the passage between the two islands the depth is about 25 feet and provides good anchorage.

Lopez Pass

Decatur Island and Lopez Island have a deep pass between them, from Lopez Sound into Rosario Strait. The northern shore of the pass has a delightful beach between Decatur Island and a forested headland. If you stay on the waters inside this beach and headland (in Decatur's southern hook) you will discover a tiny, dome-shaped island that bears exploring. There is a fascinating concrete bulkhead that almost appears to have been the beginning—perhaps—of a bridge to nowhere. The area between the tiny island and the beach bordering **Lopez Pass** goes absolutely dry at low tide, so use caution.

There is good fishing in Lopez Pass, which is used occasionally by visiting boaters after crossing Rosario Strait. There are no hazards in the pass and it is plenty deep, with the eastern entrance marked by a navigation light on the tip of Decatur.

The Three Rs

There used to be three famous little islands in Lopez Sound: **Rim, Rum** and **Ram**. In the latest issue of NOAA chart for the area, #18429, they have chosen to rename poor little Rum—which is a "Rum go!" as the English would say. It has become **Cayou Island,** named for an Orcas Island pioneer. Now, really, which sounds better to you: Rim, Rum, Ram—or, Rim, Cayou, Ram? Sometimes federal agencies are deficient in poetic soul!

Rim Island is the smallest and is fairly flat and rocky with just a little shrubbery. It is shoal off the northern shore. Someone has placed a high stick in the middle of this dot.

Rum, (aka Cayou) is the middle island; about two acres in area and is fringed with a shoal on the northern tip. The water between these two islands is negotiable, although there is a lot of kelp in the passage. Cayou is an attractive little piece of real estate with a number of small firs and junipers and a dramatic-looking snag on the north end of the island. It is a wildlife refuge, which means don't go ashore.

Ram Island is a beauty! Furthermore, it is one of the publicly-owned islands that permits visitors. There is a welcome sign on the east shore reading: 'Ram Island, Public Access Approved.' A little pebbled beach on this side of Ram is the only place to land a small boat and go ashore safely and easily.

Boaters should beware of a shoal about halfway down the east side of Ram. You can go from 60 feet of water to less than a foot at low tide in just a hundred or so feet of travel. Finding anchorage near Ram Island could be tricky. You would be well-advised to drop your hook behind the north side of Lopez Pass or in Mud Bay farther south and dinghy over.

Ram Island is fairly well-forested. There are paths that lead up across the rocks and into the trees. The south end of the island is a rocky cliff, well-suited for sitting and resting, or perhaps some picture-taking. A silvered snag sits atop a spine of rock.

A rock southeast of Ram Island is marked with a triangular day beacon, Number 4.

South End of Lopez Sound—Inside

There are two large bays in the southern end of Lopez Sound, **Mud Bay** and **Hunter Bay**, bisected by a forested peninsula. Mud Bay has two small islands owned by Uncle Sam in its northern entrance: **Fortress Island** and **Crab Island.**

Fortress Island looks like a fortress—at least it is barren and sculptured—and is about 200 yards long. It is mostly inhabited by birds and does not recommend itself to visiting.

Just to the east of Fortress Island is an islet belonging to the U.S. Fish and Wildlife Service. It is unnamed on the chart, but state DNR maps call it **Skull Island** (the same name as one in West Sound on Orcas, incidentally).

And immediately east of Skull Island is a lovely little bay lined with what—at first glance—appears to be a village of Indian tepees. However you will quickly notice that they are all sparkling white and not very ethnic. The wild Indians you will encounter are all bubblegummers from the mainland who are vacationing at Camp Norwester. There is a brightly-painted Indian totem consisting of a Red Man holding something over his head. There is also a dock with an ornately-painted dugout canoe. It would seem that the kids in camp eat an inordinate amount of shrimp and crabs because the tideflats at the northeast end of Mud Bay are filled with pots.

Incidentally, the charts show a mean rock right in the center of this little bay with a small marker a few yards to the west of this rock.

Just south of Camp Norwester there is a large bay which dries at low tides, and there are piles and snags, a rock offshore and a white daybeacon.

Mud Bay

The eastern shore of Mud Bay has steep banks, trees and little habitation. On the trip down to the south end of the bay, take note of the dangerous rock about 200

Totem and tepees at Camp Norwester.

yards offshore on the eastern side of the bay and about a quarter-mile from the southern end of the bay.

Mud Bay is appropriately named. The water is quite shallow and the tidelands extend all along the front of the pastoral meadow at the end of the bay. The bottom is—guess what—muddy!

Most of the Mud Bay shoreline is owned by the state, but is undeveloped land. This means you can stroll on the beach, walk the dog, run the kids, dig clams, whatever your heart desires. Just don't go onto the uplands.

As you circle Mud Bay and head into Hunter Bay, you will pass **Crab Island,** and you can go on either side of it. It's a half acre of flat, grass-covered rock, posted as a refuge.

Hunter Bay

We are now at the northeast corner of Hunter Bay, which may be one of the most inviting anchorages anywhere in the San Juans. Even at the height of the tourist season there is usually plenty of anchoring room. The bottom of Hunter Bay is uniform in depth—about 15 feet at low water, which makes it ideal. The muddy bottom provides good holding ground, and the forested hills around it offer good protection from all but strong northeasterlies.

There are few houses on shore and there are a number of intriguing little nooks and crannies in case you wish to row around and do some sightseeing. There is a small county dock at a road end just west of Crab Island. There is no accommodation for yachts except for brief load and unload tie-ups at the float, but there is a boat-launching ramp available adjacent to the dock. There are no amenities such as stores or gas facilities ashore.

The northwest portion of Hunter Bay has a small aquaculture float. Beyond that is a reef which extends out about 100 yards offshore. The shoreline in this area is a trifle tricky. Note that you can go from 60 feet of water to six feet in just a few yards. The reef that is indicated by a wavy line at this point is marked at its outer end with a big pipe that has been sunk into it as a marker.

Small Island

Continuing north, there are a couple more indentations and hooks along the western shore of Lopez Sound, and then you reach **Small Island**—it is. This is

Carry A Bee Sting Kit!

It seems impossible that an annoying bee sting could lead to death, doesn't it? But it can—and sometimes does. How does a little bit of bee venom cause serious consequences? Because it triggers, in some people, a massive reaction of the body's defense system, and the reaction (not the sting) can do you in.

Now, we don't want to be considered guilty of practicing medicine without a license, so we will give you a rundown on the facts. This is information we gleaned by reading several booklets and chatting with doctors. For more skinny on this subject, naturally contact your family sawbones.

First of all the question, are you allergic? The answer seems to be that nobody knows in advance. The fact that you may have been stung by bees, wasps and hornets in the past and suffered only a localized bite doesn't mean much. You can have a half dozen stings over the months and never have a serious reaction. The seventh time you get zapped you might end up in an emergency ward. Apparently the body builds up an army of antihistamines which lay dormant for a number of stings, and then suddenly the whole force of combatants can be released by a triggering incident. Then the army of body chemicals can march out and lay you low in an imaginary war against a whole hive of

stings. In short, the bee just zings you—then you kill yourself by overreacting! So much for good old mother nature knowing her business!

Here's the scenario. A bee or hornet gets mad at you for invading its territory, which might be your finger or toe. It decides to teach you a lesson. It stabs you with stinger and injects a little potion of venom. If the little hummer happens to be a honeybee, the stinger breaks off in your skin because the needle happens to be equipped with some tiny fishhooks. The bee (always the female—male chauvinists please take note) will now die. As the stingee, I am sure you will shed no tears about her demise.

You can tell if you have been stabbed by a honeybee because you will see a little black dot left in the skin. The first-aid books will tell you this: do not pinch the stinger or the surrounding skin to get it out. The bee has only given you a portion of its full shot. The rest of the venom is still in the stinger; you can complicate matters by further injecting yourself. The advice is to 'flick it off.'

Now in most cases, all that will result will be a local swelling and irritation, which will disappear in a couple of hours. But if you are allergic—that is, you've built up a whole DuPont Corporation of antibodies—you will quickly notice one or all of the following symptoms:

another of those islands owned by Uncle Sam and is tenanted by a zillion gulls. There is little moss and grass but plenty of rock. You are not allowed to go ashore, warns the sign, and you probably wouldn't want to anyway unless you want to study guano. It's shallow between Small Island and Lopez—take care if you venture through there, it gets down to just a little over one fathom.

Immediately south of Small Island there is a humongous cable installation with towers trooping down to the Lopez shoreline and disappearing into the water. This is one of the main power feeders to the San Juan Islands. The cable begins on the

1.) Itching and a rash, followed by swelling.

2.) Weakness.

3.) Swollen lips.

4.) Headache.

5.) Cramps.

6.) Difficulty in breathing.

It's that last symptom that is serious. Your windpipe can swell up and cut off your breath. Once that happens, the patient is in for some white-knuckle surgery called 'tracheotomy.' About 200 persons per year are killed by bee stings. The number would undoubtedly be much higher except that medical help is usually available in a short time. The minimum time in these life-threatening cases is one hour. If you happen to be out on one of the outlying islands, you could be cutting it close getting to a hospital.

What To Do:

We have copied these instructions from several medical books:

1.) Remove stinger.

2.) Wash area with soap and water.

3.) Apply a paste of Adolph's Meat Tenderizer (if it's available). It contains 'papain', an enzyme from the papaya which breaks down some of the venom.

4.) If tenderizer is not available, use ice compresses.

5.) Apply a tourniquet if practicable.

6.) Rest the injured part. Activity spreads the venom.

7.) Watch for the above serious symptoms indicating a systemic reaction.

8.) If reaction symptoms follow, use a bee sting kit, following instructions.

9.) If the kit first-aid doesn't improve the situation, get help from professionals.

Here's another note. If the victim has shown reaction to bee stings in the past, immediately use the bee sting kit. The reaction is likely to be more severe the next time.

Some further suggestions: treat every bee sting as a serious matter. Even if you are a big hale macho male, you might be in a world of hurt. Don't hesitate to yell for help. Other boaters in a moorage may have bee sting kits if you don't. There may be a doctor or nurse in the area. A high percentage of doctors are yachtsmen.

Don't hesitate to contact the Coast Guard on Channel 16 or the San Juan Radio Watch on CB Channel 9. They can get fast transportation if it's necessary.

And one more tip to add to your supply of healthy paranoia on the subject. Bees and hornets can sting in the so-called 'off season.' Bees hibernate during the winter, often in the bark of trees. When they are disturbed, they may not fly but just crawl around looking for a new warm hideout. They could choose you.

Now, march out and plunk down about $10 for a bee sting kit. And keep it handy.

mainland and lands on Decatur just south of James Island. Then across Decatur and Lopez Sound to Lopez. If you drop a hook in this area, you might find your anchor chain becoming very incandescent! It's also frowned upon by Opalco, the islands' power company.

Thatcher Pass

Where to go next? Well, since we're headed north in Lopez Sound, we might as well go through **Thatcher Pass** and poke our noses out into Rosario Strait, see the marine park on James Island and take a look at the bay on the east side of Decatur.

Undertakers Reef

As we head into Thatcher, we pass a neat little geographical item called **Undertakers Reef** on the northwest corner of Decatur, just north of lovely Sylvan Cove. The name is not particularly kind to the practitioners of this profession. Over the decades, it may well be that this hazard has contributed a bit to the trade, but rest assured that if it had been so named by these gentlemen, it would have been called 'Funeral Directors' Reef.

Another thing to note: Undertakers Reef is mean, sneaky and ornery. In the first place, where it rears its head, there should *be* no reef. The shoreline above it is a cliff. One would judge that the steep incline would head on down under the surface of the water to about 50 fathoms. But, instead, these boomerang-shaped rocks pop up out of about 50 fathoms—totally unexpectedly. There is a marker of red diamonds with a big number '2' off the northeast corner of the reef. There is also about 15 feet of ugly rock at high tide between shore and the marker so that the only real danger the reef poses is to boats that are hugging the shore of Decatur as they leave or enter Thatcher Pass—something that skitterish fog-bound skippers have been known to do.

Fauntleroy Point

At the northeastern corner of Decatur Island, this point with its flashing four-second light was named for a surveyor with the U.S. Coast Survey in the 1850s. According to Doug Cardle, George Davidson was aboard the survey vessel *Fauntleroy* when he was naming geographical features in this area. Cardle further states that the boat was so named because the surveyor was in love with a young lady back in Illinois whose last name was Fauntleroy. He immortalized his love by naming the point for her.

Having informed you thus, we have exhausted the store of information, useful or otherwise, about this point. Except to tell you that the white navigation light, 37 feet high, can been seen for a distance of seven miles as it flashes from the headlands.

Decatur Bay and Head

Around the corner, there is a big deep curving bay indenting the northeast shore of Decatur which deserves a name but doesn't have one. We shall call it **Decatur Bay**—just for purposes of reference. This bay extends from **Decatur Head** to the

---

Geography Tidbit

It's hard to tell by looking at maps and charts just which is the largest island in the San Juans, but Orcas has 58 square miles, winning the questionable honor by just one square mile. San Juan Island is second with 57 square miles.

Orcas also boasts the highest point in the islands — Mount Constitution, whose 2,407-foot peak offers a stunning 360° view of the surrounding water and land for miles.

"On a clear day, you can (almost) see forever" from the top of the mountain.

---

aforementioned Fauntleroy Point. It is about three-quarters of a mile long and the area shallow enough for anchorage is about a half-mile wide. At the south end of this bay Decatur Head is a promontory connected to the main body of the island by a sandspit. While it is possible for southerly winds to whistle over the sandspit and make anchorage in a storm a bit noisy, it is still a better bet than to try and anchor at the west cove on James Island Marine Park. We'll discuss that area in more detail in a bit.

Decatur Bay is picturesque. There is a small community of attractive houses, mostly vacation cottages, at the south end. Behind the hills of Decatur Head there are a couple of barge-shaped rocks and beyond them a long privately-owned dock. A marine contracting company has a dock here with some equipment moored at the float. A house on shore has a giant old propeller painted white, in its front yard.

The western edge of this bay is good moorage in fairly deep water. Note there is a threatening rock in the middle of this area. This is all private beach, so don't plan to go ashore, except for a 30-foot county road end on the west shore.

James Island

Just a hop, skip and a jump from Decatur Head is **James Island State Park.** This 113-acre primitive paradise has a couple of hazards for the novice. It is a good refuge after a stormy crossing of Rosario Strait, but if you tie to one of the park buoys on the eastern cove you may find yourself in for a bouncy night; what with swells from Rosario and wake from the ferries. If you go around to the west side, tie up at the small state park float or grab the one mooring buoy. Short of that, go somewhere else for the night. For while extolling the virtues of the island itself, we feel the moorage is tenuous.

The float is out of the water from October to May, as are most state park floats, and we decided to anchor on the quiet west side, one night in March. We set the hook

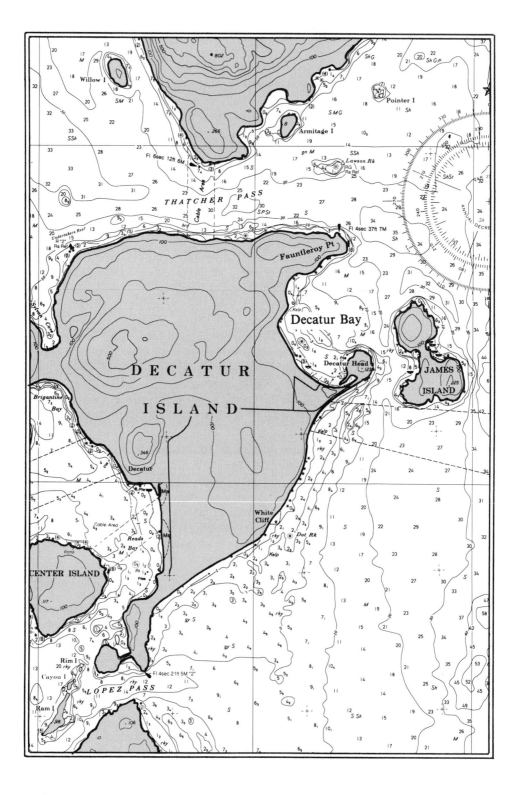

James Island State Park Dock—the only safe moorage in James' western cove. Tie here or wish you had.

securely, but 'just in case', we tied a quarter-inch spinnaker sheet to the piling on the dock as a stern tie.

It was a quiet night with no other boats about, only a full moon shining down. We retired early, knowing we had a well-set anchor. Sometime, in the wee hours, we awoke to hear water rushing past the hull and poked our noses out into the cool night air. We were fine, but the earlier low tide was now changing rapidly to a very high tide. We listened uneasily to the rushing current, checking the anchor every couple of minutes.

And then a shout from Al, and I charged out on deck. The well-set anchor had suddenly dragged; we had swung around and were within touching distance of the sheer rocky cliff on the shore of the cove, hanging away from it only by the taut quarter-inch spinnaker sheet. As Al hauled in the anchor, I started the engine and abandoned the spinnaker sheet. When the anchor was on deck, we headed out around the island and tied to a buoy on the eastern cove. There the wind was blowing about 20 knots and there were three to four-foot swells—all this at two in the morning. It was no longer a lovely night. Next day we powered back and retrieved the spinnaker sheet from the by-now tranquil little bay.

But if you can have a quiet night secure on a buoy or at the float, you will love James Island. The small beaches are steep and gravelly, with lots of driftwood. The rest of the shoreline is rocky cliffs. Trails criss-cross the forested island randomly from the low spots to the high bluffs, sometimes above sheer cliffs. There are deer that feed at dusk on the bluffs, and fishermen say fishing is good off the rocks. There are pit toilets, picnic tables, campsites and fireplaces, but no fresh water.

The little island was named for Reuben James who supposedly saved the life of Stephen Decatur in a gunboat raid into Tripoli Harbor in 1804. He became a naval hero when he took a saber slash intended to kill Decatur, according to Doug Cardle.

Jasper Bay

This delightful spot hardly deserves the name since it is just an indentation. The shore is parklike and there are a couple of beautiful homes on shore but there is not much room for anchorage.

Just about due west of the southern tip of Center Island there is an unnamed cove on the western shore of Lopez Sound. Some good moorage can be found in the southwest corner of this cove, although the water is fairly deep, about 30 feet.

South along Rosario Strait

Now that we've explored one of the lesser-touristed areas of the San Juan Archipelago, let's go on an expedition that is seldom made by Down Sound yachtsmen and is even overlooked by San Juan Islands' boaters—the reaches on the 'outside' of the south end of Lopez.

At times when the Gulf Islands, Desolation Sound and the Sunshine Coast of B.C. are a beehive of wandering pleasure boaters, the beautiful and primitive coves and beaches of the lower Lopez area have only an occasional visitor. Some of the most uninhabited and untouched areas of the Pacific Northwest are down in these out-of-the-way spots.

A trip to the south end of Lopez requires good weather because there are challenging passages to be sailed. Don't try it if there are small craft advisories or southerly winds. But, given a couple of days of promised calm weather and sunshine and a good supply of color film, you can hold your own with the doughty captains who have just returned from 'around Vancouver Island', the Queen Charlottes, or other remote areas.

So let's pick up our cruise from just south of James Island and Decatur Head.

As you head south, keep fairly offshore because of rocks below the 100-foot cliffs, including state-owned **Dot Rock** about 300 yards offshore at **White Cliff.** To the east of this is the **Bird Rocks** group, a wildlife sanctuary, and **Belle Rock** near the center of Rosario Strait.

If Rosario Strait is on its good behavior, you can make the run down to **Cape Saint Mary** just past **Shoal Bight** on Lopez in short order. Keep an eye on the marker for **Kellett Ledge** as you pass the point and head into **Telegraph Bay**, which is hardly a bay at all—just a wide spot in the road called Rosario. Historian Doug Cardle says that this curving shore got its name because it was to be the first underwater point of what was going to be a Pacific underwater cable, an idea whose time didn't arrive.

Watmough Bay

The first anchorage on this eastern shore that is of any real value is at **Watmough Bay.** Some of the boaters who come through **Deception Pass** and encounter lumpy waters in the southern part of Rosario consider Watmough a haven. It is also a

Weather Tidbit

Islanders like to keep it a well-guarded secret, but it's been getting out that we do have less rain than Down Sound.

Because the islands are in the rain shadow of Vancouver Island, the average annual rainfall here is about 20 inches, compared to about 39 in Seattle.

Even so, in our diversified islands, the rainfall actually differs from island to island, and from one part of each island to another.

It seldom snows in the islands, except for a little powder on Mount Constitution and on San Juan Island's 1,000-foot hills; and freezing is kept to a minimum.

We do have lots of wind, particularly in the winter and especially on the south shores of San Juan and Lopez, bordering on Juan de Fuca Strait.

Oodles of sun the rest of the time—just like Camelot.

last-night spot for many heading south across the Strait of Juan de Fuca the next morning.

Not everyone is that kindly disposed to the narrow, shallow, rocky-bottomed bay—especially our friends who dragged anchor far out into Rosario one night when a wind came up and their anchor didn't hold.

Nonetheless, this is one of the beautiful bays in the San Juans, with towering black cliffs on the north shore, not quite such high cliffs on the south shore and a delightful secluded beach at the head of the bay. It's a good protected spot from one of the sudden westerly squalls that appear occasionally out of nowhere in the summer months. Local fishermen consider it a haven. The water shoals up suddenly as you enter Watmough—from 60 feet to 12 feet in just a few yards. The depth averages about 14 to 16 feet at low water. The one drawback to this anchorage is that rocky bottom, and if your anchor doesn't skid across it, it might get hung up. It is wise to put a locator-line and float on your anchor so you can see when you are over it when hoisting the line.

Sunrises are beautiful in Watmough Bay.

Watmough Head

Boulder Island, owned by the Fish and Wildlife Service, is at the eastern end of Watmough Bay, just off **Watmough Head.** It is seven acres of rather barren, dome-

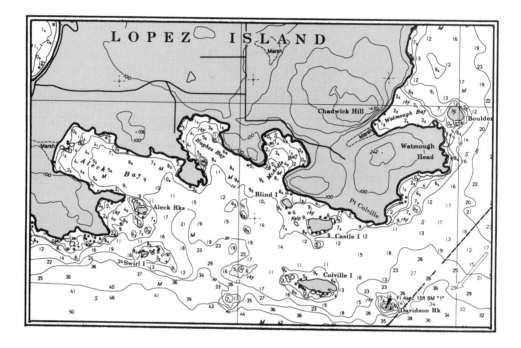

shaped rock with a vertical marker in the highest point on the island, about 75 feet.

Watmough Head, a windswept, rugged piece of land jutting into Rosario, is famous for an Indian tepee that has been there at least 30 years, according to Lopez Island locals.

Point Colville

There are beautiful sandy and pebbled beaches between Watmough Head and **Point Colville**. Since the point is owned by the U.S. Lighthouse Service, the beach is public. The drawback is that there is no good anchorage offshore. If you like a half-mile row, or if you have a shoreboat with an outboard, you can find places to pull up on the beaches, except at highest water, while you're anchored in Watmough Bay. Note the dangerous rocks just off the beach about two-thirds of the way from Watmough to Point Colville.

Colville Island

Another federally-owned island, **Colville** is a 12-acre bit of ground about three-fourths of a mile offshore that sits out in the rough junction between Rosario Strait and the Strait of Juan de Fuca. It is one of the largest bird sanctuaries in the San Juans. Lopez residents troll for salmon just offshore near Colville Island. There are lots of shoals along the south and western shores of Colville.

Davidson Rock

This rock is marked by a flashing four-second light, 15 feet high, visible for six miles and is at the western edge of the southbound Puget Sound traffic lane. It is also used as a departure marker for those heading south across the Strait from Watmough Bay. It's particularly handy during those pesky foggy days which begin showing up in August.

Castle Island

Just offshore, west of Point Colville, is **Castle Island,** and it's easy to see why it has that name. The nine-and-a-half-acre wildlife refuge towers like a castle over all that surrounds it, and the Strait offers a moat. There are some rather intimidating rocks just offshore all the way around, with a kelp-covered reef at the eastern end. There is an unnamed rocky island off the western end.

You can pass safely between Castle Island and Lopez and see the beautiful cliffs on Lopez at this point—good picture-taking territory.

Blind Island

There are *two* Blind Islands—not very good planning on the part of somebody! One is at Shaw Island and the second one, which we're interested in just now, is the little two-acre rock north and west of Castle Island. If you pass between **Blind Island** and Lopez, note that you should hug the little island to avoid a rock off the south shore of Lopez.

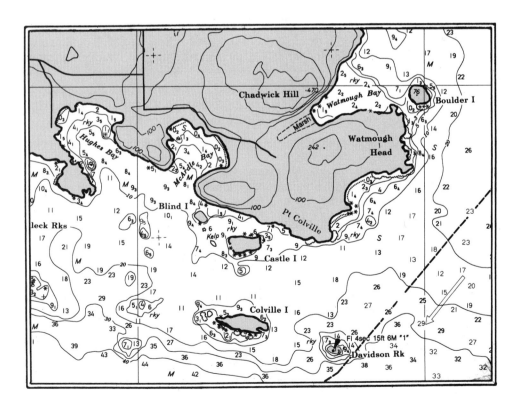

McArdle Bay

The passage between Blind Island and the towering cliffs of Lopez on the way into **McArdle Bay** offers breathtaking scenery. This beautiful bay is not much for anchorage, despite the good bottom and depths, because it is exposed to winds and waves from the Strait of Juan de Fuca. There are marshes at both the eastern and western ends of the bay, and a few houses have been built here. Gillnetters, who have been fishing on the banks and are not ready to come in and sell their fish, often ride out in McArdle or neighboring Hughes Bay.

Hughes Bay

This is almost a twin of McArdle, but you can duck farther back for protection in the west cove. On the approach to **Hughes** from McArdle there is a rocky bluff with picturesque windswept trees. The bay has a rocky bottom and is rather deep for anchorage until you are well inside; but would be a spot to ride out a southwesterly if needed. There is a small islet off the south end of this bay. There are not a lot of houses, but the shores are all posted private.

As you leave Hughes Bay headed west, look for a charming little cove in the high rocks—it has a sandy beach and a small boat house that looks like it is no longer used.

Aleck Bay

Aleck Bay is a favorite anchorage for commercial fishermen, and some visiting yachtsmen. As the chart shows, the bay runs east and west, with a mud bottom for good holding. This is a highly-prized area for homes for Lopez residents because of the spectacular view out into the Strait—in good weather they can see the Cascades and even Mount Rainier—a coveted sight in the San Juans.

The shores of the bay are rugged and rocky at the outer entrances, but the shoreline softens near the end of the bay, with forests and finally a lovely no-bank sandy beach—"the finest in the islands" according to the residents.

Aleck Rocks

This is a U.S. wildlife preserve of two islands separate at all but low tide, when they become one, at the southern entrance to Aleck Bay. There is a neat cave on the rocky shore here. Despite the fact that **Aleck Rocks** is posted "No Trespassing," quite a few young people from Lopez go out to the rocks and even party overnight according to local rumor.

There is an attractive unnamed cove that indents Lopez just west of Aleck Rocks with a small beach. The depth shoals from six to two fathoms rapidly, but it could provide a delightful daytime moorage in calm weather. Be on the lookout for a rock at the west entrance to this little cove—it's marked on the chart. In real life, you will see it outlined with copious strings of kelp.

Swirl Island

This is another U.S. nature preserve—a one-and-a-half-acre rocky island surrounded by rocks and reefs. It's a pretty name for an island, although it's not particularly appropriate for this one. The name probably came from the rips and eddies that surround it.

South Shore to Iceberg Point

From the tip of Lopez between Aleck Rocks and **Swirl Island** to **Iceberg Point**, is a coastline of jumbled cliffs and rocks—black, windswept and primeval. There are 100 to 225-foot high rocky bluffs overlooking the Strait on this land which is a lighthouse preserve.

From the tip west, you will go past an indentation fraught with rocks and reefs and on to **Flint Beach**. This is a beautiful little bay with a small barren island along the beach and a large unnamed island in the center of the bay. There is an attractive house just above a driftwood-piled shore at Flint Beach.

Since Flint Beach is covered on both charts, it is time to go back to our original chart, #18434, for the run up to Cattle Pass.

On the trip from Flint to Iceberg Point, keep on the lookout for an unnamed islet near the coastline. There is no safe passage on the north side of this islet which is surrounded by kelp beds.

Even on a calm day the restless Strait sends large breaking waves against the rocks at the base of the cliffs along this bleak, uninhabited coast.

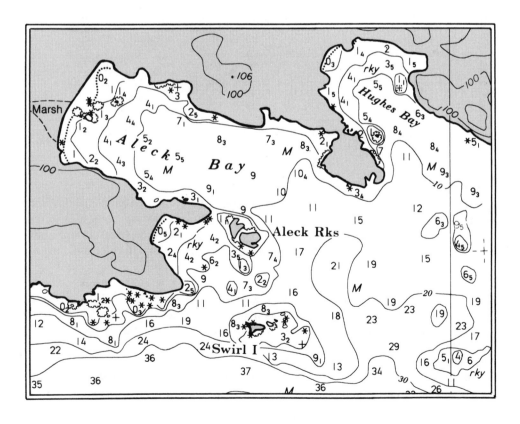

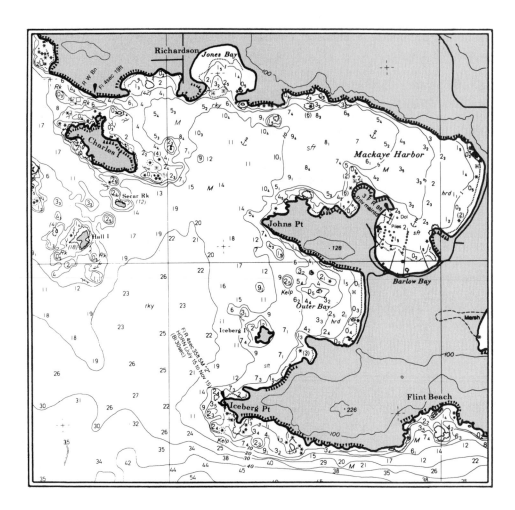

Iceberg Point

Iceberg Point with its welcome, albeit not particularly picturesque lighthouse, is a comforting sight to most sailors after crossing the Strait, for it signals surcease from what can be a rough or perhaps a foggy trip. The lighthouse beam at 35 feet above high water can be seen for five miles, and the horn blasts every 30 seconds from July 15 to November 15.

The lighthouse is set on a grassy knoll above the cliffs, with dangerous rocks and reefs surrounding it. Although the land around the lighthouse is public, owned by the Bureau of Land Management, it is inaccessible because the only land entry is across privately-owned property. The view from the knoll is spectacular.

Iceberg Island

Iceberg Island, another U.S. preserve, is at the entrance to **Outer Bay**, just inside Iceberg Point. This island is about three-and-a-half acres with a driftwood-covered

> Ever wonder about the strange name of the 'sockeye' salmon? It has nothing to do with a fish's eyes. We got it from the Indian name of the species 'tsaki'.
> — quote from THE GALLEY restaurant, Lopez, menu.

beach on the southwest side. It doesn't tower like one would expect an iceberg to do. Instead, it is flat and barren except for brown grasses and lichens.

Outer Bay

The low bank waterfront along **Outer Bay** is both public and private, with several residences and **Agate Beach County Park**. Right in front of the park there is a large moss-covered rock about half an acre in size. It is a favorite clambering place for young visitors. The park is somewhat spartan and is not for overnighting. But it has picnic tables and outhouses and a nice beach to land a small boat on. Anchoring in the bay itself, in a hard bottom of about two fathoms, is possible in calm weather. There are several rocks and reefs in the bay; check the chart for exact location if you decide to stop. The needle-shaped rock in the west end of the bay sticks up like a menacing spear. The other rocks seem to be fairly well-marked by kelp.

There used to be reefnet gear in Outer Bay during the fishing season, according to old-timers, but they are long gone.

Mackaye Harbor

As you continue in a northerly direction, you will round the bluff on **Johns Point** named for any one of a great number of men called John. Continue past rocks and reefs, giving a wide berth to the mess of stones, off a rounded bluff, just before you enter the harbor proper.

This is the home of the Lopez fishing fleet. During the season, fishboats anchor in the harbor between trips. Fish buyers ply in and out, hauling the catches and there is a fish-packing plant on shore.

Almost all of **Mackaye Harbor** is good anchorage, except for the shallows at **Barlow Bay** in the southern end. But remember, this is a commercial area and these fishermen are earning a living, so steer clear and be sure to leave an anchor light on at night.

There are several moorages in Mackaye Harbor for fishing boats and Barlow's Landing is a dock that can offer temporary moorage for visiting boaters.

Another possible overnight moorage spot is the middle float in the harbor, owned by Island Fresh Seafoods. Check at the shack at the center of the float for instructions.

An old abandoned 60-foot hulk lies on the beach on Barlow Bay. At one time, it was a respectable work boat. It was anchored in the harbor and whoever owned it did not maintain it properly. As a result, it suffered two fires and a sinking before its ignominious ending on the sandy beach. It's a favorite snapshot background.

The lovely sandy shore along Mackaye Harbor is posted private, so best stay off.

Richardson

Continue westerly out of Mackaye Harbor, past private **Jones Bay** with rocks in the entrance, and there is **Richardson**.

The store is practically an historic landmark and has long been a favorite stop for recreational and commercial boaters. This is the first fuel stop in the islands, and they carry gas, diesel and propane. And even more important, they make the greatest ice cream cones around. In fact, Richardson's store comes as near to being an old-fashioned general store as can be found in the Pacific Northwest. You can get just about everything there from food to fishing tackle to clothing to, well . . . you name it, they have it.

Richardson's serves the entire southern end of Lopez Island as well as the boaters, and is also a favorite haven for tired bicycle riders who have pedaled to the spot from the ferry landing about 12 miles away.

There is no float at Richardson's. Boaters who want to buy provisions or take on fuel and water have to tie up to the high pilings that support the wharf and scramble up the ladder, or anchor off and go ashore by dinghy.

The supplement to The San Juan Islander, 1901, wrote about Richardson in glowing terms.

"The first town which one approaches in going to San Juan County upon the steamer 'Lydia Thompson' from Seattle is Richardson. The rugged and unpropitious shores which rise before the eye from the water's edge give little evidence

Abandoned hulk in Barlow Bay

Richardson store and dock

of the fertile and productive acres of land which lay immediately inland and which constitute an agricultural district than which heart could desire no better in the world. Thus, the unfavorable conditions which upon arrival seem to fill the mind are swept away in admiration for the opportunities and scenes of progress which are seen upon all sides within the forbidding pale."

Richardson was settled in the 1870s by a man named, naturally, George Richardson. Fishing became the leading industry.

"In the fishing season the entire bay is filled with all kinds of fishing craft and the shores are lined with tents and huts of the fishermen. There never was a year when fish were not plentiful and of the finest varieties. During the summer over 400 men were here engaged in this industry. The fish running into Puget Sound through the Strait of Juan de Fuca strike this point first, and when fish are caught in no other locality, they are caught here. During the past summer when a phenomenally large run was experienced in all places, one of the purse seine outfits caught so many fish in one haul that they were unable to lift the net and were compelled to let the fish go."

And that's the way it was.

When the Coast Guard manned the lighthouse at Smith Island, the Coasties would pick up supplies for their lonely vigil, at Richardson's. It's well worth a visit.

Charles Island

You can pass between the point on Lopez just west of Richardson and **Charles Island** if your mast is less than 54 feet. **Buck Island** is at the southernmost end of a rock pile in **Davis Bay**. Stay to the south of the island. Otherwise, head back south, giving the rocks off **Charles Island, Secar Rock** and **Hall Island** a wide berth, heading well off the west side of **Long Island**—and there you are, back at **Whale Rocks** where this little trip started.

But we're not quite through. All those above-mentioned bits of rocks are a slight bit interesting, even if bleak. Hall Island, nearly two acres, and Secar Rock, less than one acre, belong to the U.S. Wildlife service.

And Charles Island is owned by the famous Scripps family—world-renowned newspaper publishers. If you are in the southern Lopez area on the Fourth of July, you will see a private fireworks display emanating from Charles Island that is one of the most elaborate pyrotechnic performances outside of Seattle.

Now if you went between Charles Island and Lopez, leaving the marker on the south side, you will pass into Davis Bay, a cluttered area of rocks and tiny islets, but that is a shortcut into San Juan Channel. Leave Long Island, Whale and Mummy Rocks to your south side and you'll be okay. Davis Bay is an area with private homes, but watch out for the rocks, especially off **Davis Point**.

That's it. We've just circumnavigated **Lopez Island**!

THE SHORES OF SHAW

Our next rubberneck trip will take us around that enigmatic little hunk of water-surrounded real estate called Shaw. The fascinating thing about this island, the geographic 'hub' of San Juan County, is that it has remained almost totally uncommercialized despite its ferry service, county roads, power, telephone and more than 100 year-round residents.

Some of the 'outer' San Juan Islands have adamantly refused to permit electricity and communication and regular ferry service on the theory that it would lead to an infestation of Seven Elevens and Golden Arches. Shaw is proof that if the people of an area are intelligent and serious about limiting the inroads of consumer-oriented businesses they can manage to do so quite well.

Shaw boasts a one-room little red schoolhouse in the center of the island which is on the list of National Historical buildings. Kids from kindergarten through eighth grade attend the school. Attendance grew rapidly from a low of three students in 1979 to ten in 1983. There is also a log cabin historical museum, a library and a semi-cloistered Catholic monastery.

As a boater, you will probably be more interested in the scenery of Shaw, named for Naval hero, Captain John D. Shaw, than in a discussion of the community's philosophy.

So let's pick up at the first point of contact that boaters have with the island as they come north up San Juan Channel.

Hoffman Cove

If you check chart #18434, you will see that once you pass Turn Rock Light in San Juan Channel, you have to alter course or you'll be headed right into **Hoffman Cove** on Shaw, which is not a bad place for a first visit. There is room for perhaps one or two boats to anchor, but it offers no protection from the wind and chop that travels

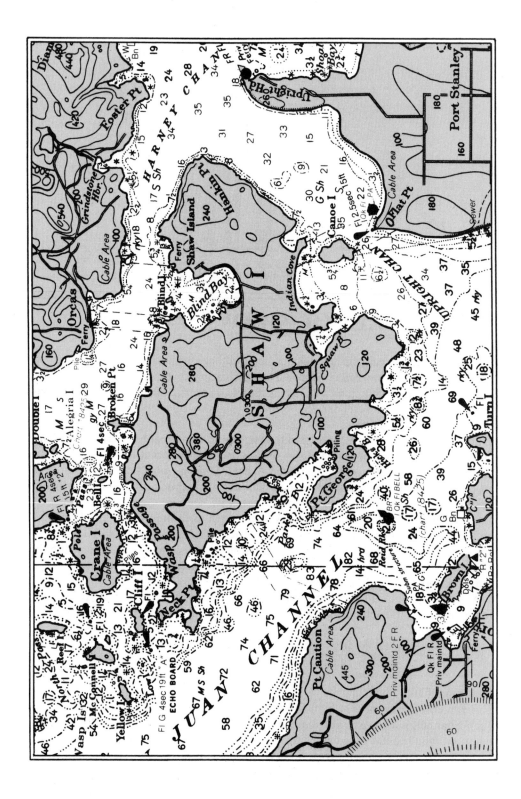

Tidbits

There are 172 islands in the San Juan Archipelago, according to the U.S. Coast and Geodetic Survey.

Officially, the San Juans include eight large inhabited islands: Orcas, San Juan, Lopez, Shaw, Waldron, Stuart, Decatur and Blakely; 26 small islands (some of which are privately-owned and inhabited) such as Brown, Pearl, Henry, Crane, Mc-Connell, Spieden, Johns, Charles and Center; 76 'tiny' islands, some of which are privately-owned and have shelters and small cabins.

But besides all this, there are hundreds more reefs and rocks which have vegetation and marine populations of their own.

northward up the channel. It is a nice little cove with a low bank gravel beach, evergreens down to the high tide line and large rocks jutting out on either side of the beach. There is one house and a two-boat boathouse in the cove, which was purchased by a Hoffman back in 1891. Several Hoffman families still live on Shaw.

Part of the shoreline is owned by the University of Washington, as is much of the forested upland on the southwest side of Shaw. Despite the fact that the University is a state institution, its landholdings on Shaw are off-limits to visitors. They are maintained as a wildlife preserve by the UW and administered by the Labs in Friday Harbor.

Hicks Bay

There are some beautiful beaches on the approach to **Hicks Bay**, the next harbor north, which is also posted by the UW. There are rocks about 100 yards off the eastern shore of this cove, but it's safe to go between them and the land. This is a favorite rookery for seals, and as we went slowly past we saw a mother seal and her nursing baby on the inner rock. Someone has built a lean-to of driftwood on the northwest corner of the cove and there is a house on the eastern shore. There is ample room for several anchored boats in the tree-lined bay, but again, it is not protected from southerly channel winds and waves.

Point George

Point George, heading northwesterly, is an uninhabited hook of land with a rocky, forested bluff. As you round the point, you come to a bay that is the favorite of many San Juan Island boaters who want to take an evening's dinner cruise.

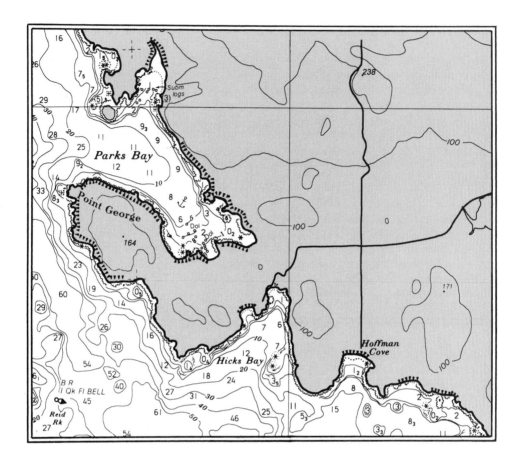

Parks Bay

Parks Bay is liberally posted with signs reading: 'No Trespassing', 'No Camping', 'No Hunting', 'No Fires'—all of which seem slightly shrill. One would think that 'No Trespassing' would suffice. It is hard to imagine how one could camp, hunt or build fires without trespassing.

Parks Bay is a quiet, secluded spot, the waters reflecting the deep green of the surrounding trees. Boaters in Parks Bay tend to be quiet also, picking up the tranquil mood of the cove itself. In a dinghy trip around the cove you can observe, at close range, the herons who stand for hours along the rocks, patiently waiting for dinner to swim past, darting their long beaks suddenly into the water. Gulls, of course, are everywhere, shouting raucously to each other, hoping for a handout, fighting over a tidbit. Whales have even been known to cruise close to the entrance to the bay, but they reject the urge to swim into the shallows.

Friday Harbor Labs has a dock in Parks Bay with a small storage shed and boats tied to the float for the use of University personnel. The small bights at the north and south ends of Parks Bay have pilings which were part of earlier logging operations.

Tift Rocks - abandoned trapper's home. Inset: Chet Tift, net mender

At the north end of Parks Bay is a tombolo that is worth inspection by small boat. There is a tideflat behind the tombolo which has a collection of drift logs.

The anchoring in Parks Bay is good in water from 12 to 30 feet deep. There is enough room for at least a dozen boats. Some visiting boaters prefer to drop the hook there instead of spending the night in the busier and noisier harbor across San Juan Channel— Friday Harbor.

Parks Bay was named for the unfortunate Hughie Parks who settled in the area in the 1880s—a much harder worker than most of his neighbors who literally drove him insane with their constant harassment. Finally, Hughie could stand it no longer and shot one of them—and another and another. When the lawmen arrived, Hughie did himself in before they could arrest him.

At the northern end of Parks Bay, a peninsula with a small rocky island at the end juts out. The tiny bay north of this peninsula is known as Post Office Bay by Shaw residents, although it is not named on any chart.

Tift Rocks

Cruising along the west shore of Shaw from Parks Bay there is a scattering of waterfront homes. About a mile northwest of the Parks Bay entrance are **Tift Rocks**. Surprisingly, many long-time boaters in the islands have never noticed Tift Rocks. They are worth a visit.

Tift Rocks were named for Bert Tift, the first postmaster on Shaw.

It is easy to see why these low rocks are posted as a wildlife refuge. Grass and moss grow from small niches on the rocks on these nearly treeless, tiny islands.

If you cruise slowly between the rocks and the main shoreline of Shaw, you will probably see whole families of seals sunning themselves. They respond with curiosity to visitors, and may slide into the water and swim out to look you over with as much interest as you show in them.

The largest and most northerly of the rocks contains the remains of an old stone cabin. Until a few years ago, the house was in fairly good condition, but vandals set it afire and the roof burned away. The thick walls of island rock and concrete still stand. Beyond Tift Rocks on Shaw there is an unnamed cove fronting on a meadow that looks appealing, but is too shallow for moorage except temporarily, at high tides.

Neck Point

On the chart, **Neck Point** looks like a piece from a jigsaw puzzle. It consists of two necks, actually: a scrawny one at the farthest point west and another huskier one that stands at right angles to the first one, pointing northwest. The uplands are low hills and there are two marshy coves at the beaches. The cove in the most westerly, footlike peninsula, is guarded by rocks and reefs, as you can see on the chart. It is not very inviting, even though it would provide temporary shelter from an upchannel (southerly) wind. There is an islet in the cove that has some vegetation on it and a wildlife refuge marker: "Keep Off".

The big peninsula is Neck Point proper. The area is a residential community and

Symbols For Reefs And Rocks

For a few bucks you can buy a very useful chart from your marine store. It's called Chart #1. It's a complete list of all the symbols used on NOAA charts. Of particular interest is Section 'O' which deals with dangers to navigation.

Most of the symbols are pretty self-explanatory, but you may have been confused by the symbols for rocks. They come in two styles: asterisks* and plus+. Rocks that 'come awash', that is, poke their ornery little snouts above the surface of the water, are indicated by the asterisk(*). Those that never get exposed are indicated by plus(+). A line of tiny dots surrounding a rock or reef indicates it is a danger to navigation. A reef that has no rocks that break the surface is in-dicated by a circle of dots.

Both type of rocks usually have some clue as to how far below the surface they might be at high tides. This is based on the 'Datum of the Chart' which is 'mean lower low water'. This information is put in parentheses: *(2) which means that the rock "covers and uncovers at the datum of the chart", plus two feet. Note: 'feet', not 'fathoms'.

Sometimes the chart will use another symbol to indicate a rock that surfaces; it is a dotted circle and the letters 'Rk' inside it. Next to it could be a number like 0_2, meaning "no fathoms, only two feet".

Needless to say, the rocks with the + sign and no corresponding figures are the ones you never take chances with!

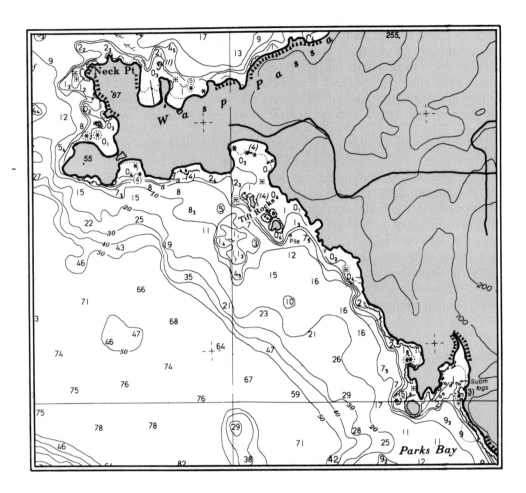

the folk who live there have a nice dock in the northerly cove. They even have a heated swimming pool back in the woods. There is a large unnamed rock marked with another wildlife refuge sign in the entrance to this cove. There is marginal anchorage for a couple of boats, but the lands are all posted, so there is no shore access, although the folks who live there are generally a friendly group. Just east of this cove is another marshy one—almost a twin of the first. Like the others, there are rocks in the entrance—one which uncovers at five feet.

Broken Point

Just west of **Broken Point** by a few hundred yards there is a cable area which is not mentioned on the charts as it is a recent installation. There is a cove and a tombolo with a house at the highest point, a cluster of low trees, and one lone tall fir. Ferries pass close to Broken Point where there is a lean-to on the western tip. The cove on the east side of Broken Point is not a good bet for an anchorage. The water is quite deep and shores up very quickly, but could offer some temporary protection in a southwesterly blow.

Blind Bay and Blind Island

About a mile east of Broken Point on the Shaw shore is the start of the scattering of rocks that extend almost one-fourth of a mile out into the passage as you approach **Blind Island**. If the Coast Guard ever finds itself with extra money to spend for navigation aids, it would do well to mark the northern limits of these rocks. They must be very well scarred from the number of wayward keels that have come to rest on them.

But before coming around into Blind Bay, it would be well to look at some of the hazards that surround this six-acre state marine park island delight.

If, for some reason, you decide to go between the shoreline of Shaw and the reefs off Blind Island, favor the Shaw shoreline, but not too closely. The local residents put through here quite blithely in small boats, but if you insist on playing chicken with the rocks, go on a slow bell, watch your depth sounder, and put someone up in the bow to look for keel inspectors. There are many. We strongly advise against this route. Some of the rocks show up even at high tide, but it's a veritable barnacle-crusted jungle at low tide.

Since the moorage for Blind Island is on the southern side of the island, the safest entrance is around the eastern side of the island. There is one nasty rock in that area

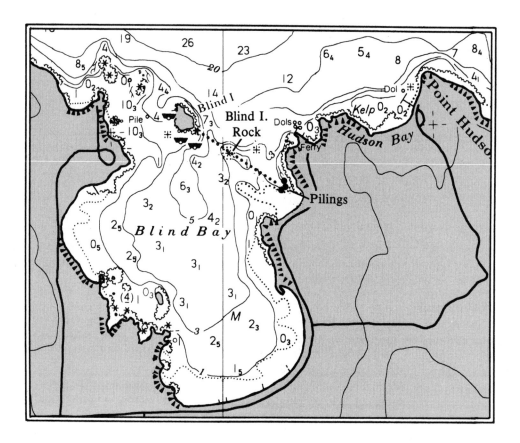

The 'Allright' aground on Blind Bay rocks

that catches a good dozen or so boaters every season. The **Blind Island Rock** (our name) is about halfway between the island and Shaw and is covered with water above a three-foot tide. There used to be a stick propped up on it, but it has disappeared—a storm may have wiped it out.

So there it is, just waiting for you. If you want to avoid finding it by the touch system, keep close to Blind Island. If you would like to know just where it is, here's how to spot it:

Look for three pilings in the marshy cove just south of the Shaw ferry dock. The rock is in a line between the northern edge of Blind Island and those three pilings. It is on the halfway point of this line.

The Blind Island Rock is usually perched on by boats coming west from **Harney Channel**. As they round **Point Hudson**, they slip close by the ferry dock to see the interesting ladies at the dock, then they head for Blind Island and one of the state mooring buoys. Next thing they know, they are sitting high and dry on an invisible platform and are calling for help on their CBs and VHFs.

Now that we've gotten you safely behind Blind Island, here's what you'll find: four mooring buoys and a beautiful bay. Note: there is a rock in the moorage area (although we couldn't locate it), so keep a short scope on your anchor line. If you find all the buoys occupied, you can anchor in 15 to 30 feet of water southwest of the buoys and closer to shore. The water immediately south of the mooring area is rather deep for anchorage, at least 30 feet at low tide. Blind Bay can be pretty choppy in a southwesterly blow as the wind blows in over the low part of Shaw Island.

Blind Bay is inviting for small boat touring along the low bank waterfront. The main island road from the ferry landing to other parts of Shaw encircles the bay and there are often retired reefnet boats beached on the eastern shore.

Although it is now long gone, there was once a fish cannery in Blind Bay, built just after the turn of the century. It was eventually changed to a fruit cannery.

Red Tide

The deadly Red Tide isn't red—and it isn't tide. It's an invisible toxin which is exuded from a kind of plankton called 'gonyaulux catanella'. We toss in the biological name of these little hummers in case you ever get sick from eating bivalves that have picked up some of this toxin—you'll want to know whodunit.

You see, good old gonyaulux catanella is not harmful to the shellfish who eat it—it just wipes out humans who eat the shellfish who eat it. It turns out that, chemically-speaking, this poison—which is called, in the laboratory, PSP, Paralytic Shellfish Poison—is just like curare. You know, the stuff the Amazon natives put on their arrows and blowgun darts. I hope you're getting the picture. It's not something you mess around with.

There may be some comfort in knowing that only 15% of the people who get sick with red tide poisoning actually die. But it could certainly make you glad you had Blue Cross, couldn't it?

It is understandable if you get a teensy bit paranoid when you are eating clams you have just dug and someone informs you that PSP is tasteless and odorless. The fact that you have taken the clams out of boiling water doesn't help—the chemical is stable in boiling water. The number of clams or oysters is not significant—it's the amount of poison present in each one. That is to say, one very poisonous clam could do you in, but a whole meal of slightly poisonous clams might just make you very, very sick.

How do you know if the clams you have in the bucket are O.K.? Before you dip 'em in drawn butter, call one of the two hotline numbers for the San Juan area. You can talk to County Health Department employees, who have the latest information locally, by calling 378-4474. Or you can call the toll-free hotline at 800-562-5632.

As a matter of fact, why don't you go up to the wheelhouse and jot those numbers down on your list of ready-reference numbers?

Now that we have given you fair warning, let's discuss some of the nitty-gritty facts.

In a lot of places, the red tide warning signs are posted late. In some places, they are left up long after the emergency condition has abated. Let's face it: local folks are not anxious to have all of the visitors scarfing up the clams. The sign you see posted may have been put up last year! When in doubt, ask.

Now, how can you test to see if the shellfish is safe? There is a simple test. All you have to have is a laboratory and a bunch of mice. You grind up the clams and inject them in the mice—then hang around and wait. That's the way the University of Washington Labs does it! Sorry, there's no other test for PSP. As a matter of fact, they record the toxicity of PSP in 'mouse units'! Really!

Now, there's a sort of down-home test for red tide toxin, but it's not very reliable. Old timers will tell you, "just rub some of the meat on your lips. If your lips start to tingle, chuck the critters out!" Recent studies have proven this test totally invalid—don't try it!

Well, that is one of the first symptoms—tingling lips and tongue. But that is followed shortly by numbness in the toes and fingers. After that—it's yell for the San Juan Aid Unit. They've got special instructions and available planes for medevac. You can get them on VHF Channel 16 or CB Channel 9.

But, what the heck, we know we are not going to dissuade you from digging clams. We don't want to. They're part of the joys of this area.

Just take the extra precaution of checking.

We want you around to buy the next book we write.

Right Shoulder, Clam Gun!

If clam hunting is your thing, the following chart of types of shellfish you are liable to find is valuable. If you are of a scientific turn of mind, you might want to invest a few well-spent bucks to buy a copy of 'Seashore Life of Puget Sound, The Strait of Georgia and the San Juan Archipelago,' by Eugene N. Kozloff—printed by U of W Press.

With this handy tome, you will be able to distinguish between a Bay Mussel (Mytilus edulis) and the California Mussel (Mytilus californianus).

Some people get a kick out of such tomfoolery.

Digging clams is a popular pastime among Washingtonians. This is one of the major reasons people go to the beaches. However, it should be noted that even though Puget Sound is renowned for its good clam digging, few high quality clam beaches are accessible to the public. Most of the beaches contain moderate to low numbers of clams. Furthermore, the clams are usually not evenly distributed but are found in scattered beds. With the exception of Manila clams and eastern softshell clams the best digging is usually at the lower tide levels.

The following is a listing of types of shellfish most likely to be found on the various beaches of a particular habitat type:

Rock Beaches

Common Names	Scientific Names	Edibility
Bay mussel	Mytilus edulis	Very good
California mussel	Mytilus californianus	Very good
Pacific oyster	Crassostrea gigas	Very good
Pinto abalone	Haliotus Kamtschatkana	Very good
Gooseneck barnacle	Mitella polymeras	Very good
Gooseneck barnacle	Lepas anatifera	Very good

Gravel - Cobble Beaches

Common Names	Scientific Names	Edibility

Manila clam
    Japanese littleneck
    Steamer clam
	Venerupis japonica	Very good

Native littleneck Steamer clam	Protothaca staminea	
Bay mussel	Mytilus edulis	Very good
California mussel	Mytilus californianus	Very good
Pacific oyster	Crassostrea gigas	Very good
Olympia oyster Native oyster	Ostrea lurida	Very good
Geoduck	Panope generosa	Very good
Horse clam Gaper	Tresus capax	Good
Eastern softshell Mud clam	Mya arenaria	Very good
Bent nose clam	Macoma nasuta	Fair
White sand clam	Macoma secta	Fair
Red crab	Cancer productus	Very good
Dungeness crab	Cancer magister	Very good
Ghost shrimp	Callianassa californiensis	Very good

Be sure you read the current Department of Fisheries Fish and Shellfish Regulations before you go clamming or fishing, since regulations may change from time to time.

When you leave the beach be sure to fill in all of the holes you have dug. Small clams on the sand pile or on the sides of the hole will be washed out and killed by predators if you don't.

Blind Island reefs

There are good anchoring grounds in the bights southwest and south of Blind Island at the southern end of the bay, but you will have quite a row in your tender to get to the island park. Note that there is a hazardous area between these two bights.

A couple of the little islands have wildlife markers on them and reefs around them.

Blind Island would make an ideal kid stop. They could play king of the mountain, or cowboys and sheepherders or whatever it is kids play. There are several nice grassy spots on which to pitch a tent, and older kids could spend the night without you worrying about them. There is no drinking water available and no garbage dump, but there is a sanikan. Four picnic tables and fire pits are in strategic spots on the island, with semi-trails connecting them. One large madrona tree dominates the ridge on the western side and on the eastern slopes there are blackberry and chinaberry trees.

There were a couple of wells on Blind Island at one time. An old hermit named Lindholm squatted on the island before it became a marine park. He built a cabin and dug two holes in the rock to find water. He must have found some, because apparently he installed an electric pump in one of them. The wire that led down to it is still there, although both wells have been filled in to prevent them from being hazards. The western well, surrounded by grapevines, has a spring that provides a small trickle of water, but it is not potable. For several years after the state took over the area, there were some old iron pots and pieces of machinery on the island, left behind by Lindholm, but most of that had been picked up and carted off by souvenir hunters.

At high tides, there are several shell beaches on which to drag up your shore boat. At low tide the only good little beach is a small niche on the northeastern side of the island. The northern slope above the cliffs would be an ideal place to have an evening picnic, watch the ferryboats pass between Shaw and Orcas on their way through the islands, and view the setting sun over Orcas.

Shaw Landing

There is a small dock immediately east of the **Shaw ferry landing** where you can tie up and get gas and go up to the delightful general store at the head of the ramp. The 'Little Portion' Store and gas dock are run by Franciscan nuns who also act as ferry agents. This is the only commercial enterprise on Shaw. The installation also offers a laundromat, post office, gas pump, and a small Catholic chapel with an adjoining bell tower.

The nuns in their brown habits, whom tourists find fascinating to watch as they raise and lower the ferry transfer span, pride themselves on carrying specialty items not found in many larger stores. They also sell jams and crafts made by nuns from Our Lady of the Rock monastery and by other craftspersons on the island.

Shaw began having ferry service in the early 1930s, when the ferry stopped at a floating dock whenever it was flagged down. Once, the dock tipped up on one side as a Friday Harbor grocery store owner was attempting to board the ferry with a truckload of cattle and pigs. Truck and livestock landed in ten feet of saltchuck, the owner and the critters swam to shore and shortly thereafter, a new ferry landing was built at Shaw. In the late 60s, the flag system stopped and regular ferry service was instituted.

As you pass the ferry installation on Shaw, you may notice the Shaw Island derelict.

For the past several years, regular ferryboat riders have been watching the saga of this poor old abandoned boat, that seems to have a will of its own to survive.

State Marine Parks - Courtesies And The Laws

We're sure that you, like we, have come into a state marine park after a long haul, dead tired, hoping to find an available buoy—and discovered that some turkey has left a dinghy tied to one to reserve it while he goes out fishing!

Did you say "There oughta be a law?" Well, there is: it's RCW 43.51.040 and RCW 43.51.060.

These codes say such reserving of moorages is a no-no. The Parks and Recreation Commission publishes what is called an 'Administrative Code', which is also the law—spelled out a little more elaborately than the RCWs. So, here we will give you the quotes from Chapter 352-12 of the Washington Administrative Code. You might use this to win bets and settle arguments.

Section WAC 352-12-010 reads:

WAC 352-12-010—Moorage and use of marine facilities. (1) No person or persons shall moor or berth a vessel of any type in a commission-owned or operated park or marine area except in designated marine park areas and at designated facilities.

(2) Use of designated marine park areas and facilities by commercial vessels is prohibited except for the loading and unloading of passengers transported for recreation purposes: Provided, however, park managers and park rangers may allow extended or night moorage at any facility during the period September 15 through April 30, inclusive, if in the manager's or ranger's sole discretion suf-

ficient space is reasonably available therefor.

(3) In order to afford the general public the greatest possible use of marine park facilities, continuous moorage at a facility by the same vessel, person or persons shall be limited to three consecutive nights, unless otherwise posted by the commission at any individual facility or area.

(4) In order to maximize usable space at mooring floats, boaters shall, whenever necessary, moor their vessels as close as reasonably possible to vessels already moored. Rafting of vessels is also permitted, within posted limits, but not mandatory.

(5) Use of any state park marine facility shall be on a first-come, first-served basis only. Reserving or retaining space to moor or berth a vessel at any facility, by means of a dinghy or any method other than occupying the space by the vessel to be moored, shall not be permitted.

(6) Dinghies shall be tied up only in designated spaces on moorage floats.

(7) Open flames or live coals, or devices containing or using open flames, live coals or combustible materials, including but not limited to barbecues, hibachis, stoves and heaters, shall be permitted on state park floats or piers only when placed on a fireproof base and the fire is located away from fuel tanks and/or fuel vents. In case of dispute related to fire safety, the ranger shall make final determination.

Nobody seems to know who owns it. It was originally up on some supports in a little rocky crevice just east of the ferry dock where there are no houses. Although the windows of the boat were all broken out, it was still a rather attractive hull, somewhere around 20 to 24 feet long. Islanders would look to see if it was still there when the ferry left Shaw. They discussed over coffee when the owner was going to come and take it away.

The Franciscan nuns are ferry agents at Shaw Landing

Several years ago, high winds sent waves into the nook and after the storm abated, the boat sank in about six feet of water just offshore. There it stayed for about six months. Then one day the hulk appeared back on dry land again. Someone had rescued it. The owner perhaps? It was pulled up on the beach to a safer spot. There it sits, high and dry and rustier than ever. There are some stout lines securing it to nearby trees, and ferry riders still speculate on its future.

Point Hudson and Hudson Bay

Just east of the Shaw Landing, past a heavily timbered area, is a bight called **Hudson Bay**. This historically named, exposed bay has an elaborate private dock called Gratzer Dock in front of an older house and a warehouse.

Harney Channel

Named for Brigadier General William Selby Harney, stationed in the San Juans during the Pig War era, **Harney** separates Orcas and Shaw. Strong currents in the passage have tossed drift logs high onto beach rocks all along the wooded uninhabited northern shore of Shaw between Point Hudson and Hankin Point.

Reefnetters

The first time you come upon a reefnet rig in the San Juans, you'll swear that it's got to be a bunch of South Sea Islanders somehow transplanted here. The boats are so bizarre and primitive-looking they seem to be a relic of another age. That's because they are.

Indians, whose staple diet was fish in this area, didn't go out in their canoes with buzz bombs and spinning reels and patented fish-pole holders. When they wanted to get fish, they wanted a mess of fish — the kind of catch you get with nets. Using various kinds of locally grown fibers, they got to be artists at manufacturing very serviceable and extensive gear. They primarily used two kinds of fish traps, those strung across streams and narrow passages from the two shores and traps that were set between two boats.

When the white man came, he caught on pretty fast and copied the red man's techniques. Somewhere in the last half century, the land-based traps became illegal because they were too devastatingly effective. But the two-boat traps were permitted to continue. This system came to be known as reefnetting because nets were strung between two boats in water that was shallow enough to bunch up the schools of fish — in other words, over a reef.

The fish swim in and follow the slanting floor upwards. They can probably see that there is a narrow opening at the high end of the system, so they keep heading forward — salmon are not very long on logic, you see.

What they don't know is that there are watchful eyes looking down into the water from the high platforms. When the bulk of the passing fish are in sight, the fishermen scurry down the ladders and help draw up the corners of the net. From then on, it's a matter of scooping up the fish and tossing them into the holds of the boats. Fish-buying boats make regular runs to the various sets and pay spot cash for the fish.

Time was when reefnetting was very productive. Those were the days when the Fraser River run of salmon was numberless. But the gradual diminution of the big salmon runs and the competition of the modern-day technology has slowed the reefnet catch to a trickle.

Over the years, the number of Indian reefnetters has dwindled to a precious few. The paleface reef men have doggedly persisted in setting up their nets, almost as if impelled by instinct rather than business acumen. The income the reefnetters realize from their ancient craft varies from almost nil to expenses-plus-a-bit.

Hankin Point

Hankin Point, a not-too-clearly-defined point of land on the northeastern corner of Shaw, marks the entry into Upright Channel between Lopez and Shaw.

Picnic Cove

From Hankin Point to **Picnic Cove**, the shoreline is forested, rocky and primitive. Eagles soar in the area, searching for their daily rations.

Picnic Cove is a beautiful little inlet with low bank and sandy beaches and a good

We've talked to reefnetters. Why do they continue to do it? They shrug — why not? They've always done it. They love it. One suspects that even if they knew for certain they would get skunked, they would still go out and set their nets. The one clue we have is the obvious eagerness and enthusiasm of the crews. It seems to be a mix of three basic human drives: it is a custom, it is a business, and it is a sport.

You can see why it gets into their blood.

moorage in about 1½ fathoms at the head of the cove. There would be good protection from almost all prevailing winds. There is a tiny tombolo at the southwestern edge of the entrance to Picnic Cove.

Canoe Island

Leaving Picnic Cove, and to the southwest of it, is a larger island—privately owned—the site of **French Camp**. You can pass between **Canoe Island** and Shaw, staying close to Canoe, and have about 35 feet even at low tide. A long, kelp-covered reef reaches south from Shaw most of the way to Canoe Island, and a kelp bed leads north from Canoe, but the two do not meet. Just take the path between them and there should be no problem.

In the summertime you will undoubtedly see a number of young people hiking on Canoe Island and sailing, rowing, or canoeing in the surrounding waters. If you get close enough to hear them speaking, you may be surprised to hear they are conversing in French. Teenagers come from all over the country to this summer camp to learn French culture and get intensive training in the language in this lovely island setting.

And although it is a primitive spot and the youngsters live in teepees, they have the best of everything. The teepees are on wood platforms and have electric heat, with outlets for portable stereos and TVs; there is a heated swimming pool, tennis courts, an archery range and a library.

The youngsters learn folk dancing as well, and often perform in summer festivals and parades on neighboring islands. A family of several dozen raccoons on Canoe Island are nearly tame and they pester the teenagers to give them after-meal handouts.

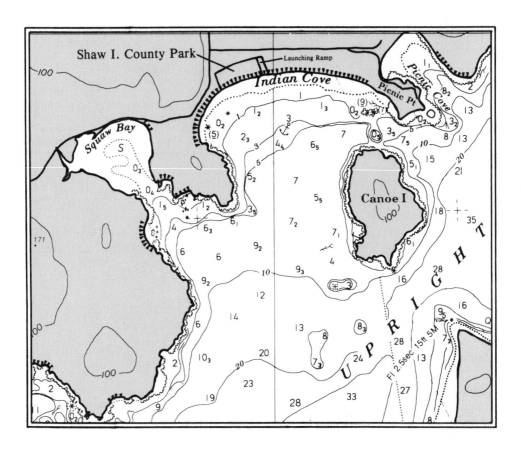

Eagles

It is a felony to kill or wound any of the protected species: Bald Eagles, Golden Eagles, Peregrine Falcons, Trumpeter and Whistler Swans. It is a serious offense even to OWN an eagle feather. Fines for killing and interfering with eagles can be as high as $10,000.

Both the National Wildlife Federation and the U.S. Fish and Wildlife Service offer $500 reward for information leading to the arrest of persons harming or destroying eagles.

It's far more intriguing just to watch them as they perch in tall trees along the shore, watching for a meal to swim by.

This is a private island and you need permission to go ashore. A local weekly newspaper carries a regular notice that there is no hunting and definitely no trespassing on Canoe Island.

If you choose not to go between Canoe Island and Shaw, but instead to stay in Upright Channel, be aware of a large kelp-covered rock 200 yards off the southwest tip of Canoe Island. It is well-marked on the chart and is obvious by the sailor's friend—kelp.

Indian Cove

Indian Cove is the site of the **Shaw Island County Park**, a 64-acre island paradise and favorite beachcombing spot for islanders.

The park begins about halfway along the shore of the semi-circular cove—at the boat-launching ramp, which is simply a paved strip down to the beach. To find the launching ramp, look for a red house with long, paneled windows trimmed in white and flanked by tall trees.

The county park beach is one of the best in the islands: a great place to launch canoes, kayaks, rowing boats of any kind, as well as a sensational place for cooped-up kids to let off steam and run and play.

On the beach is a gigantic, spherical-shaped rock. Behind that and up a grassy bank, you will find a picnic pavilion: look for the green walls and white roof with a high flagpole in front of the picnic shelter.

Picnic tables are plentiful and there are eight campsites and fresh water. Shaw Islanders hold some of their picnics and get-togethers at the park during the summer. The 'Round Shaw Row' begins and ends there the second Saturday each August and attracts scores of rowing, pulling and paddling boats of every description.

High point for kids, both grown up and pint-size, is a one-rope swing: a gigantic manila hawser with a jerky knot in the end. It dangles from a branch on a big old tree above the sand. A good push and you soar out over the waves one minute and back among the trees the next.

Naturally the park has a couple of county-code privies—bring paper, you never know.

There is considerable space for anchorage in Indian Cove in a good sandy bottom. While islanders love it, it is not a popular place for passing boaters, perhaps because it is exposed to southerlies—or maybe they just don't know about it.

Squaw Bay

You can hike from Indian Cove to the eastern shore of **Squaw Bay** where the sandy beach holds the summer sun's heat. If you're hardy, you might enjoy a swim in the late afternoon. But Squaw Bay is too shallow to offer much moorage. It is an interesting place to visit by shore boat. There is a lovely meadow at the northern end of the bay.

As you leave Squaw Bay headed southwesterly during fishing season (July to September), give the half-dozen reefnetting gears a wide berth, so as not to spook the salmon. The boats and their nets are well marked with buoys. As you curve past the rocky southern end of Shaw, you will find you have circumnavigated the island and are back at Hoffman Cove.

Shaw's swing for swingers?

68

AMONG THE WASPS

Doug Cardle, the Lopez Island historian, says that the **Wasp Islands** and **Wasp Passage** were named by the explorer, Navy Commander Charles Wilkes, in about 1838, after a warship that fought in the War of 1812. They weren't named after those pesky little stinging insects.

Even if the area hadn't been given that name as a memorial, it might have been applied by latter-day boaters who found the passages between Shaw and Orcas very annoying. There are rocks and reefs and islets and shoals which require skippers to sort of slalom through the spots unless they want to stay in the main channel of Wasp Passage.

The ferries, bound to and from Anacortes, Friday Harbor and Sidney, B.C., and various other stops, ply through this passage, but there is plenty of water for you to slide past them. Every once in a while, the ferries will encounter a tug with a few sections of logs in tow and the passengers will be treated to a display of seamanship that resembles brinksmanship.

Private boats leaving the Port of Friday Harbor and heading for the 'outer islands': Sucia, Matia, Patos, Waldron and the others—usually head north-north-west, just skirting Neck Point, between Low Island, and Shirt Tail Reef, which has a very conspicuous marker—a green diamond on a concrete pylon. Then they make a couple of doglegs between **Yellow** and **McConnell Islands** and scoot up past Jones Island. **(See chart inset.).**

Shirt Tail Reef

The **Shirt Tail Reef** marker, which has a flashing green four-second light, does indeed mark some nasty rocks north of it which are visible once the tide is down to two feet. Many novice or visiting boaters tend to get disoriented in the area and the reef is a boon to local marine repairmen.

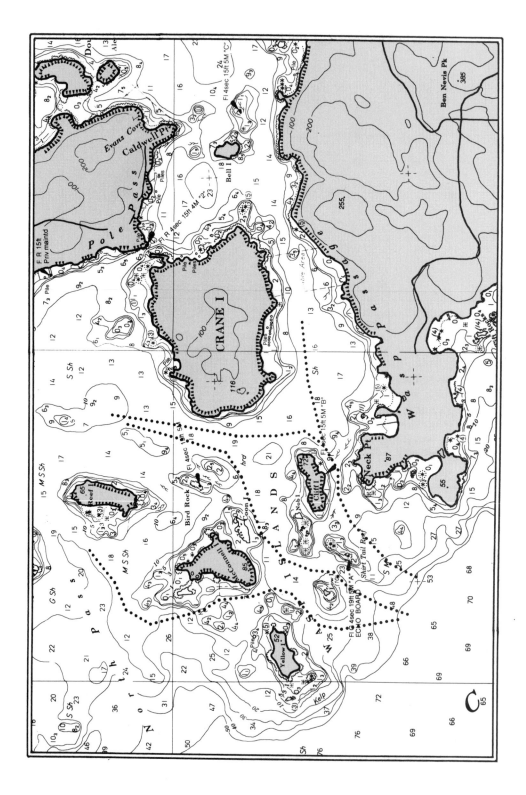

Low Island

Low Island is just that: a low island covered mainly with grasses. You can pass close to its eastern side when heading north between it and Shirt Tail Reef, but it is foul off the western shore. As you head north, note and note well the submerged rock off the southeastern shore of Yellow Island, another well-known keel-kisser. From Low Island, head toward the southwest point of McConnell in order to give a good clearance to the Yellow Island Rock. But you also have to keep off the northwest tip of McConnell, and then you can go back on your north northwest heading and it's clear sailing—or clear powering if you insist.

Passage

If you're heading for Deer Harbor, from Friday Harbor, you have a choice of several passages (see chart inset):

1. Go between Neck Point on Shaw and Cliff Island, then keep Crane Island on your right and head straight in.

2. Go between Shirt Tail Reef and Low Island, continue on this heading until you are near McConnell and Coon Island, head east a bit, and then pass between well-marked Bird Rock and Crane.

Kayakers enjoying Wasp Passage during a calm morning.

3. Or go between Yellow and McConnell, pass the northern end of McConnell and then past **Reef Island** through North Pass and on in.

4. Or make up your own combinations of the above. There is considerable nastiness around that cluster of rocks known as **Nob** and **Cliff Islands**. Local boaters can tiptoe between them by staying close to Cliff Island, but unless you have need to, don't try it in a deep draft vessel.

Let's Not Hype Hypothermia

When you're cruising San Juan Islands waters and you get into tight situations you might find yourself remembering all of the baleful things you've heard about how fast people can die of hypothermia if they fall overboard. Phrases like "If you don't get picked up right away, you're a goner!" get kicked around. We've heard estimates on survival time in the saltchuck from five minutes to 15 minutes.

Well, we think it's time to talk turkey — cold turkey — about hypothermia in local waters. What are the facts? We think that exposure is a serious matter. A person who finds himself in the water needs prompt rescue — he does not need panic back on board! And, above all, he needs to avoid personal disorientation.

Let's look at the facts: in 50° water — the average temperature in the San Juans including winter — you can last up to four hours, even if you are wearing only light clothing!

If you are floundering around out there, waiting to be rescued, you are probably in greater danger of being hurt or drowned by an improperly handled rescue boat than dying of exposure. This means that you want the people who are still on board to make a nice easy 180° turn and come up to you at dead slow speed, out of gear, and as close as practicable. You can help them by remaining calm yourself.

Your first big problem is to stay afloat. Now, you have probably thought that wearing a life jacket was too wimpy for good old seafarin' you. So you've got to tread water. This exercise wastes body heat so you now only have two hours to be rescued.

Have you learned 'downproofing?' That's the technique that says you can float better if you put your head down into the water. If you learned it — forget it. That's the advice of the survival experts in the United States Coast Guard. Keeping your head wet will cut your survival time exactly in half.

Good sense dictates that if you can possibly do it, pull your shirt or jacket up over the top of your head.

If you're a swimmer, even a good swimmer, don't strike out for shore unless it is very close by. The best swimmers can get eight-tenths of a mile, average swimmers only 100 yards, before you use up all of your heat — and sink. A good rule of thumb: the distance to shore is twice as far as it looks.

Stay put!

Navy doctors recommend what is called the H.E.L.P. position — the letters stand for 'Heat Escape Lessening Posture'. It isn't hard to remember — it's the fetal position — all huddled up. It's the way you warm yourself up when you crawl into a cold bed at night. In the H.E.L.P. position, if you can find a way to

Cliff Island

Cliff Island marker displays a couple of black diamonds and is far enough out to warn you of the ugly rock near shore. In this part of Wasp Passage there are few homes on the heavily forested Shaw shore. Coming up on the left, Crane Island has summer-type cabins above the beaches. We checked to see if we could find the pilings shown on the chart to be in the little bight on the southern shore of Crane, but none were visible.

stay afloat, you now have up to four hours to hitchhike.

And now a word for the folks who are still on board and are going to rescue the person overboard. Needless to say, if someone falls in, you should YELL LIKE HELL! Be sure the person at the helm hears it! And you people still aboard make sure someone keeps an eye on the person in the water all the time.

Second thing: throw something that floats overboard. Throw a whole bunch of somethings! Life jackets, of course. Flotation pillows, naturally. Fenders. Empty plastic jugs. Styrofoam ice chests. Wooden or tubular deck chairs. Plastic tackle boxes. Oars. Your own jacket and hat if they float, the person may be able to add them to his or her clothing. Watch your aim, of course. If you're towing a dinghy, cast it loose.

In other words: litter the water. Anything that will float will help the person float. The things he or she can't get to will mark the spot.

Now a tip to the helmsman. Of course, the worst thing you could do is chop the throttle and coast. You can't make a decent turn that way. But let's be sensible—that's the first thing you are going to do as an instinctive reaction—unless you are some kind of real cool head at the helm.

If you do put the boat into idle, remember—you have time to be careful.

Don't go astern—boats back up far more slowly than they go forward. Besides, you are coming at the guy with a spinning prop. Keep her in forward gear and make a good efficient half-speed turn. If you can see the floater's head, he or she is probably safe for a few minutes, at least. Come up on the person dead slow. If he or she is conscious, allow some space to toss a line or reach a boat hook out to him or her. Be careful not to run up over the person—remember how you lose the mooring buoy when you get too close to it?

If the person in the water isn't able to cooperate, somebody's got to go in and help, somebody wearing a life jacket and warm clothing. It might be a good idea to take along a spare flotation device.

What about a lifeline? It probably isn't a good idea to tie it to the rescuer. Better he should hold it in his hand and let somebody on deck pay out the slack. Don't worry if the line isn't a heavy mooring line, it won't take many pounds of pull to tow a couple of floating people alongside.

One more tip—which you've probably already thought of—don't be bashful—get on the VHF and yell 'MAYDAY'. The Coast Guard may not be able to get a boat to you in time, but there are bound to be a number of boaters in your area who will rally around to help.

As you pass Crane, heading eastward, you can encounter some devilish currents and tide rips in the area of the cable crossing. There is a rock off the eastern end of Crane Island and the chart shows deep enough water to pass between it and Crane, but the line of kelp discouraged us from trying to make it through. Too often kelp can indicate hidden rocks. The chart makes the pass look worse than it actually is. Just hug the Shaw shoreline staying in at least four fathoms.

Crane Island was apparently named for cranes, however, since there aren't cranes in the islands, whoever named it must have mistakenly named it after seeing a heron.

Bell Island

You can easily pass between **Bell Island** and Crane, Bell and Orcas, or Bell and Shaw. The marker, just east of Bell, is marked with green diamonds and there is a lot of kelp nearby. Keep well south of the marker.

Several of the smaller islands in Wasp Passage are owned by the U.S. and are marked restricted as wildlife refuges. **Low** and **Nob Islands** are among those, and are less than an acre in area.

Nob Island is a beautiful little high-domed island with many trees and dramatic snags—some of them look like giant deer antlers.

McConnell, Reef, Crane and Coon Islands are privately owned. **Reef Island** has real, boat-holding reefs on the west side—watch your depth and chart to avoid them.

Who Was Charlie Wilkes And What Was His Bag?

He was a navy commander who spent only three days in the San Juan Islands in July in 1841. The U.S. Congress had sent him on an exploration which was rather ambitious: to look over the area, make soundings, and put some names to the geographic features.

In 1848, he produced a chart he had drawn of, (get this): 'The Archipelago of Arro, Gulf of Georgia, Ringgold's Channel (now Rosario Strait), Oregon Territory'.

He called the San Juan Islands 'The Navy Archipelago'.

It was, he said, comprised of 25 islands. He ran down the roster of famous American naval heroes and named everything in sight.

Mt. Constitution was on Hull's Island — now Orcas. It had two deep indentations: Ironsides Bay and Guierierre Bay — now East Sound and West Sound.

Rodgers Island was the name he gave to the island that the British had called San Juan.

East of Rodgers Island was Chauncey Island which now has the alias of Lopez.

Some of the names he dreamed up were rather romantic. In his history of his travels, he has this:

"(President's Passage) passes into Ontario Roads between Rodgers and Chauncey Islands and Little Belt Passage; on the north, the waters flow through Frolic Straits into Ironsides Bay, and around the Macedonian Crescent ..." (the last three names were taken from historic British Navy Ships.)

'Macedonian Crescent'! 'Frolic Straits'! Where are you now, where are you now?

'Dream cabin' on the beach at Coon Island.

Coon Island

This is one of the most delightful private places in the San Juans. There is a plea-sant passage between tiny Coon and McConnell, and the smaller island has a dock in this two-fathom passage. On the north side of Coon you will be treated to one of the most attractive scenes in the whole San Juan area: a neat little beach with a modest cabin. It is one of the settings we look at wistfully every time we pass it.

Yellow Island

Yellow Island is owned by the Nature Conservancy and is open to the public for sightseeing. This remarkable island gets its name, probably, from the brilliant fields of golden buttercups which carpet the southern slopes of the island each spring.

Lew and Tib Dodd purchased the island in 1946, and lived a halcyon life in a log cabin they built of driftwood planks. It nestles among the rocks between the beach and the forest on the south side of the island overlooking Wasp Passage and San Juan Channel. Farther around to the west they built a guest house and a primitive sauna which was recently torn down. The heavy-beamed, low-ceilinged, main cabin was not only built but furnished from tide-given lumber and other treasures. The cedar shake roof was hand-hewn from driftwood cedar chunks.

Lew never left the island for more than short trips to Deer Harbor or Friday Har-bor for mail and groceries, and never to stay overnight. He died in 1960 at the cabin, and his ashes are buried at his favorite island spot, Hummingbird Hill. There is a charming and heartwarming tribute to the departed owner. It is a bronze plaque, set in rock on a high promontory, with a poem by Don Blanding which expressed the feelings Dodd had about life. We were tempted to print it here, but decided that might diminish the emotional impact of coming upon it in its natural place.

Tib lived alone on the island for six months each year until 1978. She rowed or ran a small outboard boat to Deer Harbor for her groceries and mail until she was in her late 70s.

Yellow Island was purchased by The Nature Conservancy in April, 1980, and it has since been open to the public on a limited basis. It is not a picnicking and camping area, but is simply for nature lovers to enjoy. Brilliant red Indian paint brush, blue camas and the spectacular buttercups cover the island's meadows in wild disarray at the peak of their spring blooming. Hummingbirds dart among the flowers to get their share of sweet nectar. Visitors may wander the many trails interlacing the island, but are asked not to stray from the paths as the fragile island shows every footprint.

There is no dock or public mooring buoy in the little cove on the southern side of Yellow Island, the best moorage. Spits extend from both the east and west points of the island, and the western side is foul about 300 yards offshore. Drop the hook in the south cove where the water is safe and fair, the bottom sandy, and is good holding ground. Row ashore where you will be greeted by the island's caretakers and enjoy the original beauty of the San Juans in this microcosmic island.

Bird Rock

Another major marker in the Wasps—north of Wasp Passage—between McConnell and Coon, Reef and Crane Islands—is **Bird Rock**. Marked with an orange diamond mounted on four cans on the rock, the reef extends north for about 100 yards and is hidden at all but the lowest tides. Surrounded by kelp beds, it catches its share of unwary boaters. Keep clear of the kelp and you'll avoid the reef.

The Dodd home on Yellow Island

OUTLOOK INN
ORCAS ISLAND, WASHINGTON

ORCAS - THE TREFOIL ISLAND

It would be an oversight to discuss the geography of an area without talking about the people who inhabit it. And it is important for visitors to get some feeling for the people.

So let's wade courageously into a sea of glittering generalities about the folks of Orcas Island, variously called the 'tourist island' and the 'big island'—it is, after all, one square mile larger than San Juan.

One of the encouraging facts of such an endeavor is that no matter what an observer would say about the folks of that trident-shaped island (unless it was too scandalous), there would be locals who would agree as well as disagree, which is one way of saying there is less homogeniety about Orcasites than there is Lopezians.

Partly because the island is spread out, like a flattened but bumpy orange peel, there are several little population centers which have individual characters. For example, folks who live in the village of Olga do not often come into contact with the people from Deer Harbor, unless there is an island-wide public meeting of some sort—or maybe a high school football game.

Major shopping is done in the village of Eastsound, which is at the head of East Sound, although there are several stores in the other communities. There is no easy access from sea, however. There are no docks or floats for transient boaters. All you can do is anchor out and dinghy ashore. The business community of Eastsound has discussed for decades the necessity of putting in some kind of a facility so they can compete with Friday Harbor for the boaters' dollars, but nothing has been done, possibly because a bad winter storm might wipe out such an endeavor.

It wasn't always that way, for in the late 1800s there was a wharf extending far out into the Sound for steamers and early day ferries to load and unload passengers and goods.

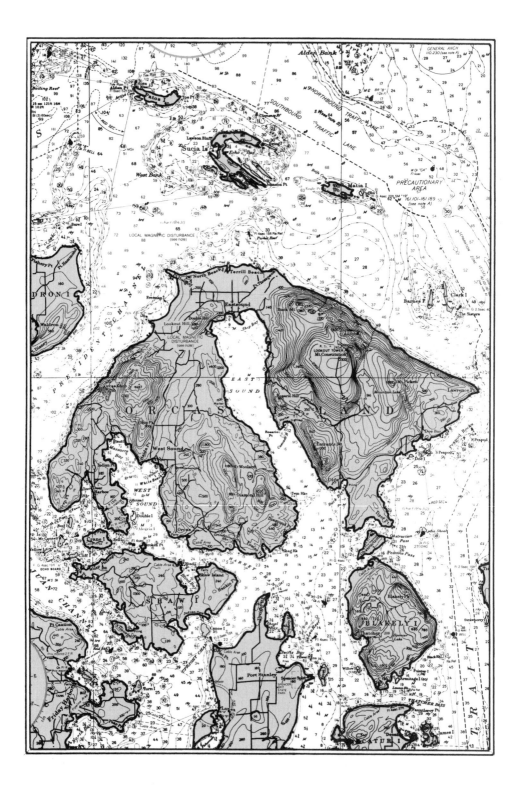

Turtleback Mountain Thermals

On warm days, the air over Crow Valley in the low area east of Turtleback Mountain on Orcas becomes heated and rises to the top of the mountain. At this point, it mixes with the cooler air and creates 'thermals' which cause avalanches of wind to come down off the north side of the mountain. These winds can be strong and very capricious. Sailing along the northwest shore of Orcas, especially in the late afternoon, can tax a skipper's talents. It will be calm for a moment, and then come whistling up to 20 knots. The wind will come directly down off the mountain for a bit, then without any hesitancy, change direction by 20 or 30 degrees. If you want to train your crew to make quick sail trims, this is an ideal place for it. If you want to avoid the capricious winds, you should stay at least a half-mile offshore.

Eastsound is the heart of Orcas Island. The schools are there, and the library, the banks, movie theater, marvelous historical museum, the sheriff's office, nearby airport, medical center, dentist, service stations, drug store, shopping center, bakery, grocery store and specialty shops, restaurants and lots of real estate offices.

There are four post offices on Orcas, a further factor in dividing the island community. The daily ritual of 'getting the mail' tends to create a sense of community when folks all meet at the central post office in Friday Harbor or at Lopez or Shaw. But Deer Harbor, Orcas village, Olga and Eastsound all have separate post offices and there are even four zip codes on Orcas.

The ferry lands at Orcas village, which is convenient for the ferry captains. But, once ashore, the driver who lives in Doe Bay has almost an hour drive to get home. Because the roads are winding, particularly around the several mountains, the speed limit for all of Orcas Island is 35 miles per hour. (It's 45 miles per hour on all the other islands.) In winter, when the infrequent snow comes, the roads can become almost impassable.

Back in the 'good old days' prior to World War I, Orcas Island was renowned for its orchards of apples, prunes and pears. Fruit-growing was a prime island industry. When eastern Washington growers began to work harder, the orchardists on Orcas found their markets had been usurped and commercial fruit-growing came to an end. There are still thousands of fruit trees on the island, uncared for, but still producing excellent yields.

But times change, and now the largest number of people on Orcas work in tourist-related jobs, the main Orcas industry. A growing number of cottage industries are springing up around the island—pottery, jewelry, woodworking, boatbuilding, weaving, and other wool-related ventures, to mention a few.

The major employer on Orcas—Rosario Resort—has in recent years opted to employ Asiatic 'boat people' in many of its service positions.

As the fame of the island continues to grow, the demand for vacation and retirement housing burgeons and real estate has become a major business.

Like the other San Juan Islands, the educational and net-worth levels of the residents is much above statewide averages. Outstanding, even nationally famous representatives of almost all of the professions and arts have retired—some in early middle age—on Orcas.

The days of coping with the inconvenience of transportation island-wide will have to come to an end. Then, the dream of some of the Orcas folks: a shuttle ferry across Eastsound, a ferry dock with service to the mainland from the eastern leaf, or better highways—will materialize.

And while Orcas did not have the tempestuous start of the Pig War, as San Juan Island did, it early became a resort island, with tents blanketing the Crescent Beach shoreline well over a century ago with mainland folks trying even then, as now, to escape from urban pressures on an island.

And, of course, for centuries past the Indians came to Orcas from all over the West Coast to enjoy the more laid-back life in the islands—a tradition that will apparently continue indefinitely.

When you study the profile of Orcas Island, you are reminded of one of those Rorschach ink blots. Two deep sounds nearly cut the island in thirds, leaving similar, but not duplicate by any means, land and water masses on either side. Orcas has some of the most delightful anchorages and some of the most cantankerous expanses of seawater to be found anywhere.

There are tiny coves and bights, almost pristine and untouched, resorts to suit the most sophisticated tastes; stretches of primitive, uninhabited, densely forested coastline where steep cliffs add to unpredictable thermal winds, and equally unpredictable currents that can carry boaters far off course.

Since we've arbitrarily decided to make all of our projected cruises from San Juan Channel, let's do Orcas clockwise, starting at ...

Spring Passage (Use Chart #18434)

Beginning at the southwestern tip of Orcas, **Steep Point**, we begin to head northerly in **Spring Passage**—a deep passage less than a half-mile wide which runs in a north-south direction between Orcas and Jones Islands. This western shore of Orcas is steep and forested, with rocky bluffs and only a few houses which have been built

Exploring tidepools

in what often look like inaccessible, isolated spots. There is a shallow in the northerly portion of Spring Passage at 5¼ fathoms which is known for good bottom fishing in the otherwise deeper channel, which averages 11 to 35 fathoms.

We once caught a 23-pound red snapper on this rock. It isn't easy to find the spot, however—we still have trouble getting it on our depth sounder. We suggest you strike an imaginary line from the white beacon in the passage to the visible shoreline on Orcas. You are looking for the surrounding depth of about 80 feet. If you are too deep, drift a bit ESE until you get the right reading. We also recommend you get a currently hot cod jig at one of the local marinas. Another tip: local fishermen

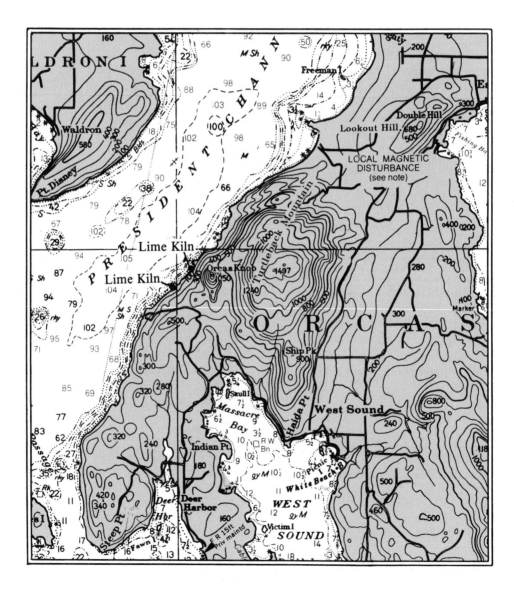

Some Thoughts on Kids & Life Jackets

Kids are critters with wonderful agility and sense of balance, right? So are dogs and cats. Practically every boater who cruises regularly with a hound or tabby on board will tell you that they do fall overboard; they misjudge distances, they lose their footing, they do dumb things. Adults do dumb things. Kids dope off. The big difference is that youngsters usually have a parent around to keep an eye on them and participate in the never-ending battle to keep them in life jackets.

Several years ago we heard a horror story about a young boy who was drowned and we still get nightmares about it. This incident involved some very capable sailors including a well-trained boy. He always wore his life jacket when he was on deck. Always, that is, except for one terrible, fatal moment.

The story is that he took the jacket off when he went below to use the head. The pump on the thing wouldn't work, so he got a bucket with a line to get sea water to flush it out. He was only going to be on deck for a minute. He went to toss the bucket over. The bucket caught a wave, the line snaked out faster than he had expected, it must have caught him around the wrist—in a moment he was gone. For some reason, the person on the helm didn't realize he had been on deck. By the time they missed him, it was too late. He was never found.

That's all we know about the story. It may not even be true. But it sounds all too possible.

That's why all kids—even young teenagers—wear life jackets when they are on our deck—even to bring up a cup of coffee for the person on the helm. A lot of times, we have to be insistent and upset tolerant parents. If a visiting tad goes to his folks and wails, "Dad, do I have to ...?" we get the adult off the hook: "It's a rule. You obey it or you stay below." If the papa or mama doesn't agree, they stay ashore from then on.

Now, here are some suggestions. First of all, you don't have to load the kid down with a big old cork jacket. We wouldn't like that either. When we adults work the foredeck, we wear a float-coat or a Stearns-type vest. The float-coat is fine for bad weather. The Stearns-type vest is a good compromise for warm weather. So, have a couple of them on board if you regularly take kids out.

Secondly, if it's your own boat and they're your kids, you owe them the example of subscribing to the rule yourself. If you pick up a PFD when you leave the cockpit, the kids won't think you're being unfair.

It seems, too, that when small kids are playing below, they should be allowed to shed the things—particularly if they're the bulky kind.

Sure, it's a drag to be constantly checking and reminding. but it's got to be worth it.

After all, kids are kinda hard things to replace.

say, "Get the proper spot, fish for 15 minutes. If you don't get a fish in that length of time, you can be pretty sure they aren't biting for some reason. They're down there, though!"

West Side Orcas Island

As you make a northerly circuit of Orcas Island, starting in Spring Passage, you will find you are in for about four miles of breathtaking, but mostly uninhabited coastline.

The mountains on this northwesterly side of Orcas come almost straight down to the sea in many places, and they are responsible for some of the often tempestuous thermals, which can be so confusing to boaters.

Occasionally you will see boats hovering just offshore, fishing. But there are few coves or moorages until you near **West Beach**. You will also note that chart #18435 peters out on you just abaft Orcas Knob and you need to switch to #18432.

The chart shows an unnamed bay just northeast of the 48° latitude line. Known locally as **Cormorant Bay**, it is the site of the former Totem Council of Girl Scouts Camp, and is now privately owned. The chart shows a dolphin and a rock which bares at a three-foot tide in the center of the cove.

There is a log breakwater and dock in the south end of the cove, and a large house which was once the camp's headquarters. You could probably dart into this bay for a brief time to ride out a storm, if need be—but you won't hear the Girl Scouts singing around the campfire. On the other hand, nobody will try to sell you cookies!

Just beyond the next tiny point on the chart, there is a county road end which you can spot with binoculars. The road end is public access, but the uplands on either side of the access area are privately owned, so your beachcombing is limited to just the road end beach. As there is no anchorage in this place, it is of interest only if you have a small boat to pull up on shore. The road end does not have a launching ramp, but you could probably put in—or take out—a kayak, canoe or small rowboat, hand-carried, of course.

Lime Kilns

Cruising along this remote stretch of Orcas' west side, with its steep, forested

Limestone Mining On Orcas

Lime became a big business on Orcas just about the turn of the century. The 1901 supplement to the San Juan Islander describes the fledgling industry in glowing terms:

"The development of the west side of Orcas Island has been greatly stimulated by the operations of the Island Lime Company, and when this institution reaches the position of importance and activity it is destined to enjoy, the people of this county will realize the wonderful possibilities of the future.

"The representative and leading institution engaged in the lime industry upon Orcas Island, and the second largest in this county (the largest was the Roche Harbor Lime and Cement Company on San Juan) is that of the Island Lime Company, located at the west side of Orcas Island near Deer Harbor. This company was organized and began active operations in April, 1900, and has been running continuously since that time. It employs about 15 men and is producing over 25,000 barrels of lime per annum."

The article goes on to explain that the lime is said to be the purest manufactured commercially in the world—99.15% pure carbonate of calcium—and carries the brand name Imperial.

Old lime kiln on Orcas' west shore

"This company, although of very recent introduction into the commercial world, has been so successful in its operations that its product is finding a large and growing demand in San Francisco and Honolulu—so much so that with present facilities it is unable to meet the trade with a sufficient supply. Preparations are now underway to enlarge the plant and meet demands— the active management of the plant is in the hands of Mr. W.B. Auger, a gentleman of high business ability and capacity, and one not to be deterred by any obstacle in introducing his product in any field and let the business world know the superior quality of the article he manufactures. He is one of San Juan County's most active and professional businessmen and deeply interested in the advancement of the county's industrial and commercial interests."

Although lime kilns are mentioned occasionally in Orcas Island histories, we were unable to find the reason for the demise of the Island Lime Company which began with such enthusiastic support from the community. All that is left are the picturesque remains of the west side's once profitable lime kilns.

Lover's Cove graffiti

bluffs can be intriguing, and as the water is deep, you can go close inshore almost all the way.

About 1¼ miles north of Cormorant Bay is the first of two abandoned lime kilns. You can locate it on your chart by looking for the 500-foot unnamed knob, about a mile southwest of **Orcas Knob**. There is a notation offshore on the chart which reads 'M S Sh', referring to the sea bottom characteristics. Draw a line from the top of that knob to the letters on the chart and along that line, on shore, is the relic kiln.

As you cruise past you can see part of the stone chimney has fallen away, exposing the masonry of the inside. It's a real photo subject. You can also see the remains of a shack on the beach. Up above it and slightly to the north is the ruins of another shack and tumble-down fence.

Just a little under a half-mile from this old kiln, you will find another one. You will see it on the first real shoreline you have encountered beyond Cormorant Bay. There is an old log shelter just beyond it on the beach.

About the turn of the century these lime kilns were big business and there were great expectations for their growth which for reasons we don't know never materialized.

Lovers Cove

Lovers Cove is a lovely spot and one of the few possible anchorages along this stretch of the Orcas west shore. Try as we will, we cannot find any explanation for the name. It must have been coined in a previous generation when young people didn't have drive-ins for their cars—or, horrors—campers!

This trysting place would attract only the hardiest of amorous couples—it involves a long hike over some very high ground. By the time they got to the spot, they would likely be so pooped they would have to content themselves to holding hands. It does have one thing going for it—it would be private.

It also has one of the few bits of graffiti in all of the San Juans: someone has spray-painted the words 'Lovers Cove' on the outermost rock. A reef extends out from shore to the rocks which are visible even at high tide. There is a nice beach in here and the spot is a favorite one for scuba divers as well as lovers. About 500 yards north of Lovers Cove, in the next bight, there are three log dolphins and a cabin on the beach. This is the first real habitation in the three miles from the public access road near Cormorant Bay.

West Beach

West Beach is a resort on a gently curving sandy beach with housekeeping cabins,

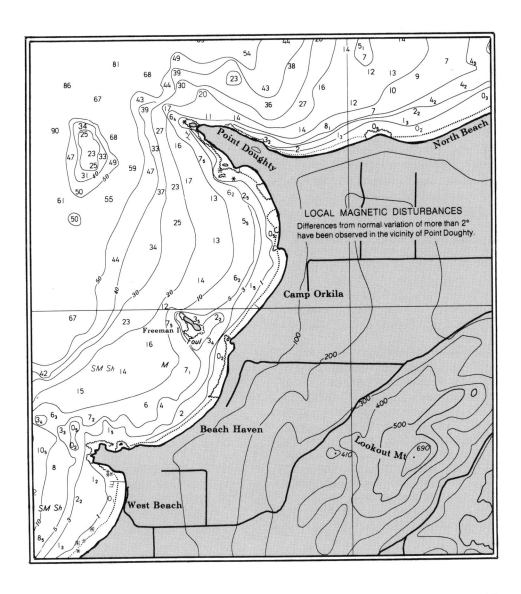

trailer accomodations and a campground. There is a road leading in and the spot is a favorite for summer visitors by land or sea. A long dock extends out into the water and you can stop by for gas, seasonal or overnight moorage, boat rentals, water and boat launching. The resort also has a grocery store, ice, bait, outboard repairs, scuba air, propane, laundry, showers and restrooms. There are mooring buoys owned by the resort. The resort owners boast "the finest fishing in the San Juans".

Peninsula

As you cruise northeasterly, you will notice both on the chart—and by looking—a peninsula just beyond West Beach. A kelp-covered reef extends several hundred yards offshore. Notice the depths here: 0_2 and 0_5, which means two to five feet at mean lower low water. If you are running close in, you should watch your depth sounder and stay in between 50 to 65 feet if you want to avoid the shallows—and running aground.

This little peninsula is tipped by a remarkable series of ramps and walkways built by an elderly pair of gentlemen. They wanted a convenient path to their waterfront

Orcas Island Indians

Very early Orcas settlers were the Indians, and the wonderful 1901 Supplement to the San Juan Islander claims that only Orcas had an important Indian history.

"Of all the islands, Orcas is the only one with important Indian history and some contend that there are traces here of the prehistoric people of North America. When the white men came upon the scene here the Indians of the flathead tribe inhabited the land and many tales of bloody encounters with the Stickeens, a warlike race of British Columbia, were told by the old men and women. A special mention is made of these matters in the sketch of East Sound and West Sound. Many stone relics—tools and vessels—have been picked up in various places, and implements of bone curiously wrought, and countless flint arrow and spearheads have been found. This is more especially noticeable at East Sound and the country between there and West Sound."

Ethan Allen, a former Orcas Island school superintendent who later moved to Waldron Island, left his Indian artifacts to the Orcas Island Historical Museum where they are housed in a special room. The fascinating museum is well worth a visit.

Edith McLachlan, a lifelong resident of Deer Harbor, writes of the early Indians on Orcas in an enchanting little book called 'They Named It Deer Harbor', which is filled with Deer Harbor history.

She said that when the first white men arrived in Deer Harbor there were Indians living in long houses close to the beach at the head of the harbor. The houses were anywhere from 40 to 100 feet or more long, and 14 to 20 feet wide, built of thick cedar planks.

"The core of the social structure of the family was three generations and they all lived together in the long houses," she wrote.

Indians of the San Juans were mostly Lummis, a peace-loving tribe, but Orcas was the battleground of many fights with the warring northern tribes of British Columbia who wanted to capture the hard-

where they could enjoy the scenery. One of the old fellows is confined to a wheelchair, so the covered ramps are in the nature of a facility for the handicapped.

There has been a storm of controversy over these walkways. Some of the neighbors have objected to their presence and the county planning commission has been trying to persuade the men to make them a trifle less conspicuous, perhaps by removing portions of them.

Just around the hook from these ramp-covered rocks there is a reef with barren rocks visible at low tide as indicated on the chart. This beach has a gently sloping bottom which would make convenient anchorage on calm days.

Beach Haven

Beach Haven Resort is tucked back along this low bank waterfront. There are vacation cabins with boats, motors and mooring buoys for guests only.

Freeman Island

Freeman Island is a one-third-acre island offshore between Beach Haven and

working Lummis as slaves.

"One dark night men from a northern tribe landed on the north shore of Orcas Island, probably at what we now call West Beach. The brave Northerners succeeded in greatly surprising our Indians. Another battle was at West Sound Bay. There the northerners practically annihilated the insufficiently equipped tribes. The Orcas Island Indians nearly became a memory in that one great battle. Massacre Bay, now West Sound Bay, was named after this battle. Also from this battle came the names of two islands in Massacre Bay, Skull Island and Victim Island (now both state park land).

"An early tradition states that Skull Island was named by early explorers or settlers who had visited the island and had found numerous bones, skulls and many skeletons. Victim Island, it is said, derived its name from early settlers who claimed that great torture was inflicted on one of the Orcas Indians by the northerners before they made off with most of the canoes and the young women.

Massacre Point (now Indian Point) was named from that great battle."

Indians in the area lived on fish which they caught both in traps and reefnets, and by hunting and gathering plants. "They picked berries, wild roots (camas, garlic and onion), which they roasted and dried. They dug clams and oysters, hunted deer and snared wild fowl by means of nets stretched on poles near the shores. Herring eggs were obtained by weaving branches about a rock and letting the herring spawn in the artificial nesting places; then the branches were lifted out of the water. These branches were then placed in the sun so that the eggs could dry," McLachlan wrote.

Other Indians came to the islands during the summer, mainly to gather berries and wild roots and to hunt enough food to tide them over during the winter. And some stories have it that Indians came to the islands just to relax and enjoy — they were the first tourists.

Camp Orkila. It's owned by the U.S. Fish and Wildlife Service, but is not posted so you can go ashore there.

There is good anchorage in muddy sand between Freeman and Orcas in about 20 feet of water, then row to Freeman. The beaches are rocky but you can land the dinghy and then search for a spot to climb the steep island sides to reach the trails across the top. It is a bit of a challenge to find the best way up the cliffs, but there is a spot on the west side where you can scramble up rocky sand and reach the island's narrow spine.

Since Freeman is close to the YMCA camp at Orkila, and the kids paddle out there, the paths on top of the island are well-worn. Steep 20 to 30-foot cliffs rim the perimeter of the tiny island and it is pinched in at the middle by two ravines. It would not be an easy island for the very young or the very old to enjoy firsthand.

But it is none the less charming, with a knoll on the western end with a great view north toward the Strait of Georgia, Waldron, Patos, Sucia and the Canadian Gulf Islands. There is a bench mark on the top of this knoll, just before it gives way to the rocks below.

At the cinched-in waist of the island, there is a steel pipe about two-feet long driven into the earth. Its purpose is not clear, but perhaps it was for a mooring at one time. There are stunted trees, including madrona, firs and cedars on the island, as well as a good supply of underbrush.

Tide pools abound on the surrounding black rock beaches, with only one sandy beach on the eastern edge. It would be good to think that Freeman Island had something to do with humanism, but the island was actually named for a sailmaker, S.D. Freeman, on a ship in the Charles Wilkes expedition.

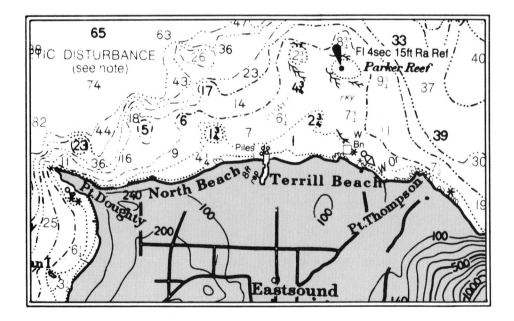

Freeman Island - public land

Point Doughty

Point Doughty, at the N.W. tip of Orcas, is a 60-acre Department of Natural Resources Park with a major drawback—there is virtually no access. There are no trails or roads in from land, so the only way to get there is by boat. But the area offshore is fraught with rocks, swift currents, kelp and constant waves to discourage all but the most determined small boater. On a calm day at slack water you could anchor south of the point and dinghy in, but landing is difficult. Some kayakers and canoeists do use the camp occasionally, which has picnic tables, campsites, a pit toilet, fire rings, but no water.

Some of the kids from nearby Camp Orkila hike to the camp on a private trail, making Point Doughty practically their own campground.

North Shore

The North Shore of Orcas, from Point Doughty to **Point Thompson**, has several resorts: Glenwood, North Beach Inn, Smuggler's Villa and Captain Cook, formerly Bartel's. In addition to the resorts, the low bank waterfront along Terrill Beach makes the north shore prime residential property.

The resorts all offer moorage of some sort for guests, but they are not your basic, drop-in marinas.

Glenwood Inn, the most westerly resort in this stretch, has housekeeping cottages and mooring buoys for guests. North Beach Inn has similar arrangements. Next in line is Smuggler's Villa which is a condominium resort with moorage privileges for boats up to 28 feet at adjacent Smuggler's Villa Marina.

Captain Cook, formerly Bartel's Resort, has opted not to provide a full-service marina.

If you are one of the avid fishermen who used to rent boats at Bartel's, you pro-

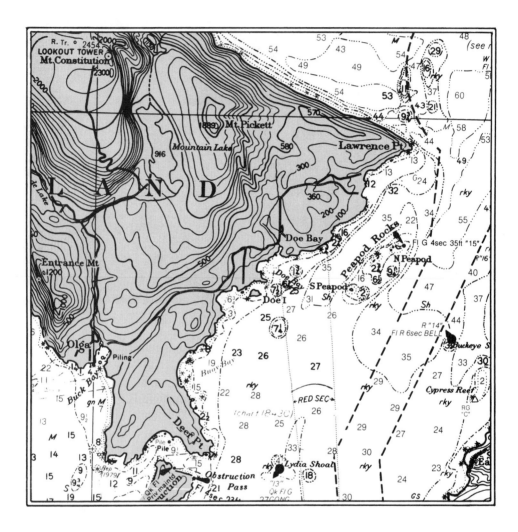

bably have fond memories of the place. Islanders still refer to the place as Bartel's.

Just offshore about a half-mile is **Parker Reef**, well-marked with a flashing four-second light mounted at 15 feet and a radar reflector. This is the boundary of the shallows which extend all along Orcas' north shore. There is good fishing in this area.

The rocky reef extends about 110 yards in all directions from the light except on the east side where it extends about 160 yards. Kelp covers the area between it and the shore and there are several shoal spots within the ten-fathom curve, both south and west.

Point Thompson

From Point Thompson east to **Raccoon Point** and on to **Lawrence Point**, Orcas again becomes steep and forested with no bays, bights, coves, beaches or good mooring spots, and because there are no roads into this steep northeast coast, it is virtually uninhabited.

Raccoon Point is the only named spot along this entire coast which tumbles from the 2,500-foot top of Mount Constitution to the sea in less than one mile. Strong, gusty winds often sweep this area.

Lawrence Point

Lawrence Point is the easternmost tip of Orcas and is known for both its good fishing and its rough waters. An unnamed shallow bank just off the point accounts for both reputations. The point was named by Wilkes for Capt. James Lawrence who pleaded "Don't give up the ship" as he lay dying in the War of 1812. (His men gave up anyway.)

At one time there must have been a cable from the mainland that rose out of Rosario Strait at Lawrence Point. You can see a weather-beaten old 'Cable Crossing' sign on shore.

Around Lawrence Point and to the southwest is a good-sized indentation—we hestitate to actually call it a bay—the chart shows a road end and a chimney, with shallow water a fair way offshore. On shore there are a dozen cabins with a boat launch.

This is the site of the former Sea Acres resort which about 30 years ago was a

Beachcomber's treasures

Killer Whales

You probably already know this: killer whales are not killers (at least not of people) and they are not whales — they are a member of the same family as dolphins.

It's rather hard to write about these creatures without getting a bit rhapsodic. You can easily go overboard comparing them to another form of mammal: homo sapiens — you and me. They are warm-blooded, air-breathing, bear their young live, and family-oriented. They communicate with each other by singing — no matter that their melodies are more discordant than even punk rock.

Now, you must understand, what we're giving you in this little feature article, is not totally scientific. We intentionally avoided going to the headquarters of the Whale Watching society for information, because we didn't want to learn more about our finny friends than we could handle. Like the subject of eagles, San Juan Islanders have a pretty good layman's grasp of the habits of killer whales.

In short, don't use this information if you are about to write a dissertation for a degree in Marine Biology.

Probably the most fascinating bit of lore about these non-fish is the generally accepted notion that they have a rather high degree of oral communication. However, in human terms, they sing to each other rather than speak. The music they make is a hodgepodge of clicks and squeals and "whoomfs". The reason it is considered song instead of talk is because there are clearly-defined rhythms and repetitious phrases. Some of the students of this whale communication say that various pods have unique melodies. Further, they say that each year they have a favorite 'pop tune'. After a season or two on the 'hit list' the orcas will pick up another series of phrases and

it becomes the 'new top pop'. (Sounds like human teen-agers, doesn't it?)

There are those that say that these melodies are varied so as to call attention to 'good fishing' or 'a menace' or the desire to 'just reach out and touch someone'. It doesn't take much imagination to compare it to a human glee club out hunting rabbits.

Killer whales, like the other dolphins, tend to strike up acquaintances with two-legged mammals. They even show a willingness to learn tricks suggested by human trainers. If you don't believe that — go to Marineland and watch them perform.

Since the law strictly protects them from harm by people, they often show an interest in slow-moving boats. We've actually had them make a torpedo run on the 'Sea Witch'. They cut through the water at about 20 knots in our direction. Just when we thought they were going to go right through the hull and end up in our forepeak berth, they made a shallow dive and came up on the other side.

We're here to tell you that it can be an awe-inspiring experience to see an animal the size of your boat zoom by a scant two feet beneath the keel. We have also discovered they have an uncanny sixth sense that tells them when boat occupants do not have a camera at hand, or are out of film.

Incidentally, the law forbids chasing or harassing killer whales.

If you spot a single orca or a pod of them, you can contact the tracking teams by calling 1-800-562-8832 — a toll-free line. Since you might not want to spend the money for a ship-to-shore phone call if you want to report a sighting, the custom around here is to go on VHF Channel 16, the calling and distress fre-

quency, and ask for any boat at a dock in the vicinity.

Explain that you want to report a whale sighting. Usually someone will come back and volunter to get the information and use a dockside phone to call the team. (Remember to switch to a working channel, of course.)

If this brief introduction to killer whales piques your interest, you might browse on over to the Friday Harbor section of this guide and read up on the Whale Museum in Friday Harbor. When you get in town, you can drift up and get as much more information about the creatures as you can handle.

thriving establishment. But somewhere along the years the resort closed down and all the cabins were sold off so the whole place is privately-owned—mostly by mainlanders.

Peapod Rocks

About a mile south and ever so slightly west of Point Lawrence is the **Peapod Rocks State Parks Underwater Recreation Area**—a favorite spot for scuba divers. You're not allowed to go ashore on the low-lying rocks—which don't seem very inviting anyway. But the seals love the rock islands and the waters around them, full of more rocks. Peapod Rocks are posted 'No Trespassing' to protect the seals and nesting birds.

But divers can explore, although they should be wary of the strong underwater currents.

A flashing green four-second light marks the northeast side of North Peapod. The islands extend almost a mile in a basically north-by-south configuration with South

'Sea Witch' moored at Doe Island Park

Peapod at the southern end—clever idea. They were named by someone in the Wilkes expedition who may have been a vegetarian.

Doe Bay

Due west of South Peapod is **Doe Bay**, at one time the site of a planned community called Polarity Institute. Like many of these experiments in communal living, it aroused considerable suspicion and comment among Orcas Islanders, even though it was isolated on the far eastern shore of the island. After several years of integration into the community, a number of non-members began to express approval.

The group moved to California in 1982, and the area was sold and turned into a resort. There are older cottages, camping, mineral baths and a mooring buoy and boaters are welcome. Doe Bay affords space for several boats to anchor in 12 to 20 feet of water. The mud bottom should hold ground tackle well, but expect the typical Rosario Strait swells. It's especially rough in southeast storms.

Doe Island State Marine Park

As you continue southwesterly from Doe Bay, you will find delightful **Doe Island**, a 6.5-acre state marine park. It's one of those places you're sure was made for you alone.

It's a magical little spot: tall trees, unspoiled beaches, all the flora and fauna you're supposed to find in the San Juans—and a romantic quality in the peace and quiet of the woods and shores. Trails crisscross the island, ending up on shores filled with driftwood treasures and myriad sea life. Views in every direction are picture-perfect.

The cove west of Doe Island on Orcas is privately-owned and there are a number of private mooring buoys in the area which can make it difficult to find a spot to drop anchor.

There is a small park dock and float, with just room for one boat on each side of the float. Four campsites, picnic tables and pit toilets accommodate the campers who arrive by boats. There is no fresh water and no garbage drop, so be prepared by bringing your own water and trash bags.

Waves and swells from Rosario Strait can make tying up at the float a bit rolly at times. Nevertheless, Doe Island Park is a great stopover for the kids and dogs to run off some steam while adults relax with an easy island hike.

At this juncture, we should ask the reader to take note that this book is the product of the labors of two writers, Al and Jo. Al is a thoroughly civilized human being who eschews all forms of exercise more fatiguing than dental-flossing. Jo, on the other hand, is an 'outdoors' type who skies, bikes, swims, hikes and otherwise indulges in energy-intensive activity.

This digression is felt to be necessary because of the inclusion of such apparently self-contradictory phrases as the one above: "... relax with an easy hike." Clearly, this is *ipsa loquitor* a logically indefensible proposition. (Al.)

Boats can pass between Doe Island and Orcas in two fathoms—but we recommend using your depth sounder.

Buoy Bay

About a mile and a half south of Doe Island is **Buoy Bay**, a curving bight flanked by reefs. There is no public land here and anchorage would be less than satisfactory because of the exposure to the lumpy waters of Rosario Strait.

Deer Point

From Buoy Bay to **Deer Point**, there are a number of tiny indentations and shallow bights, ending at the nearly uninhabited peninsula of Deer Point. If fog or inclement weather tempts skippers to hug the shoreline, be on guard against a number of rocks and reefs just offshore all the way from the bay to the point.

Obstruction Island

Obstruction Island sits squarely between Orcas and Blakely Islands and the two passes it creates are favorite entrances to the San Juan archipelago from the north or east.

Lydia Shoal in Rosario Strait is due east of the northern pass. We've been by Lydia Shoal a number of times and we can assure you there is nothing worthwhile to be seen there. It isn't marked as a wildlife refuge because even the birds think it's a bummer.

Obstruction Island has few homes and there are virtually no reliable anchorages along its shores. There is a dock on the Orcas side of the pass which is for Obstruction Island residents only.

Peavine Pass is to the south of the island. It has a 'reported' rock just off the northern shore of Blakely Island in about 30 feet. We have never found it, but we once encountered a sailor visiting in Friday Harbor who needed a scuba diver to check the bottom of his boat. He had found the rock, he said, which meant he had an awfully deep keel, a vivid imagination, or else was too close to shore.

In heavy seas on Rosario Strait, ferries occasionally go past Obstruction Island, although they normally enter the islands through Thatcher Pass to the south of Blakely. This is a good tip for private boaters. Rosario Strait in both strong southerlies and northerlies can become very formidable.

Obstruction Pass

Obstruction Pass is the wider of these two channels. Except for **Brown Rock** near the northern shore about halfway through the pass, it is clear and fair. It also offers one of those all-too-rare conveniences in the San Juans—a public boat-launching ramp on Orcas. It takes sharp eyes to find it however. Look for the road leading down to the beach and there it is. There are a number of private homes and several docks on the Orcas Island side of the pass.

Many years ago, we know not when, there was even a ferry landing at "Obstruction Pass Landing" at the end of a long wharf, according to the Washington Writers' Project.

"At Obstruction Pass Landing, the ferry docks at the end of a long wharf on Orcas Island, its terminal. The name *orcas* is of Spanish origin; Commander Wilkes (1841) renamed it 'Hulls's Island' for Commander Isaac Hull of the U.S. Frigate *Constitution*, but the original name persisted."

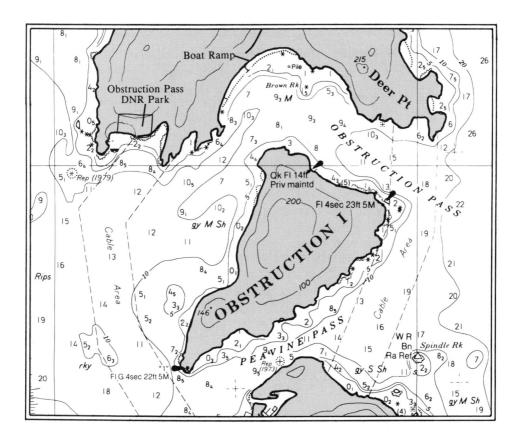

Obstruction Pass Park

The northerly pass has another advantage—the fine Department of Natural Resources marine park: **Obstruction Pass Park** on Orcas Island.

The state has provided two mooring buoys in this pleasant bay, but there is ample room for a half-dozen boats riding on the hook. The gently sloping beach is superb: pea gravel and sand—great for running and playing, wading, and even swimming if you are part polar bear. It also offers good beachcombing and a marvelous old tree leaning out over the beach that provides both shade and a good sitting space.

There is a campground ashore with several campsites including one large group site. There are numerous trails from the beach, one to the trailhead and car parking area about a quarter of a mile away. There is a garbage drop, but no drinking water. A big sign provides information about the madrona tree.

The park also provides a good anchorage in a northerly blow which can whip up the waves in East Sound just west of the point or back in Rosario Strait. The water stays relatively calm in the little bay.

East Sound

Venture now west from Obstruction Pass and into **East Sound**—a chameleon-like

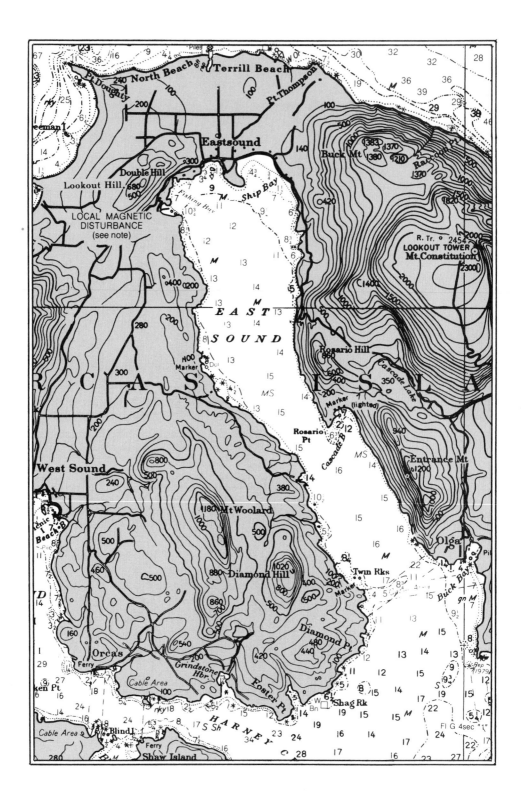

Olga Village and dock

body of water. It can be glassy calm—or blowing a veritable gale from north or south—within minutes of each other. The waves build up and the sailing can be exciting while it's dead calm elsewhere in the islands.

The village of **Eastsound** is at the far northern end of East Sound (note the spelling differences). Winds tend to blow either straight from—or straight at—the village six miles into this fjord-like channel with its steep, forested sides, especially on the eastern shore.

Olga

The first indentation heading north is the charming community of **Olga** at **Buck Bay**. There is a county dock and float at the road end. You may shop at the Olga store, which carries groceries, books, magazines, gifts, general store merchandise, even including a limited amount of clothing—and a deli besides.

Just kitty-corner across the street is the Olga Post Office. And a short walk up the road will take you to the Orcas Island Artworks. This wonderful large old building features all types of island-made crafts, such as yarns and wools, pottery, jewelry, woodworking, some clothing and many gift items. While you're shopping, the delicious aroma of home-baked breads wafts through the shop from the restaurant in the building. The meals are outstanding—even the islanders love to eat there.

You can't stay overnight at the dock according to county rules, but you can anchor offshore—one of the few refuges from the sharp and capricious northerly winds in East Sound. There is a picturesque grassy meadow at Olga, surrounding the bay.

Buck Bay

Part of the Olga community wraps itself around Buck Bay, a tideflat and old

Rosario Resort - the former Moran Mansion - a luxury stop

booming ground. Be careful anchoring at Olga as there are cable crossings at the northern end of the bay.

Rosario

Once you leave Olga and round the bluff to its west, giving a fair berth to the rocky point, the next moorage is at **Cascade Bay**, site of well-known Rosario Resort. As you make the two-mile run from Olga, you can look up at **Entrance Mountain**, a steep 1,200-foot high peak which rises virtually straight up from the water. There are no obstructions and the water is deep all the way to within about 100 feet of the shoreline. However, watch your chart and depth sounder if you go in that close.

The water is five to nine fathoms deep in Cascade Bay. The resort has placed mooring buoys for guests in the relatively shallow waters—and they are not free. It is barely possible to drop an anchor in Cascade Bay without running afoul of the mooring buoys. If a southeast blow makes up, you will have no protection.

If you choose to go into the Rosario marina, pass between the riprap breakwater on the left and the dock on the right and you will be assigned a protected slip.

Rosario, touted as the largest resort in the state, is a truly lovely spot in an incredible setting: on a rocky point at the foot of steep, forested hills. The elegant hotel with restaurant, pools, cocktail lounge and other amenities, was once the private home of Seattle shipbuilder Robert Moran. Many boaters find the luxury resort a welcome stop. They tie up for the night to enjoy the three heated swimming pools, jacuzzis, dinner, dancing, tennis, pipe organ concerts and a dressed-up night out while the kids swim and go horseback riding.

Rosario has a grocery store at the marina for all kinds of supplies, including fishing tackle and fuel.

Griffin Rocks

The stretch of East Sound north from Rosario is fairly similar to that between Olga and Rosario—fjord-like steep, forested slopes with no moorages. But the area softens finally at the cove just south of **Griffin Rocks** and the shoreline changes. Griffin Rocks are detached from the shoreline. One is large, maybe half an acre—with a couple of fir trees and brush. The second rock, closer to shore, is much smaller and has little vegetation. The rocks are just north of a small private bay which offers little protection from winds.

These little islands have a spot in Orcas Island history as, "They were a burying ground for the Indian tribes whose custom it was to put the dead in their own canoes and place the canoe among the branches of the scrub juniper trees which grew there. A log that lay on the point north of the harbor had its limbs lopped off and each decorated with a human skull of which there were over a score." (From the James Francis Tulloch Diary.)

Coon Hollow

Coon Hollow is a little geographical pockmark on the eastern shore of East Sound just north of Griffin Rocks. It is shallow and does not offer refuge—except for raccoons.

Ship Bay

Just ahead is shallow, curving Crescent Beach at the head of **Ship Bay**. A couple of tumbledown empty cottages still stand across the road from the beach—remnants of early day summer cabins. The beach is now a privately-owned aquaculture farm and is no longer open to swimmers and beachcombers.

East Sound from Buck Mountain

Eastsound

After a quick look at beautiful **Crescent Beach** (don't go in too close or you'll find yourself neighbors with the clams and oysters) head west around forested **Madrona Point** into **Fishing Bay** with the village of Eastsound at its head. There is an old dock there, the former Standard Oil dock, now private. If you want to go ashore at East-sound—and you probably will—you'll have to drop the hook and dinghy into the tiny bit of beach. Anchoring is pretty good between miniature **Indian Island**, known locally as **Jap Island** and the dock. We wouldn't advise going around the island except by dinghy—at low tide you can walk out to it from Eastsound beach. The island is used every 4th of July as the launching pad for the Orcas fireworks, which light up the summer sky invoking lots of "oohs and ahs" from onlookers on shore and in the bay—a popular spot to anchor for that patriotic weekend.

Indian Island is just a half-acre rock with not much except grass. It's owned by the Feds—feel free to wander or picnic on the spot.

West Shore Of East Sound

After you up-anchor at Eastsound Village, you can follow the western shoreline of East Sound back south to Harney Channel. First spot to look into is the tiny cove of **Judd Bay**. It's a small bay with a booming ground and a log skid. Local boats are usually anchored there, taking up the space, but there is room for a couple of extras in a pinch.

There are a fair number of homes in this area, but as you head south they become scarcer. The prevailing northerlies or southerlies sweep any of the minor indentations and there are practically no refuges or anchorages.

Due east of Rosario Hill the chart lists "dolphins" and "marker". We could not

Seals enjoying the sun

find any dolphins and the marker is probably a benchmark and not a navigation aid.

Just north of Dolphin Bay note a summer cabin with a dock that is cantilevered out over the water. It is built on top of a big log that is secure on the shore.

Look north-northeast, over the Rosario Resort complex and up to the top of the mountain, and you will see a fire-watcher's tower atop a high trestle. Since watching fires from such houses is now virtually a thing of the past, we assume this is no longer manned.

Next along this shore is **Dolphin Bay**, which scarcely deserves the title of bay. It would never be considered an anchorage and apparently gets its name not from the playful species of mammals, but from several log dolphins near the shore which indicates that it was a log dump at one time. The old logging road must have been improved because there are several houses on the tiny beach.

Just south of Dolphin Bay you will spot a small rock, possibly one-quarter acre—with a few tufts of grass on top of it. Farther along there is a long dock extending from the shore and a rock just south of it, considerably larger than the previous one. There is a tiny bight just south of the large offshore rock, and then a giant boulder appears on shore WNW of Twin Rocks.

Twin Rocks

Twin Rocks are two similar half-acre islets belonging to the U.S. Wildlife Service. They have no trees or shrubs, just grasses and bracken with no visible marker. The chart shows you can go behind them, but we didn't try, mainly because we were there at an extreme low tide with 30-knot northerly winds blowing down East Sound and didn't want to take any unnecessary chances.

Just south of Twin Rocks is a long, gently sloping shoal that ranges from 4 to 8

fathoms and extends nearly a half-mile into East Sound. There is no problem crossing the shoal even fairly close to shore at **White Beach**.

White Beach to Grindstone

From White Beach south, Orcas has several tiny bays and coves with both vacation and permanent homes tucked among the forested bluffs. While there are few offshore rocks, it is still better to stay reasonably in the 10-fathom curve as you pass **Diamond Point** and head toward **Shag Rock**.

Shag Rock is marked by a beacon and is often used as the start for Orcas Island Yacht Club Races into Eastsound. You can easily pass between Shag Rock and Orcas.

The first real cove on this part of Orcas is **Guthrie Bay**, a neat little harbor that could be a good anchorage except in a southeasterly. The bay ranges from seven fathoms at the outer portion to one fathom at the inner end—and then you're on the beach. The western shore of Guthrie down to and around **Foster Point** is foul with offshore rocks, so keep clear as you round the point. Homes dot the area.

The next section is from Foster Point to Grindstone Harbor—don't hug the

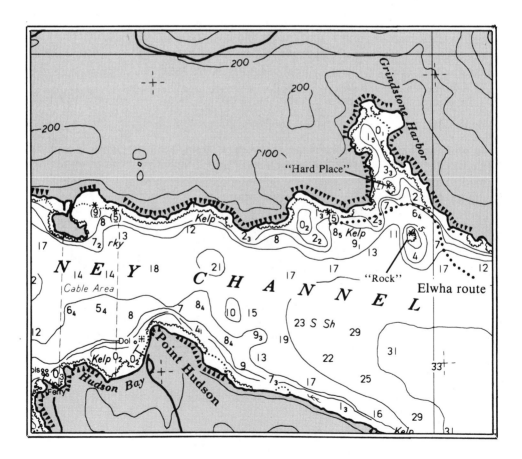

The 'Elwha'—now allergic to Grindstone Harbor.

shoreline too close, but the only real offshore obstruction is the rock at the entrance to Grindstone Harbor.

Grindstone Harbor

There is an unnamed sound that is formed by the intersection of Peavine, Obstruction Passes, Harney and Upright Channels, and East Sound. This is a well-traveled area and boats wishing to radio position reports have to resort to a reference to land features.

The middle leaf of Orcas Island is separated from Shaw Island by Harney Channel. The eastern boundary seems to be from Foster Point to Hankin Point.

Just west of this boundary line lies **Grindstone Harbor**—infamous Grindstone Harbor. We'll tell you about that story later. It is not really a harbor—the term implies that boats put in there to dock. They may have, at one time, when a grist mill was located there—hence the name.

Nowadays, Grindstone is a cove which is surrounded by private properties. It is a marginal anchorage—most of the upper waters are too shallow for cruising yachts. There is a tiny islet that sits in the center of the entrance to the cove, but it is visible at all but the highest tides.

There is another peril, a submerged rock in line with the visible rock and the end of the cove. It is far enough out into the fairway to justify a warning buoy, but there isn't one. It is surrounded by kelp, but the beds extend for quite some distance between the underwater rock and the islet. To be safe, avoid the kelp beds and stay close to the east or west shores. Possibly the handiest way to find the passage between the reef and the islet—which we think of as 'a rock and a hard place'—strike

Orcas Ferry Landing

a line from Foster Point to the edge of the tombolo at the S end of Orcas (just east of the ferry landing).

For many years, there was a resident seal in Grindstone Harbor. He used to make himself at home on the floats in the harbor—he could have been mistaken for a pet dog. He would put on something of a show for visiting boaters. We haven't seen him recently—he may have moved.

By far the most famous denizen of Grindstone Harbor is a charming lady who got herself dubbed on TV as the "Siren of Grindstone Harbor". It was she, the story goes, who tempted the skipper of the ferry *Elwha* to make the risky trip into the harbor. The gallant captain said at the time that he wanted to show her how her house looked from the water. She protests that she was horrified to discover that he was really going to gunkhole in there with a 382-foot ferryboat!

If you study the chart, you will see that it is barely possible to get a vessel of 73-foot beam through the narrow passage. A careful captain could probably go through the spot at slow bell, stopping when he had cleared the reef to swing the stern around. Rumor has it that the feat had been accomplished safely at least once in the past.

This daring skipper tried to negotiate it at about 17½ knots! Looking at the chart, you will see that he had to make a grand concourse turn in order to avoid the depth marked 2.3 fathoms—that's 15 feet. The *Elwha* draws a little more than 17 feet!

The Friday Harbor Journal of October 5, 1983, quoted a gentleman who lived just above the fatal reef.

He looked out of the window and remarked, "Here came the *Elwha* full bore! It got about a third or a half of the way in the harbor and went right between those rocks and then headed directly across the harbor ... I wouldn't dream of cutting inside that kelp bed with my outboard. The ferry went about 300 yards and then hit the two-fathom reef with a terrific crunching noise. It sounded like thunder ... it must have raised that boat about two feet out of the water.''

It could be said that this proves that the days of chivalry are not dead—but they can leave a daredevil captain with considerable egg on his chops!

Orcas Landing

Just east of the ferry dock at Orcas, you will find an unnamed bay. There is an extensive private moorage there called Bayhead Marina, which does not invite transients. Although there is space outside the marina to anchor—and many boats do—it is not comfortable because the ferries churn up the waters quite a bit.

The village of Orcas is the point-of-entry for residents and tourists alike as the ferries dock there. Just west of the ferry dock is a fuel dock and, in summer, a series of floats for public moorage. It is possible to tie up at these floats overnight—we have done it. But you will have a restless night if you do. The ferry wake and wake from passing boats thrashes the floats to the point that it is hard to walk down them when they are working. It is an ideal spot to tie up to meet invited onboard guests. It is a great place in the islands to stop for ice and groceries. Another needed facility—a liquor store—is there at the dock. It is, we think, one of the most homey and charming liquor stores in the state with a wood stove, rocking chair and giant teddy bear. Shoreside, there is the historic Orcas Hotel, which offers some overnight accommodations, a coffee shop with dining room, and a cocktail lounge. There are some small shops, boutiques, childrens' shop, etc. During the summer months, there is a fast-food eatery above the ferry dock.

Crow Valley is a gentle farming area

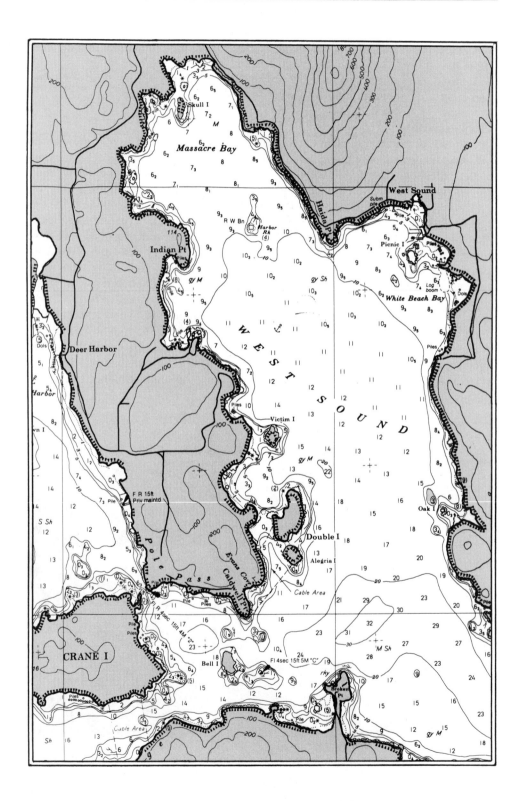

West Sound

The three-mile long body of water just west of the ferry landing is West Sound. It is about one mile across at the narrowest point. Unlike Eastsound it is not known for its freakish winds. There are several favorite anchoring places in the Sound.

Oak Island

The first noteworthy feature after rounding the point west of Orcas Landing and heading into **West Sound** is tiny **Oak Island**. This remarkably pretty half-acre island has, naturally, one large oak tree. There is also a large fir and several other small evergreens on this miniature, privately-owned bit of rocky land. There is a narrow pass between Oak Island and Orcas with only three feet of water at low tide. The little bay on Orcas opposite the island is in reality a marsh and offers no anchorage.

For the next one-and-one-half miles the eastern shore of West Sound is rugged and cliffed with many attractive homes nestled among the trees on the bluffs.

White Beach Bay

White Beach Bay is an old booming ground and dolphins still remain with an occasional log boom. There is another indentation at the northern end of White Beach Bay which is also an old logging dump. It is fronted by privately-owned **Picnic Island**. Tucked in just north of **Picnic Island** is West Sound Marina.

West Sound Marina

Mike and Peg Wareham and their son and daughter, Ian and Betsy, have operated this facility for many years and it's pretty complete. In addition to permanent moorage, they offer transient moorage, gas and diesel, all kinds of repair services, haul-out and shipwright services, some free moorage time while visiting their ship's store or the nearby West Sound Store and Delicatessen, which is within walking distance. West Sound Marina is well-protected from all but west winds, which usually aren't too strong anyway.

Cruising past West Sound Store (the dock in front is private, so don't tie up) **Haida Point** juts out. It's a bit shoal a couple hundred feet offshore. **Harbor Rock** is halfway between Haida Point and **Indian Point** on the western shore and is often used as a mark in Orcas Yacht Club sail races.

Massacre Bay

Massacre Bay is the northwestern third of West Sound, and although we may tend to rave about the beauty of the islands, it's a temptation hard to resist, especially in a spot like this. On the eastern shore, the hills rise steeply to 900-foot high **Ship Peak**; a combination of forest, rock and grassy spots overlooking West Sound. And at the northern end of the bay is delightful Skull Island.

These macabre names, such as **Skull, Victim** and **Massacre**, originated from battles of the local peace-loving Indians of the Lummi tribe who resided on Orcas, and Indians to the north. The island was the battleground of many conflicts and invasions from the British Columbia tribes. These northern Indians fought continuously with the island Indians, with their goal to capture the Lummis for use as slave workers.

Heading north into Massacre Bay there is a small bight on the eastern shore with a

Gladys

A poignant story involves the Warehams of West Sound Marina, and Gladys Prince, a great 'old lady of the sea' with a lifetime of boating experience.

Gladys had lived alone aboard her old 36' cruiser, the 'All Right', for many years in the San Juans, and was affectionately cared for by a great many boaters.

When she was 76, Gladys suffered from an illness that blocked out her normal sense while cruising in northern waters; she was caught in a storm in Georgia Strait, ran the boat on the rocks near Lasqueti Island and ended up in a Nanaimo hospital, after a long, disoriented cruise. Her son towed the 'All Right' from Nanaimo to West Sound where the Warehams repaired the boat and kept a watchful eye on Gladys, making sure she had plenty of their home-cooked food, among other things, and warm clothing.

While Gladys stayed anchored out near the marina most of the time, she did take off on a couple of cruises and ran her boat aground twice. She ran on the rocks in Blind Bay at Shaw on Memorial Day, 1982, she admitted "she should have known where the rocks were". Betsy and Ian Wareham helped free the boat and towed it back to the marina. In July, thinking she was heading west and north to Reid Harbor on Stuart Island, she ended up across the Strait of Juan de Fuca on the rocks at Protection Island. A friend took her back to West Sound.

On July 18, Gladys apparently slipped into the water while boarding her dinghy from the 'All Right'.

Peg saw Gladys' dinghy bouncing on the beach that Sunday afternoon—not tied up as it usually was. Gladys' body was floating in the water near her boat. Betsy said it was not the first time Gladys had fallen in and the family had fished her out.

Gladys, who never wanted to trouble anyone, repeated not too long before she died—something she had been saying for years: "Well, my dear, someday I'll just wrap this old anchor chain around my neck and slip over the side."

That's not exactly the way it happened, but almost, and now Gladys, who never wanted to trouble anyone, is forever 'all right'.

rock in the center and several private docks—not the best spot for a moorage.

But we found one of the most attractive anchorages in the whole area. It is the little bay north and east of Skull Island, actually at the head of Massacre Bay. There is a well-marked rock just north of the island that is shoal for quite a distance all the way around. Just beyond that is a rock which bares at low tide. We anchored between the tiny island and the Orcas shore and finally fled about two hours before low tide when we found we were in about 5½ to 6 feet of water with large rocks appearing all around us. With a 4½-foot draft sailboat we were a bit nervous. So our advice is: keep to the east of the tiny island.

Skull Island

Now for the good news. Skull Island is owned by the state and is an 'unimproved marine park'—meaning it is in its natural, primitive state, with no toilets, water or campsites on any of its 3.5 acres. It is an island to fall in love with. There is a small crushed-shell beach on the eastern side where you can drag up your shore boat and do a little bit of beach and tide pool exploring. There are bracken and juniper and wild rose thickets. The view of the grassy slopes of **Ship Peak** and **Turtleback Mountain** from Skull Island is spectacular. The eastern shore of Skull Island has some

Massacre Bay from Skull Island Park

shoals. You can walk around the island and delight in its Eden-like nature, daydreaming of owning just such a piece of property for your very own. You can circumnavigate the island in a fairly large boat, but we'd advise doing it only at high tide.

Just west of Skull Island is a private dock and a tiny bay—filled with rocks—explore that one only by water in your shore boat.

Western Shore of West Sound

The western shore of Massacre Bay has a larger bay which provides enough area and good depths for anchoring with the high ground on Indian Point offering protection from southern winds. Note the rocks and small islands near the shore.

South of Indian Point is another bay bounded on the southern end by a peninsula. This entire area is a fair anchorage, but the shore is all private.

Victim Island

Next is **Victim Island,** another little four-acre unimproved spread owned by State Parks. And while it is indeed a beautiful little island, it is relatively untouched. The lack of a good cove nearby for anchorage probably accounts for this. There is one small shell beach on the southeast side near a reef marked by a ten-foot pipe with a small square card on top. It is not easy to climb the rock face off this beach. The rock is crumbling and makes for insecure footing, unless you are a sure-footed kid, an extremely agile adult, or a mountain goat. By going counterclockwise around the rocky shore, you can find a slightly better path for climbing a little farther along.

Once on top of the island you will find it fairly primitive. There is a sketchy path around the perimeter. It's a great place for kids to explore. There is a meadow on the north side of Victim Island that would be a nice place to picnic, but you would have to pull your boat up onto the rocks—and then, of course, clamber up.

The channel between the island and Orcas has some rather ominous rocky patches at about 6 feet at low water. When we came through, we had a friend up in the bow who shouted occasionally, "more left," "now hook to the right" and suchlike encouraging phrases as he peered through the clear water at the boulders.

We anchored in about 15 feet of water at the north end of the channel. The depth went from 50 to 15 feet in just a few yards. We let out a lot of scope and backed down until the hook caught and held. We were over 15 feet where we ended up, but the anchorage was in good holding ground. We wouldn't have wanted to trust it overnight, however.

Camp Four Winds

The little bay just north of Victim Island is the home of Camp Four Winds, for summer adventures for youngsters. They sail around the bay in little sailboats and have a great time.

Just south of Victim Island on the Orcas shore is a palatial estate that was once owned by the Kaiser family. It was purchased recently by a member of the Whittier family who have, for years, had love affairs with the B.C. Gulf Islands and the San Juans. There is an impressive boat house on the waterfront at their establishment.

Pole Pass History

The configuration of Pole Pass has changed dramatically over the years to its present shape. Up until 1960 there was a flat, rocky island in the center of the pass and the pass actually got its name from a pole erected on that rock. Indians stretched a net made from cedar bark, kelp and grass, from that pole to a tree on the shore of Orcas. As ducks flew through the narrow pass in fall and winter evenings, they were stunned when they hit the net and would tumble to the water's surface where the Indians could paddle out and scoop them up. Thus the name, Pole Pass.

In 1960, that little island in the center became the northeast end of a riprap jetty off Crane Island which provides Crane Island folk with a good sheltered moorage.

There is a story that in the mid-forties two Orcas men saw a pod of Orcas — known then as blackfish — swim through the pass. The pod was so big it took them 45 minutes to swim through, strung out as they were from Orcas Village at Orcas Landing, to beyond Steep Point. There are still reports of whale sightings through the narrow pass.

The Coast Guard has provided a light at Pole Pass — a light flashing red every four seconds, which stands 15 feet above high tide and is visible for four miles — it has been there since 1933.

But before that date, the light was there only by an agreement with the captain of the boat on the main run. Back in 1833, William H. Cadwell, a homesteader, agreed to hang a lantern at the pass on the nights the 'S.S. Libby' went through the pass. Twice a week, there was a mail run from Port Townsend to Semiahmoo, now known as Blaine. Cadwell received free transport of his farm's produce in exchange for the service.

Five years later, the government installed a kerosene-burning lantern with a red globe which had to be lit nightly, and Robert McLachlan became keeper of the light, passing the job to his son, Kirk, after his death in 1907.

By 1933 the Department of Commerce relinquished lighthouses and shore lights to the Coast Guard, and in 1949 the Pole Pass light became the familiar red flashing light.

Double Island

About 400 yards south of Victim Island is **Double Island**. At one time this island and the one to the south of it were paired. Orcas folks still call the second island **Little Double**, although the official name, as you can see from the chart, is **Alegria**. Both islands are private.

On the northeast corner of Double Island is a cairn of white-painted rocks with a small upright pole to mark the spot.

The passage behind Double Island is used by locals who know how to locate the quarter-fathom shoal in the middle of it. At high tide most boats can negotiate it by using depth sounders. Use caution, it is shoal and rocky there. There is a rock marked by a red flag on the northwest corner of Double.

Alegria has a beautiful home on the southeast corner with an elaborate hoist for small boats.

Wasp Passage

Proceeding south from these two islands you will pass **Evans Cove,** which is not more than an indentation in the shoreline, down to **Caldwell Point.** Shoal water marked by kelp appears in this area, but we've never had any problem—just avoid the kelp. Between Caldwell Point and Pole Pass in this section of Wasp Pass there are a number of vacation and full-time residences along the shore. Several have private docks. The Crane Island shore has a number of rocks and shoals.

Pole Pass

The narrow passage between Orcas and Crane Islands is **Pole Pass.** The name dates back to early days when Indians used to suspend nets across the pass from high poles on each island in order to catch birds.

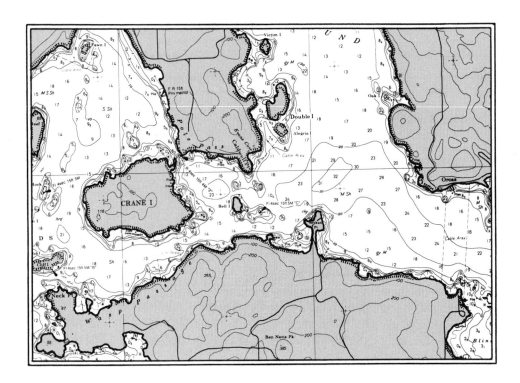

Village at Deer Harbor

When the currents are running high, Pole Pass might qualify for the term 'rapids' for a short distance. It is only about 75 yards across and the water is plenty deep, even at lowest tides, but stay in the center. As you approach Pole Pass from the east, swing wide to avoid the kelp which extends south from the point on Orcas where the flashing red light is. Then aim for the center.

Ferry captains piloting the smaller boats, such as the *Vashon,* on occasion edge their vessels through the narrow pass en route to Sidney or Friday Harbor. We were on board one day on such a trip and reactions of the passengers were worth the trip. All the passengers could see were trees to both port and starboard. When they stood up, they couldn't see water on either side. Only by going to the side windows and looking down along the topsides can water be seen. Passengers wondered if the skipper had lost his marbles and was running aground. However, no ferries have ever gone aground in Pole Pass and it does make for interesting conversation in the lounges.

Crane Island

The **Crane Island** side of Pole Pass has a breakwater and moorage for local boats just inside. Crane has a fair amount of shoals off its northeastern tip and along much of the northern shoreline, so give that area a wide berth. Crane is all private and even has a private air strip. Crane Islanders travel to Deer Harbor for their mail and other shopping-type activities.

Deer Harbor

On the eastern shore of Deer Harbor is a long dock and the grand estate of the Isaacson family who owned the now-defunct Isaacson Iron Works in Seattle. The dock has a privately maintained light at the end.

This eastern shore is sometimes known locally as the 'Gold Coast' of Orcas because there are so many vacation homes of wealthy mainlanders in the area.

Deer Harbor Resort is on the northeastern shore of Deer Harbor. The popular resort offers moorage, fuel, groceries, ice, a restaurant, gift shop, swimming pool, cabins and cocktail lounge. There is also a post office in Deer Harbor.

A few hundred yards from the resort there is an honest-to-goodness dance hall which draws young and old alike from all over the islands and has for many years. Another restaurant is farther on up the road.

Deer Harbor is also a stopover for the Santa Ship from Victoria each Christmas time.

Cayou Quay

Just across the bay from the resort is a private marina, **Cayou Quay**. It was named after the family of one of the four first settlers of Deer Harbor—men who came to hunt deer for the Hudson's Bay Company in 1852.

Fawn Island

Leaving Deer Harbor, heading west is another tiny island, **Fawn Island**, privately owned. There is no problem passing between Fawn and Orcas, but Fawn is shoal at the southern end with large rocks.

Orcas Island is steep and rocky with a few homes on the cliffs. Edmond Meany in his book, *History of the State of Washington*, writes, "Along the western cliffs of the shady green cove are feldspar deposits which reach 60 feet in thickness and 300 feet in depth. Feldspar is used in glazing pottery and manufacturing glass, but the demand has not justified development at this point."

The cliffs rising steeply from this westernmost portion of Orcas reach 425 feet and it is possible to sail fairly close to shore along the area.

You have just arrived back at Spring Point—Orcas Island has now been successfully circumnavigated.

TO THE OUTER ISLANDS

The State Marine Parks at Sucia and Stuart and Jones Islands are almost as well-known to the thousands of Northwest boaters as their own home ports. To a lesser extent, the smaller parks at Matia, Patos and Clark are also favorite spots. Folks in the San Juans think of these as the 'Outer Islands' and islanders often avoid them during the height of the tourist season. After Labor Day, however, local cruising groups will rendezvous in Echo Bay or Prevost Harbor for 'overnights'. No matter how many times we have visited these places, we keep finding new things. Since we have poked into the less well-traveled spots, we are going to share some findings and impressions with you.

We'll help plan a cruise that begins with leaving the inside waters of the San Juans through Obstruction or Peavine Pass—off Orcas' southeast shore, and act as tour guides in a big circle sweep beginning with the Sisters and ending on Stuart.

Heading northeast from Obstruction Island, you will travel past Doe Island State Marine Park just off Orcas Island which we explored earlier, past Peapod Rocks Underwater State Parks, around Lawrence Point, and then head in a northerly direction to Sisters Islands. That's about a seven-mile run from Obstruction Island.

Sisters Islands

Let's start with **Little Sister Island**. (It's sort of a stepsister.) **Sisters Islands** consist of one big island and two quite small ones, all in a cluster, immediately southeast of Clark Island.

All of the Sisters Islands are owned by the U.S. Wildlife Service. They are posted with refuge signs and discourage visitors.

Have you seen the baboon's face on the southwest corner of Little Sister? It has been sculptured by the winds and waves. Even if you don't make it out, you will find a lot of photo possibilities on this remarkable island.

Sisters Islands comprise about six acres. It's okay to go between Little Sister and

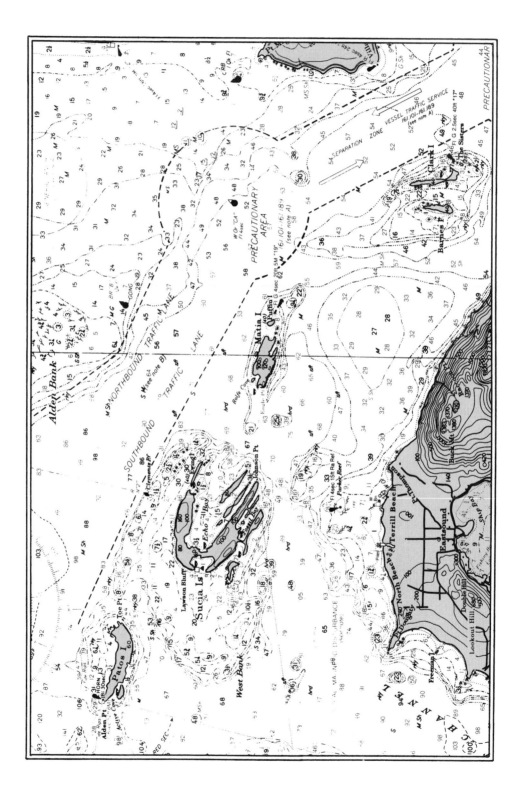

East side beach of Clark Island State Park

the two tagalong sisters to the south of the biggest Sister, but we wouldn't risk threading our way between the three rocks in that cluster.

The passage between Sisters and Clark Island is fair and passable.

Clark Island

Approaching from the south, between Clark and Barnes Islands, we notice that Clark Island, a state marine park, is about a mile long and shaped like a string bean. About one-third of the way along the island, it narrows to less than a hundred yards across. There are paths leading through the woods from the moorage on the west side to the one on the east side. Campsites with tables, stoves and pit toilets are scattered about this 55-acre park but there is no drinking water. The campsites on the west side are in the woods, while many of those on the east side are among scrub above the high tide drift logs on the no-bank beach. This makes it a great spot for families with young children—no banks to tumble down and easy to keep an eye on the kids.

There are a half-dozen mooring buoys on this long bight on the eastern shore of Clark. They are quite a distance from shore because of the long shallow beach and can catch swells from this combination of Rosario Strait and the Strait of Georgia. As you look out onto the Strait, you will notice a wicked-looking reef in the southerly end of the approach to this moorage. It looks like small rocks on the chart, but it is really a large reef. If you approach Clark on the eastern shore, you will do well to stay a hundred yards or so offshore and keep an eye out for this reef. As you will see from chart #18430, it is detached from a whole clutter of rocks at the southern end of the eastern bight. There is room for a large number of carefully anchored boats in addition to the mooring buoys along here.

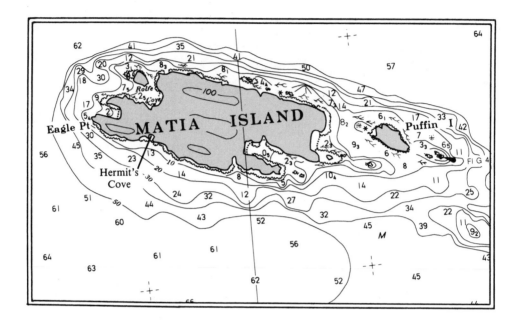

On the west side of the island, in a passage between Clark and Barnes, there are three mooring buoys. The pebbled beach is attractive. This is a fair refuge if you can catch a buoy, but it offers little protection from southeasterly winds. Near the north end of Clark Island there are a number of rocks just offshore, so give them a wide berth. Wilkes named Clark Island for Midshipman John C. Clark, who was killed in the Battle of Lake Erie.

As if you might not have enough information about Clark, we'll tell you one last thing: State Parks implemented a 'Pack-out-your-own-garbage' program at Clark and Doe Islands. The program eliminated the amount of litter and refuse to be hauled from these two islands by park rangers. However, the park managers noted that boaters took their garbage along and dumped it at Sucia Island to help overflow the garbage containers there.

Barnes Island

Barnes Island is private and offers no refuge or attractions for the cruiser. There are a number of rocks off the northeastern tip so stay clear of that area as you pass by. Doug Cardle claims that Barnes Island was named by Wilkes to honor one of his naval heroes, but we prefer to think it was named after an early sheriff, Ellis 'Yankee' Barnes, who was appointed in 1855. He served in Whatcom County, which at that time included all of the San Juan Islands.

Georgia Strait

Three and a half miles northwest from the tip of Clark you are in the southerly arm of the Strait of Georgia, running parallel to the southbound Puget Sound Traffic Lane. It is interesting to notice that the term 'Puget Sound' is used for this area although the U.S. Coast Pilot identifies 'Puget Sound' as the area from Everett to Olympia. It distinguishes between Puget Sound and Admirlaty Inlet which begins at the southern shore of the Strait of Juan de Fuca.

Puffin Island

Puffin Island is U.S. Lighthouse territory just off the southeast shore of Matia. The island is long and slanting and looks like the upended keel of a giant sailboat. The light is not on the main island itself, but is on one of two rocks to the east of the island.

The channel between Puffin and Matia has some no-nos that should be considered if you want to go between them. Incidentally, the Coast Pilot says you shouldn't try it, but there are a couple of nice coves and beaches on the eastern extremity of Matia, and boaters do it all the time. Going from south to north, give the eastern end of Matia a wide berth, and then swing around to avoid the rocks at the west end of Puffin. The water is plenty deep—just avoid the rocks off the ends of both islands.

Matia Island

Matia Island is a fascinating marine park on the edge of Georgia Strait, located north and east of the north shore of Orcas Island.

Matia, Spanish for 'no protection', is correctly pronounced Ma-tee-ah. But it is often called May-shah, Matty or Maytee. The islanders seem to prefer 'May-Shuh'.

'Hermit's Cove' on Matia

Charles F. Chapman: Shape Up

Some day I'd like to corner old Charles F. Chapman and read him the Riot Act.

I would start by admitting that I was raised on 'Piloting, Seamanship' and 'Small Boat Handling'. Just like I raised my kids on Dr. Spock. Thanks to him, I know how to tie a carrick-bend with a double becket. And I have learned how to display a quarantine flag on a 200,000-ton freighter.

Not that I ever do any of those things, you understand, but I do know how to. All in all, it's a very useful book. No boater should be without a copy.

"But when it comes to anchoring, Charles," I would tell him, "you are ricocheting off the wall. I don't know where you do your cruising but I want to tell you that here on the West Coast you have made for countless sleepless nights for me and a number of my boating friends with your wacky chapter on dropping the hook. Let me give you a f'rinstance."

One summer as I was serving as foredeck ape aboard the little sloop 'Sea Witch', my gal's chilblain express, we went into the bay at Newcastle Island, just off Nanaimo. That's a marine park and there was a swarm of boats already set for the evening. Zo eased us into an open space about a hundred yards in diameter and the sounder registered 30 feet. She rounded up into the wind and gave me the signal to consign that mass of steel to the Jones' locker. It went down over the bow roller with an impressive splash. I payed out another 75 feet of line and belayed it.

"Back 'er down, Zo!" I yelled to the helmsperson. The trailing line began to leave little ripples as it was taken up. In a few seconds, the ripples stopped and the line snapped up bow-string tight. Nothing short of Force Eight was going to dig up that hook. I waved a signal and she killed the engine. We were secure.

I went over the calculations a second time. We had about a hundred feet of scope. (That Pecksniff, Chapman, says that the word 'rode' is improper.) That meant that as the currents changed during the night, she would cut a circle of some 30 yards in radius. That would keep us well clear of the neighboring boats as we all do-si-do'd around. With the hook down, it was time to go below and get the bottle of eel-bite medicine.

About a half-hour later, a sleek 30-foot power boat, built of — and burning — petroleum byproducts, came into the area. It moseyed into an open space

The island is about one mile long and a quarter mile wide with several bays and indentations along the rocky shores.

State Parks has a float and dock at **Rolfe Cove**, two mooring buoys, six camp sites, solar pit toilets (an innovation), drinking water and trails. Five acres around Rolfe Cove, a tiny bay on the northwest end of the island, belong to the state. The rest of the island is posted as U.S. Wildlife Refuge land. While it's not illegal to walk on the overgrown trails, they don't encourage it; and you can't camp on federal land. There's a tiny cove just northeast of **Eagle Point**, with two fathoms for anchorage and space for one boat—it's open to westerlies, however.

But it was not always like that on this 145-acre wonderland. Once upon a time, Skookum Tom, a B.C. Indian, hid out there. Tom was suspected of murders in both

halfway between us and a big ocean-going ketch. The skipper sprinted to the foredeck and down went the anchor. Then line began to pay out like he was fishing for halibut. I looked at Zo. She was staring at the scene in wide-eyed disbelief. The rope continued to reel out. Finally, he snubbed it off.

"Ye Gods!" said Zo. "Another Chapman-ite!"

I hailed the newcomer. I tried to make my voice sound casual.

"Ah-h-h, how much are you putting down, skipper?"

"Oh, eight to one, naturally." He waved jauntily to me and disappeared below.

"Straight out of Chapter 6," I sighed. I knew it would be a sleepless night. I decided to limit my wassailing to one gin and tonic.

It was not only a sleepless night — it was a hellish night! That little Melmac Momser drifted around in a swath that took him over other anchor lines and under other transoms. Several times in the wee hours we heard a loud thud as his shiny hull caromed off ours. I would stagger out of bed, muttering phrases which sorely jeopardized my chance at an eternal reward, and came above to shove him off. Not once during the night did he come out on deck to see what mischief he was doing. No, I am sure he was sound asleep below, secure in the knowledge that he had done the Chapman-thing.

No, don't bother to hunt for your copy of the book. I will quote chapter, line and verse for you the commandment on anchoring.

Page 102: "What is the proper scope? Under favorable conditions, 5:1 might be considered a minimum..." (Don't laugh, I'm not making this up) "...under average conditions, 7:1 or 8:1 is regarded as satisfactory."

So, I'll look Charles right in the eye and ask him: "Where in the name of sweet suffering Siwash are you going to find a moorage in Pacific Northwest waters capacious enough to accommodate a number of boats swinging in 500-foot circles?

"Furthermore, where did you ever get that figure of 8:1 for scope, the Farmer's Almanac?"

I should also tell him that there are a lot of local skippers who would delight in seeing him swinging from a yardarm at the end of a length of anchor-line — tied of course with a carrick bend with a double becket.

Canada and the States, and Matia made a perfect hideout. He could see if waterborne police from either country were approaching by looking towards Georgia Strait to the north and Rosario Strait and the shores of Orcas to the east and south. He would then head into the forest in the opposite direction from whichever group tried to track him down.

Tom vanished into the shadows of history and the next—and last—full-time settler was Civil War veteran Elvin Smith. He fell in love with the island and moved there in 1892 to spend the rest of his life.

Although Smith was called the 'hermit of Matty's', he was anything but a recluse. He rowed his skiff every Saturday the 2½ miles to Orcas Island. There he socialized with his many friends, collected his mail and did his weekly shopping.

Little Matia Island

He built a small cabin on Matia, cleared a five-acre plot inland for a garden and orchard. He stocked the island with sheep, chickens and rabbits, even though he was a vegetarian. Seafood was easy to come by, so he netted fish and cod to his heart's content. Occasionally, old Civil War buddies would be his guests for extended periods of time.

Smith eventually abandoned his oars for an outboard motor. But even so, as he reached his 80s, his trips to the mainland became less frequent.

In the stormy winter of 1920, Smith's friends on Orcas became alarmed when they hadn't seen the old man for over two months. They sent a party to the island to search for him.

They were shocked when they found him, gaunt and haggard. Smith was near starvation after the hardships of the winter. His vegetables and fruits were gone, his 'store food' used up, and for some reason he was not gathering seafood. His only skiff had smashed on the rocks during a storm. The stranded old man welcomed his friends.

He returned to Orcas with them and tentatively agreed to build a small cabin on Orcas before the coming winter—no small feat for a man in his mid-80s. In the meantime, to satisfy everyone's concern, he agreed to have an old buddy return to Matia with him for the rest of the winter of 1920.

So on a calm February day, Smith and his new island-mate, George Carrier, loaded Smith's new boat with supplies from Orcas. The two climbed aboard the heavily-laden, flat-bottom skiff, pulled the starting rope on the 2½-horse outboard, and chugged out onto the glassy surfaced sea toward Matia.

A friend on shore watched as the small boat bobbed across the gentle swells headed toward the indistinct line of a tide rip. Soon he could see nothing in the growing dusk. The putt of the outboard was lost in the sounds of the suddenly growing winds and waves.

Worried about the two old men in the small open boat, the Orcas friend decided to make sure they arrived safely. He couldn't reach the Coast Guard, but did make contact with a Captain William Harnden of Sucia. Harnden went to Matia and searched the island and all the surrounding waters to no avail. There was no sign of the boat or the two elderly men. It wasn't until spring that some Indians found part of a wrecked boat in the sand at Gray's Point near the Canadian border—Smith's outboard motor still attached.

With this story in mind, we sailed back once again to Matia. We walked south and west from Rolfe's Cove where we had anchored. We wandered across downed logs, through brush and vines that cross the ill-defined trail. We soon found the remains of old floor planking, mellow with moss and decay. Nearby was a tiny orchard of cherry and pear-apple trees. We walked through chest-high China berries and bamboo and then suddenly burst out on the shores of one of the most glorious coves we have ever seen.

Facing the north shore of Orcas, this tiny, nearly landlocked bay is everything anyone could ever want. The crescent-shaped pebble beach is flanked by dangerous rocks at the opening, and yet it offers almost total protection—almost unseen—from the 'outside'. How many times had we sailed past and never noticed this wonderful spot!

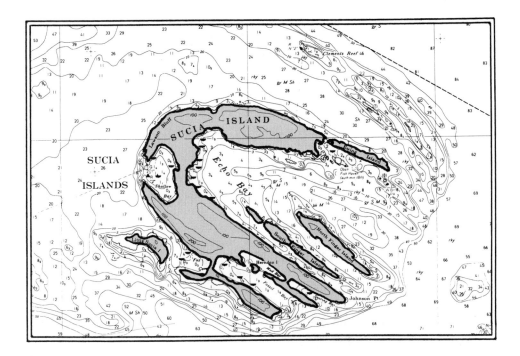

We hiked in and found the remains of an old barbed-wire fence, more cabin or shed ruins, chicken-wire fencing, and more tiny refuge bays along the shore. All the while we marveled at what appeared to be virgin timber with towering cedars. On much of the island the sun never seems to strike the forest floor.

There are spots with no underbrush—and others where it is heavy. We found ground cover of ivy, blackberries and salal. There were magnificent stands of fern—brilliant green under the tall firs—searching for sun. Other parts of the island were chest-high with berry vines where the trees thinned out.

Back at Rolfe's Cove, we rowed the shore boat through the passage inside a tiny rocky island off the north point of Matia. We passed through a lot of kelp, but never did see bottom. The ranger told us later you could take a larger boat through that tiny pass if you really wanted to. Being confirmed shallow-water chickens, we haven't done it.

Both Matia and its tiny rock satellite have wondrous sandstone rock formations, carved through the eons by the waves of Georgia Strait constantly pounding against the soft rock.

We left Rolfe's Cove, silently envying Elvin Smith and his nearly 30 years living as a hermit in paradise.

Sucia Island Marine Park

The word 'Sucia' means 'dirty' in Spanish. It is legend that the early Spanish explorers laid that name on these islands because of the reefs. But that seems hard to believe. We think Sucia got a bum rap. In an archipelago where there are a considerable number of keel inspectors lurking just below the surface to drum up business for rescue boats, shipwright and caulkers, good old Sucia deals a fairly honest hand.

This is not to say that every year a number of boaters don't get hung up high and dry off Ev Henry Point which is the southwestern tip of Fossil Bay. Incidentally, it's time to do some of the work that NOAA overlooked. That long strip of land which is on the south shore of the island and extends in an easterly direction for about .6 of a mile, is **Ev Henry Finger**—even though it is unnamed on the charts. The end of this peninsula is Ev Henry Point. Who was Ev Henry? We'll tell you in a bit, if you don't already know.

First, some basic geography of the area.

Sucia Island State Marine Park is 562 acres composed of **Sucia Island, Little Sucia Island, Harnden Island, Ewing Island** and a sprinkling of islets called **Cluster Islands** but are not so designated on the chart. Incidentally, the chart you want for Sucia, Matia and Patos Islands is #18431.

There are two off-limits islands in this area: **North** and **South Finger Islands**. They are privately-owned. The rest is all state park land.

The isolated coves and bays once served the Lummi Indians in their seal-hunting days, and later made excellent hideouts in the mid-1800s for smugglers of Chinese laborers, wool and opium. Still later, the islands played a large role in rum-running during the liquor prohibition period of the 1920s and 1930s.

The first homesteader on Sucia was Henry Wiggins, who moved to the **Mud Bay**

Remains of the old cistern at Sucia

area in 1860. Tucked in behind Harnden Island, the Wiggins' family raised cows, fox and sheep as well as fruit trees and other crops.

From 1900 to 1909 about a thousand workers operated a rock quarry at Fossil Bay. Large barracks and cookhouses were built above the present maintenance shop in Mud Bay, where there was a dock. All this was left behind when the sandstone rock, used to pave Seattle streets, was found to be too soft.

The Harnden family moved to deserted Mud Bay in 1920 to live in the old quarry workhouse. Harnden built his famous boat, the *Tulip King*, which ran excursions between the islands. In 1929 the family returned from a vacation to discover all their buildings had burned down, and they left the island soon after. All that remains of their endeavors is a stone water cistern and chimney ruins.

Private logging operations existed on the island sporadically from the late 1800s until 1955. Numerous tree stumps are found along the old logging roads which today are trails and park maintenance roads.

In the early 50s a dashing skipper named Chris Wilkinson lived on **Harnden Island** and redubbed it Christmas Island. He had a 50-foot ketch, the *Orcas Belle*, and he took landlubbers out on it for romantic cruises of the San Juan Islands. The unofficial name never took, apparently, because it is still called Harnden Island.

In the late 1950s, Ev Henry of Seattle, a man who fell in love with Sucia, organized a successful effort to acquire 319 acres to save the island from commercial develop-

Sculptured sandstone at Sucia

ment. He initiated a fund drive among Puget Sound yacht clubs to buy the island for the asking price of $25,000. This led to the formation of the Interclub Association of Washington and to the preservation of Sucia. The island was then donated to Washington State Parks.

Sea animals, such as clams and snails, were fossilized in sediments from nearby highlands more than 65 million years ago. The beds were bent into open folds which were later eroded by glaciers and ocean waves to reveal the layered and folded rock, carving out softer layers which formed Echo Bay. The sandstone borders of Sucia's many bays, beautifully sculptured, show where wind and waves have eroded the less-resistant stone.

"The Sucia Islands have a peculiar formation, owing to alternating strata of rock, one resistant, the other yielding, to erosion by sea water. Fossil Bay, at Sucia's southern end. is rich in paleontological specimens: a clay bank here once yielded the perfect foreleg and hoof of a tiny prehistoric horse; these specimens were sent to the Smithsonian Institution." That authentic bit of information is courtesy of the book *Washington*, revised.

Take your hiking boots/running shoes to Sucia—there are six miles of hiking trails and 3.5 miles of rustic logging roads that you can wander at will. Explore for yourselves this spectacular island in all its beauty. Take your swimming suits, too. We'll tell you of a warm water bay suitable for swimming.

And for those naturalists, Sucia is a gold mine. There are numerous varieties of waterfowl such as great horned owls, harlequin ducks and the great blue heron. Bald eagles soar over rocky cliffs and dip into the water for a dinner of whatever fish rise near the surface.

Tide pools offer limpets, oysters, clams, crabs, sculpins, starfish, snails and a myriad of other critters.

Swimming about are bottom fish such as cod and snapper, salmon and Dungeness crab. Do remember to observe fishing limits, and carry a punch card if you salmon fish.

State parks has implemented a recycling program for bottles and aluminum cans at Sucia, Matia, Stuart and Jones Islands. It has been moderately successful and most boaters observed seem to use the containers to help keep littering to a minimum.

Now, let's do a nose count of the bays. Starting at the southwestern extremity, we have Fossil Bay, which has its own little adjunct, Mud Bay; just east of Fossil is Snoring Bay; rounding Johnson Point there are three channels which lead into Echo Bay; out of Echo Bay to the northeast is Ewing Cove (not named on the chart); swinging out around the forbidding northerly shore of Sucia, you round gently to the northwest shore and pass Lawson Bluff at the entrance to Shallow Bay; continuing westerly out of Shallow Bay is Fox Cove, located behind Little Sucia Island.

'Amphitheater' - an abandoned quarry at Fossil Bay

Fossil Bay

Let's discuss the various moorages and anchorages. We'll start with the most popular of them all—**Fossil Bay**. A nice, wide channel brings you down into the area of the mooring buoys and floats.

If you can't catch a buoy or don't want to tie up to a float, the bottom is excellent for holding, and there is room for at least a couple of dozen more boats riding at anchor. The controlling depth in this bay is nine feet at low mean water, so 30 to 40 feet of scope ought to take care of you unless there's a blow out of the southeast. It doesn't happen often, but Fossil Bay (and Echo Bay also), because of the shallow water, *can* make you think you've decided to spend the night in your clothes washer. In the winter, we've seen boats at the only remaining float in this harbor slammed into it by whitecapped waves. We've been caught in blows that prompted us to hoist the hook and fight our way out into the teeth of the storm, sails well-reefed for safety.

There is a detached float which is tied up to pilings in the western end of the bay near the sandspit. You can tie up to it during the summer. As in many of the marine parks in the islands, most of the floats are taken out in mid-October and not put back in until May because of the winter storms. The beach at the end of the bay is shallow and sandy and is a place to swim if you have Eskimo blood.

Mud Bay is no dice for anchoring—it goes dry at low tides.

Fossil Bay is Eastman Kodak's dream. We can think of no place that offers more picture possibilities. During the height of the tourist season, the clicking of shutters can sound like crickets. And no wonder! We have been into this bay dozens of times. It is as familiar as the parking lot of our favorite grocery store. And yet we always find new photo angles. The quarry just behond the main dock looks like a giant Greek amphitheater, sunlight and shadows creating constantly changing patterns in the hewn rock. Sinuous and flesh-colored madrona trees are everywhere—they almost look like a tableau in a ballet. Kids—splashing, climbing, exploring—tempt even the hardest-hearted shutterbugs.

Sandstone rills and cliffs can be breathtaking. The action of water on the soft stone and the soluble salts that were trapped in them in early geological periods have created shell-like swirls interspersed with pockmarked rocks that looked like petrified sponges.

On a sunny afternoon, you can go over the rock outcroppings like studying a tapestry, looking for traces of things that once lived and were entrapped. You can certainly understand why the place is called Fossil Bay.

If you are ambitious, or just tired of being cooped up in a boat, you can go for a hike on one of the many trails. There is a big Parks Service map of the paths near the ranger's cabin off Mud Bay which details the trails.

The park map at the head of Fossil Bay suggests a hike out the Ev Henry Finger to visit a memorial to him located at the end of the peninsula. If you decide to take this trip, take some advice from us.

First, even though it's tempting, do not go along the beach on the southwest side of the finger and plan to climb up to the top of the land farther along. You can get up there in one or two places, but it's not recommended for armchair mountaineers. Take the path on the narrow spit that separates Fossil Bay from Fox Cove and let it lead you up. It's a trifle steep in places, but nothing like the other way.

There is a panoramic vista from Ev Henry Point on Sucia.

About halfway out the finger (at the knuckle, shall we say), you will see signs showing that the trail becomes a circle farther on. You have two choices: if you are very hale and hearty and believe in aerobics, take the southern trail and go counterclockwise. If, on the other hand, you are partial to gentle grades and wooded paths, take the trail above the Fossil Bay side.

On our first visit to the Ev Henry Memorial, we decided to make the circle by staying to the right on the rugged southern trail. After we had gone up and down ravines and edged along high goat trails on cliffs, we began to wonder if it would all be worth the trip. We wished we had asked somebody in authority, "Just what *is* the Ev Henry Memorial?"

We trudged and climbed, tripped and skidded, all the while speculating on just what it would look like. Suppose, we wondered, we get there and discover that it is the *Ev Henry Memorial Clorox Bottle?*

Of course, the views from this trail *are* grand. You can see Orcas Island and Mount Constitution in the distance. The surf, crashing onto the rocks below, is a little intimidating but very dramatic.

Eventually, you will get to Ev Henry Point and you can see why they decided to make it the spot at which they honored this farsighted gentleman.

Is the Ev Henry Memorial a plastic bottle? We're not going to tell you. We have to leave *some* mystery in this book!

Snoring Bay

So it's "Up anchor, boys, and away!" to **Snoring Bay**. Now, what about the name? One writer says that it was called that by Park Service officials who came to inspect and found one of the rangers sound asleep on the shore.

We have our own private theory: Snoring Bay is so small that only a couple of boats can anchor in there at one time. And they will be so close to each other that the people on one boat can hear the people on the other boat snoring.

The bay offers two park department mooring buoys and there are a couple of campsites on shore. The bay has steep cliffs on both sides and there is no protection against an up-strait blow.

Echo Bay

Next let's explore the big one—**Echo Bay**. You have your druthers on the way into it. There are two narrow corridors, both free of obstacles, and one ultra-wide entrance. The passage between South Finger Island and Sucia is the most picturesque because it is so narrow. If you make the entrance at night or in a fog, be careful because some big boat skippers like to drop the hook in this channel as it is usually fairly calm.

Echo Bay has 14 buoys but no dock. As you can see from the chart, these buoys are strung along the northwestern shore of the bay. It is often rolly even in calm weather because the swells come in off the Strait and break up when they 'feel the bottom'. If you do not get a buoy, you may opt to anchor as close to the westerly shore as you can , behind Finger Islands, to get a little protection from the winds. If this area is crowded, and it often is in the summer, you will have to choose between fairly deep water—30 to 40 feet in the lee of S. Finger Island—or ride the bumps in

Delightful Ewing Cove in Echo Bay

shallower water in the northerly area. The bottom is usually good for holding, although we know of a number of folks who have dragged there in a southeasterly blow.

There is a lot of good sandy-pebbly beach at the end of Echo Bay that is tempting to swimmers, but not for long, because of the cold water. Beachcombing is wonderful in the drift logs, or you can examine the sandstone rocks firsthand. There are campsites, water, and pit toilets in this area and roads and trails nearby.

The northern wing of Echo Bay is rugged and offers little landing beach. There is a reef just offshore at the head of the bay which is mostly covered at all but fairly low tides. Just west of that reef is a rock that is pretty ugly and can be covered—find both of these on your chart if you intend to pass along this shore or anchor here.

The cliffs on this side are spectacular, though. If you stay close to shore and watch your depth sounder, you can pass by some very fascinating rock formations. As a matter of fact, we are going to bring you back for an exploration of some of this area in our next anchorage report.

Ewing Cove

This is now our favorite spot in the Sucia area. There are only four mooring buoys here and space for anchored boats is limited. But the spot is choice, we think, unless it's blowing a southeaster.

First of all, there is an intriguing string of islets that form the southern boundary of this cove—**Cluster Islands**. One of them looks like a teakettle with a spout, so naturally we named it **Teapot Rock**. These little islets are a great place for kids of all ages to roam—there are no real dangers to be encountered.

China Rock where smugglers reportedly hid their human contraband

If you're a scuba diver, the area is also great. About 10 years ago, an old wooden hulk, that had once been the 40-foot *Lady Alyce,* was sunk off the entrance to provide an underwater reef for a fish habitat.

There is a pebbled beach at the head of the cove and above it is a path that leads along the top of the finger nearest Ewing Island. It has a view of Clements Reef, just offshore in the opposite direction.

Another hike we suggest is along the shoreline that will take you from Ewing Cove to the head of Echo Bay. There are a number of tiny inlets and coves that offer an inexhaustible chance for hunting for rocks and fossils. On one of the rock outcroppings on the beach we saw something soft and jet black imbedded in the rock. When we dug at it with a penknife, we discovered it was charcoal. We tried to figure out whether it was the remains of some prehistoric campfire or the result of a forest fire.

Incidentally, state law prohibits digging fossils out of the rocks unless you are part of an archeological or geological team with state permission.

On this trail you will pass through an old apple orchard. There are no longer signs of human habitation there. Somebody once lived there and planted the apple trees.

Was it the Wiggins family, or the Harndens, or one of the quarry workers who wanted fresh fruit?

North Shore

You can't pass between Ewing Island and Sucia, as the pass is suitable only for shore boats, so when you leave Ewing Cove you must head south and around the reef before heading back in a northwesterly direction to continue circumnavigating the island and end up in Shallow Bay. This side of Sucia is deep offshore, and you can pass between the island and **Clements Reef** which always feels like such a lonely spot. Fishing is good out near the reef and that makes the trip more interesting.

Shallow Bay

Head past the 160-foot high, forested bluffs, past **Lawson Bluff,** and into the crab-shell-shaped bay. The entrance to the bay is marked by two beacons. The green square marker on the left—#1—marks the reef between it and the Lawson Bluff shore on the north. The red triangular marker indicates shallow water on the right side. Stay between the two and you are in a favorite anchorage—a good spot in all but strong northwesterly blows.

The state mooring buoys are all in the northern portion of the harbor as the southern part drops to just three feet at minus tides in much of the area.

There is a marsh just beyond the southern beach and the trees in it have all died

Sandy shores make good playing at Shallow Bay

137

Smuggling and China Rock

It's common knowledge that the San Juan Islands have a long, colorful and, some would say, occasionally seamy, history of smuggling. Small wonder — this is a natural area for smugglers to use.

There are untold numbers of tiny coves, bights and bays, even caves, where smugglers could hide out. And with so many islands, overhanging trees, notched-out hideaways and even large rocks, smugglers could find lots of room to hide their fast boats — boats far faster than the government cutters used to chase them ... at least much of the time.

As far as we can figure, smuggling started with illegal booze about the time the Americans and British set up their camps back in the mid-1800s. That particular product reached its peak during prohibition, and if we are to believe what we read, we may still find bottles of white lightning on the sea bottom where it was hastily dumped before a 'revenuer' caught up with the smuggling vessel.

But liquor wasn't the only commodity to be smuggled. There was also Canadian wool and silk, and we've all heard of the sheep farmers on San Juan Island whose winning ram would 'grow' several hundred pounds of wool each year, at least when it was being declared, as opposed to the normal amount of fleece of maybe 10 pounds or less.

In recent years the San Juans still have a share of illegal drugs crossing the border, and that continues to be a concern of customs officials.

But perhaps the most heinous of all smuggling was of human beings — Chinese in the late 1800s.

Large numbers of Chinese entered the country legally to work as laborers in unskilled jobs on the railroads or the canneries. But by the time some 300,000 Chinese were here, Congress passed a law in 1882 making it illegal to import any more. However, there were many who still wanted to enter to be with friends or relatives, and after they reached Canada, were willing to pay whatever the cost might be to enter the U.S.

One story, told by Dave Richardson in 'Pig War Islands' and Bryce Wood in 'San Juan Island,' is that one smuggler left some Chinese 'temporarily' on a rock in San Juan Channel as the feds came looking for them. The hapless Orientals were found much later near starvation, apparently existing only on clams on a reef then named China Rock.

(Bryce Wood identifies the reef as "probably Half-tide Rocks near the south end of Griffin Bay.")

According to the diary of Orcas pioneer James Frances Tulloch, a famous smuggler named Kelly smuggled whenever he was out of jail. "It was claimed by his friends that on one of his trips with a load of Chinese he was fast being overhauled by a revenue cutter and he killed the Chinese and threw them overboard, then let himself be overhauled and examined." (From 'The James Frances Tulloch Diary', by Gordon Keith.)

In another smuggling yarn, a number of Chinese were found in the bottom of Kelly's boat, sound asleep, as the officials greeted the boat when it landed at the Kanaka Bay shore. That was the end of their shortlived stay in the U.S.

Well, all this is by way of an introduction to China Rock. That's not the same China Rock mentioned earlier. This is the enormous rock in Shallow Bay on the west side of Sucia. This rock is one of those eroded sandstone giants; it sits on the edge of the beach and then goes far back into the woods. There are ledges and caves and hidey-holes that snake all through the rock. It is probably 35 to 40

Dragon-shaped rocks guard China Rock

feet high and extends back at least 100 feet.

In the water immediately in front there is even a dragon-like rock sculpture that looks as though it belongs in an Oriental temple.

The trees are tangled and the woods make many of the shallow caves difficult to see in the dim light. What a wonderful place to hide contraband!

It's easy to imagine the scene: the fast little sloop maneuvers into Shallow Bay, ducks behind the northwestern point, and in the dark, everyone speaking in hushed tones, all the Chinese are rushed onto the shallow beach. They run along the edge of the water, the smuggling skipper knowing that their footprints will be erased by the high tide later than night; then they reach the comparative safety of the enormous rock.

The smuggler urges the Chinese farther back into the forest and into the caves where they will never be seen and can wait until they can be picked up and safely taken to Seattle or other ports in the area where they can find jobs.

It makes for exciting fantasizing as you stand there surveying the rock, and possibly has some semblance of truth. How else did this labyrinthine sandstone get its name?

from saltwater intrusion—they are ghostly silver. At first glance, you might think there is a moorage beyond the beach with hundreds of white-masted sailboats. The swamp is a wonderful place for amateur biologists and photographers.

Shallow Bay has several things going for it, and if you love to swim, you have found one of the few warm water spots in the San Juans. Shallow Bay warms up enough in the summer to allow swimmers time for honest-to-goodness swimming. Not as warm as Desolation Sound perhaps, where the water gets up into the 70s in the summer, but warmer than the normal 50 or so degrees in most of the San Juan Islands.

There are several good beaches in Shallow Bay, but the one on the northern shore is beautiful sand along the no-bank upper beach and the perfect place for little kids to play at the water's edge and for anyone to swim. The beach on the eastern shore is a bit steeper and pebble-covered.

Against the northeastern shore lurks the enormous, patently evil-looking China Rock. Shadows engulf the huge rock as it extends back into the woods. A dragon-like sandstone sculpture guards the side of the rock as it might the entrance of an ancient Chinese temple.

The accepted theory for the name is that smuggled orientals were hidden in the holes in the rock to escape detection from the Customs and Immigration authorities back in the mid-1800s.

China Rock is an enormous eroded sandstone giant.

On one visit, we found an ideal hidey-hole in one of the lower interstices which must have appealed to children, in it we found a cache of shells, cans, bits of seaweed and driftwood that had been hidden out of sight. No doubt some child had deposited

Lovely Shallow Bay on Sucia Island

140

The split rock at Fox Cove - a climber's challenge

carefully picked-up beach treasures in that niche after being told by a stern father-captain, "You can't bring that junk aboard the boat."

The idea was so marvelous that Al reached into one of the deep holes and hid a quarter. "I wonder if it will still be here when someone else visits the place?" he said.

If you find it, tell us the next time you see us in Friday Harbor or out sailing. You might even decide to play the game too, by leaving small change in the various pockets like an Easter Egg hunt for the tads.

Now you've had a swim, taken pictures of each other hiding in China Rock, left a quarter in a tiny hole and played on the beach—time to take off for more exploring around Sucia Island.

Fox Cove

Fox Cove is the next little bight around to the south. It's formed by Sucia on one side, and Little Sucia Island on the other, with the head of the bay a spit between Fox Cove and Fossil Bay. (This spit was formed by sediment left from the melted glacier—same as the spit between Echo and Shallow Bay.) There are several park mooring buoys in Fox Cove, fire pits, campsites, water, toilets, trails, etc.

You can enter Fox Cove from the northwest and find a good anchorage, or through the narrow and somewhat hazardous pass between Sucia and Little Sucia. Somewhat hazardous, we say, because reefs extend from both shores on the southwestern entrance and the water is about two fathoms with lots of kelp.

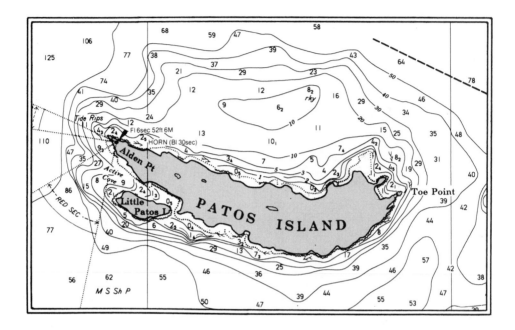

This cove is another great area for the kids, with sandy beaches, sandstone caves to play in and easy access to all the main island trails. Dinghy out to Little Sucia and hike around the place. It's isolated and primitive and a wonderful place to watch gorgeous sunsets out over Boundary pass and the Canadian Gulf Islands.

Patos Island

You can't leave this area without a quick trip over to **Patos Island**. When son John and his Ann sailed from Sucia to Patos, he left this entry in the log book: "The fog lifts and we're on our way from Sucia to Patos. No wind at all, so we idle on over. As we came to the shelf between the two islands, we cut the engine and drifted while I fished. Caught one five to six-pound snapper, a two-pound rock cod and another five to six-pound cod of some sort I've never seen before. We let him go!

"Anchored with two other boats in Active Cove and one left, so we picked up his buoy later. It's beautiful here. We walked around the old lighthouse and buildings, found a private beach for bathing and saw many eagles. Quite a spot for the San Juans."

But he didn't wax quite so lyrical in the middle of the night when the boat began rolling. By 1:30 a.m. a strong wind was blowing through the cut.

"At 2 a.m., I decided to stay up as the winds built up. By 4 a.m. we had two-foot waves breaking the anchorage, there was only 11 feet of water under us and it was getting rather uncomfortable."

By 5 a.m. they powered out into the northerly, reefed the sails and sailed to Stuart Island.

This is only by way of what can happen at Patos.

When we were at Patos it was lovely and calm, but we anchored for only a short time in **Active Cove** as the buoy was taken and we didn't want to risk getting caught that night in the same weather John had found. But we were there long enough to see the now-automated gleaming white lighthouse at the tip of **Alden Point**—its fog whistle shrill, even on clear days. We were anchored in Active Cove where the tide rips can be swirling suddenly after a flat calm. There is an old pier once used by the Coast Guard but it is in disrepair.

We wandered around a bit and got some of the feeling of this isolated, far-north state marine park.

Patos has some wonderful tales, best memorialized in Helene Glidden's book, *Light on the Island.* Helene grew up on Patos where her father was lighthouse keeper at the turn of the century. She tells of smugglers, shipwrecks, storms, tragedies, and her large family living on the remote island, with warmth and tenderness.

President Teddy Roosevelt even went near enough to the island on his ship to dip the colors to his old friend, Helene's father, who manned the lighthouse at Alden Point.

There is little protection on Patos Island, except for Active Cove. There is a tiny bight inside **Toe Point** at the eastern end of the island and there are a couple of other little bights and indentations along the island's forested shores, with trails through the woods.

It's a nice place for a short visit, but we wouldn't want to live there.

State Parks does not plan any overnight camping areas on Patos because there are eagles on the island and they don't want to disturb them.

Active Cove, by the way, was named in honor of the U.S. steamer, *Active,* which was active in survey duties around in the Northwest in the 1850s and 1860s according to Doug Cardle. And Alden Point as named for the *Active's* skipper naturally, Lt. Commander James Alden.

Patos Island automated lighthouse at Alden Point

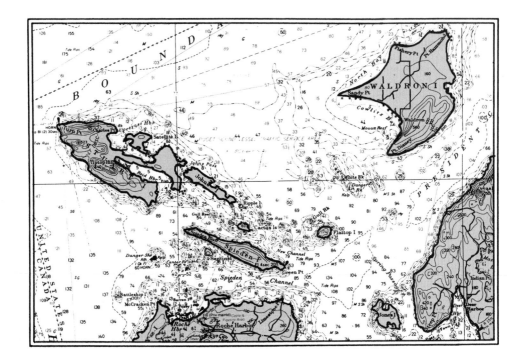

Waldron History

(From a Monograph by Charles H. Ludwig of Seattle, dated 1959.)

There's a strange turnabout in the history of Waldron Island. It was, for centuries, a summer tourist spot. About the turn of the century, the landholders appeared and tourism disappeared.

The early summer visitors didn't call it 'Waldron' though. They called it 'Schishuney'—by that they meant 'the place to fish with a pole'. The visitors came from Orcas, Lummi, Lopez and San Juan Islands. They boated in from Vancouver Island, Skagit and Whatcom county areas. They were the Lummis, the Saanich, the Songish and the Samish tribes. They were an easy-going, convivial group of peoples. They canoed to Schishuney in the spring, summer and fall. They camped on the beaches and fished and gathered shellfish. Occasionally, they hunted deer, elk and rabbits for a change in meat diets. The fields provided camas and many varieties of berries.

Life would have been idyllic for these listless foragers, except for the occasional visits of two tribes from the northern reaches, the Kwakiutl and the Haidas. They came to gather a crop of another sort—human. No, the white man did not invent slavery on the North American Continent.

For centuries the peaceful tourists coped with the frequent raids. Sometimes they managed to hide in the heavy forests and the towering rocky crags. Legend has it that they even fought and won some pitched battles with the invaders.

But the devastating white man fire-sticks made the contests unequal during the first part of the 19th century. The northern Indians found they could trade hides to the Russian traders and receive muzzle-loaders. They would descend on the little island paradise in 50-man canoes, kill the males who resisted and take away the male captives, their wives and children.

Like all other predators, however, the warlike northerners took care never to completely destroy the tribes; they were too good a source of loot and manpower.

When the white man first arrived in the mid-1800s, order was again established. The contact with the strange pale humans soon became almost as devastating as the Haida raids. When the new interlopers discovered the beauty and natural resources of the island, they began to stake out claims and tourism rapidly vanished from the island they now named 'Waldron'. The name came from one of the members of the Wilkes Expedition—Thomas W. Waldron, a captain's clerk from the brigantine *Porpoise.*

To this day, Waldron Island is off-limits to casual visitors.

History records the story of the first white resident of the island. His name was James Cowan. He built a small shack at Cowlitz Bay. In March of 1868, friends from the adjoining islands sensed something was amiss with Cowan. He had not been seen for some time, no smoke rose from his chimney. On a calm day, they sailed over to check on him. They found his body buried under some brush. The settler had been shot in the back.

His murderer was never discovered. Some said that an enemy from San Juan had

County dock at Waldron Island's Cowlitz Bay

done him in as the result of an old grudge. Others remarked it was undoubtedly the work of notorious old 'Skookum Tom', a renegade Indian who had been accused of a number of murders in the islands.

In 1870, the worldly goods of the victim were sold for $350. They consisted of two two-year-old steers, two one-and-a-half year-old heifers, five other calves and a bull. Added to this inventory was an unspecified number of pigs and poultry and 160 acres of crop land.

By 1870, there were four families living on Waldron: Edwin and Jeannie Wood, John and Elizabeth Oldham, and two bachelors, Benjamin Hunt and John Brown.

John Brown (not an assumed name, we are told) took it in his mind to drain a marshland to convert it to a planting field. He imported a crew of Chinese and Indian laborers, whom he paid the munificent sum of 25¢ per day to dig ditches, some of which had to be 40 feet in depth. When the land was finally dried, it began to sprout weeds. Brown, who did not have much knowledge of soil cultivation, burned the area to get rid of the weeds. Well, it burned and burned. When it finally went out, the fire had destroyed all of the peat and it was virtually worthless. He went 'back to the drawing board' and died soon after.

Ned Wood had, earlier in his life, fallen victim to gold fever. He hitchhiked a ride from the Eastern U.S. to Panama. Then he walked up the coast of Central America for hundreds of miles until he found a port with a ship that would transport him to California. He found no gold in California; so undaunted, he wandered up to the Fraser River in 1852 where gold had been struck. He blanked out on that strike, also. When he didn't make a killing in gold nuggets, he discovered his fortune lay in iron—blacksmithing and shoeing horses for miners.

With something of a stake, he heard the siren song of the islands and came to Waldron Island to till the soil. It is possible that he bent the truth a bit in the retelling of his experiences, because the word went out that he had a cache of gold hidden somewhere on his land.

He died without leaving a will or a clue to his cache. To this day, people still prowl his land with metal detectors looking for the horde. Little matter that legend has it that it's all a chimera. After all, when someone sets out to find hidden gold, the last thing in the world they want to hear is that it's all a figment. Human nature has changed little since the 1850s.

The land of poor old murdered James Cowan was bought by a gentleman named Sinclair McDonald. He was another gold-hunter who had lucked out.

Sinclair was an enterprising individual. First, he built a log cabin which was nominally a post office. Then he became a postmaster. His next undertaking is called by historians, 'The Lucy Bean Affair'.

At the turn of the century, commercial enterprise of a more ethical cast came to Waldron. At that time, the city of Seattle wanted to pave Yesler Avenue and it needed stone blocks.

Two Tacomans, George Savage and George Scofield, discovered that Point Disney could provide a 200-foot thick layer of sandstone. They set up a quarrying operation and imported about 150 laborers—tough and skilled white men. They were paid the mind-boggling sum of $1.50 per hour—an instant fortune for those

Lucy Bean Story

Shortly after the end of the Civil War, Sinclair McDonald, who lived at Cowlitz Bay, built a small house which became the island's post office. Charles Ludwig, the Waldron historian, tells the story of postmaster McDonald and the saga of Lucy Bean.

No one knows for sure whether McDonald actually perpetrated the scheme, but Waldron became known as the center of the Lucy Bean Missionary Post.

Ludwig writes, "... large packages of used clothing began arriving from the east addressed to 'Lucy Bean, c/o the Waldron Island Mission'. McDonald forthwith began a lucrative trade in selling these to Indians who frequented his place.

"The 'mission' prospered until the day that a committee came out from the east to investigate it for the contributing member churches. When they found that the island was completely devoid of the flourishing missions described in Lucy Bean's letters, the source of supply for the first attempt at private enterprise on Waldron came to an abrupt halt."

days. The jobs had exotic names: powdermen, tool sharpeners, coyote hole drillers, donkey engine operators, cablemen, bull cooks, storekeepers and an assortment of various quarrymen. They lived in a big bunkhouse about a mile-and-a-half from the stone face and they had to climb to work along narrow footpaths where one misstep could bring on a funeral.

At the beginning of each operation, the drillers would hang like spiders from ropes tied to a tree at the top of the cliff. When they had drilled 60 feet into the rock, they would shift to one side and drill another hole at right angles to the first. This second hole was the 'coyote hole'. Once it was completed, the laborers would pad their shoes with gunnysacks to avoid sparks and they would form a human chain of powderbag handlers. Once the coyote hole was filled, the cap would be placed, the wires strung and everybody would take cover. When the handle of the generator was plunged, the whole face of the cliff would blow off and avalanche down its face.

Then the cutting crew would go to work shaping the 6x6x12-inch rectangular blocks which would be loaded onto a barge to be shipped to Seattle.

Some of these blocks are still to be found on the Queen Anne counterbalance.

The bubble burst one fine day in 1906. The pavers in Seattle found that concrete was superior to paving stones and they canceled the Waldron contract.

The union boss on Waldron got wind of the change and absconded with all of the funds for the payroll. He also highgraded all of the chow. The next morning, the workers showed up for work to discover they had been had. Some of them stayed on trying futilely to cut and sell stones. Later, a few settled down on the island to become solid citizens.

There remains one more illustrious name in Waldron history—'old Ethan Allen'. This character is not to be confused with the Revolutionary War Hero who captured Fort Ticonderoga.

Ethan and his wife Sadie migrated to Waldron in 1895 and homesteaded a claim just south of Mail Bay. He and his wife taught school on the island for a while. Then Ethan became superintendent of schools for San Juan County. During his tenure, which lasted many years, he would row from island to island to check on the welfare of the outposts. He once claimed to have rowed 'ten thousand miles' on his tour of duty.

He was an avid collector of Indian artifacts. His contribution is still visible in a special 'Ethan Allen Room' in the Orcas Island Historical Museum.

A guidebook to Washington State says: "It contains a large collection of artifacts gathered over a lifetime by a descendant of the Revolutionary War here, comprising more than 3,000 items including arrowheads, spearheads, Indian baskets, pottery, stone dishes, grinding implements, paint pots, ornaments and ceremonial pieces."

Now that we have given you a sort of Readers' Digest rendition of the story of the island, we can begin our description of the significant features visible from the water.

Cruising Waldron Island

With chart #18432 before us, let's look at this historic old island. We shall begin our cruise at Mail Bay on the eastern shore of the island and follow the clock hands around. When we say 'cruising around Waldron Island', we really mean 'around'. The people of that rock are textbook xenophobes. (Xenophobia—fear of furriners.)

It is their notion that if strangers should be allowed to roam at will on their land, they would massacre all of the cattle, cart off all of the women and steal all of the produce; in short, emulate the ancient Haidas.

Or, what is even more horrific, they might be tempted to buy property and set up a Waldron-Hilton. They firmly believe that the fact the island has no electric power, no water district and no telephone would not deter almost immediate Carmel-ization of their island paradise. As a matter of fact, they are fairly fixed in their belief that tourism, anywhere in the islands, is an open invitation to the devils of epidemic suburbanization.

At this point, your two correspondents—myself, Al Cummings, and my colleague Jo Bailey-Cummings, beg to file separate reports on the character of the Waldronites.

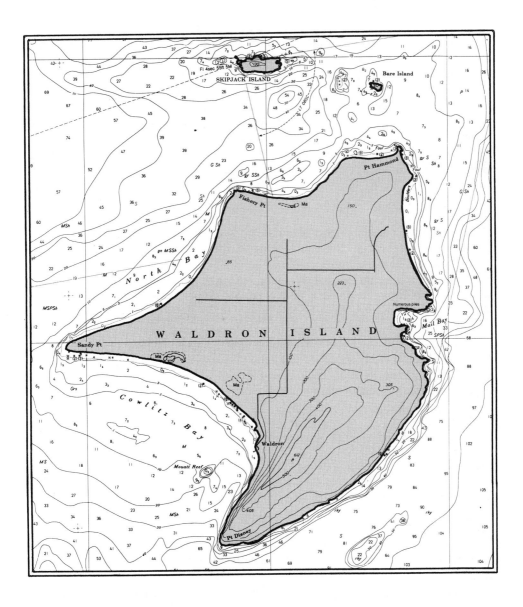

Ms. Bailey-Cummings has a number of friends on Waldron and has even been treated with civility on her infrequent visits.

I, on the other hand, had only one friend on Waldron. We loved him. He died a few years ago. I frequently refer to the place as 'that Churlish Isle'. If you ever visit the place for some reason—do not mention my name.

Okay, my choler vented, let us set about noting the geographic features of this bastion.

Mail Bay, on the eastern shore, is one of two possible refuges in the coastline of Waldron. It could accommodate about a half-dozen boats at the hook in waters that vary from 40 to 11 feet. Part of the northern sector has the hazard of subsurface pilings which are mentioned but not indicated on the chart. Other pilings may be seen on the vestigial point and it tends to bisect the harbor. These are probably the remains of old docks built by early settlers. It was in this bay that Enoch May beached his boat in 1878 to deliver the first mail pouch. The residents shortly gathered on the beach for the first mail call. The actual post office building was soon constructed in the middle of the island to provide more convenient access to the settlers. Mail Bay was the closest shelter for the rowboats that had to cross President's Channel from Orcas. It is also an escape point from the frequent squalls and tricky currents of the passage.

Point Disney

The two-mile coastline from Mail Bay to **Point Disney** is rugged and cliff-dominated. There is no shelter on the entire southeast profile. Fishermen occasionally try their luck just offshore.

Point Disney was named in 1841—long before the birth of the father of Mickey Mouse. It got its name from a sailmaker, Solomon Disney, who served aboard Wilkes' ship. They must have been scraping the bottom of the barrel for names about that time!

This is the site of the historic sandstone quarry. We've tried to pick out some of the coyote holes that are supposed to be still visible on the terraces of the quarry, but could not spot them. Let us know if you find them.

It's a majestic headland, though, well worth a photo or two.

Cowlitz Bay

Cowlitz Bay is the shallow bight around the corner from Point Disney. In later years, and before the dock was built by San Juan County engineers, there was a stick that protruded from a crack in the rocks on the south side of Point Disney. There was a coffee can tied to the end of the stick. The mail boat would hover beneath it and the mailman would cram it with the thrice weekly delivery. Remember—there was no 'junk mail' in those days. One wonders what disposition was made of the old Sears catalogs.

A researcher says that the bay got its name from a boat owned by the Hudson's Bay Company which carried on fur trade with some of the Indians who summered there.

Mouatt Reef, in the mouth of the bay, never goes dry and has only three feet of water above it at MLLW. It is host to a good crop of kelp.

The county dock is located at the eastern edge of the bight. On the chart, you will see the legend 'Waldron'. It does not indicate a town or village or even a cluster of buildings. It is the terminus of a county road, however.

At the end of the dock you will see a two-story building. It is owned by some off-island people, we have heard they are artists who use it as a workshop.

If you look carefully to the right of the white building, you will see a log cabin. This is the present post office and meeting place for Waldronites.

On the dock you will see a small shack, probably used for storage by the local boaters. It has a light duty boom and block.

400-foot high Point Disney

There is a float of about 25 feet that remains in place year around. It is there for the mail boat and the other county boats as well as off-loading of supplies for the locals. Any delivery of heavy equipment is accomplished by the beaching of a power barge.

On one of our visits to the island (we had been granted permission) we moored the *Sea Witch* to the county dock. In order to observe protocol we went up to the post office and told the postmaster we were expected. He told us the mail boat was due some time that day and suggested we find some other place for our boat. There was a dinghy riding on a buoy about 50 yards off the dock. We could tie to that buoy and we were told to use the dinghy to get us back to the dock.

After visiting the schoolhouse, we came back to the dock about sunset. We discovered, to our chagrin, that the dinghy was no longer at the dock. There was our transportation back home, riding out there in the bay. We went back to the post office to inquire. There was nobody around.

It was winter, so cold that even the skipper-person of the *Sea Witch*, who has Prestone instead of blood in her veins, was not willing to swim out to get it.

We went back and combed the beach for something that would float. We found an old rowboat on the shore. When we lugged it down to the shore, it promptly filled with water. We dutifully hauled it back to where we found it.

Further along the beach, we found another old boat. We dragged it down to the water's edge and discovered that it leaked copiously, but with bailing could probably transport us.

There were no oars around. We found two pieces of driftwood to serve. We clambered in, rowed a bit, bailed a bit, rowed a bit, bailed—etc. Eventually, we got out to the sloop, dead tired and soaking wet.

We got aboard, fired up the engine and towed the boat-shaped sieve back to the dock. Then we returned the rowboat to its gravesite, I said a few profane words of requiem to it, and we departed.

Gentle reader, you may now see whence comes my unstinted animosity to this pearl of the archipelago. If you have any enemies, send them to me and I will sell them a contract as exclusive supplier of welcome mats for Waldron.

Notice the small marshland and tide pool off Cowlitz Bay as you near **Sandy Point**. This was the location of the home of the first white settler, James Cowan, who was done in by 'person or persons unknown'. It was called 'Tule' (pronounced 'too-lee') in the old days.

Sandy Point was named, and this will come as no surprise to you when you see it, after the nature of the shoreline.

North Beach is such a beautiful strand that one can almost understand the Waldronites' fierce sense of territoriality. No resort developer could see it without lusting for it. Our departed friend had a picturesque cabin just above the high-tide

---

Eagles

If you should decide to add eagle-watching to your sightseeing when you are in the San Juans, we can give you some information that is helpful. First of all, we will quote from The Audubon Society, Field Guide to North American Birds—Western Region. We will try not to tell you more about the symbolic American bird than you want to know.

It is one of the hawk family—the biggest. It can develop a wingspan of as much as 96"—that's eight feet wide, friends. Its body can range from three to four feet long. The bald-eagle isn't bald—you probably know. Like all of us, it gets a little white on the pate with advancing years. In the case of the eagle, that's from its adulthood, which it reaches in five

years. Youngsters are almost completely brown in color except for the leading edges of their wings which are white. As they age, they molt white feathers on their heads and black feathers on their underside wings.

As for the voice of the eagle being heard throughout the land, prepare for a disappointment: it makes a kind of loud mousey sound. Audubon's book says, "quite weak for so magnificent a bird." And all along you thought they flew around crying "E pluribus unum", didn't you?

Eagles are compulsive nest-builders. They enlarge their private homes from year to year until the things get so top heavy they break the limb they are at-mark. We think of this shore as 'North's Beach', because his name was North Burn. He was one of the sons of the beloved vagabonds of the islands, Farrar and June Burn.

In the years before his demise, North owned a little amphibious craft which he called his 'Tonka Toy'. Although he was physically handicapped, he was a demon-driver when he got at the controls of his seagoing duck. He would roar down the beach, bouncing over drift logs, cutting wheelies on the packed sand, and then head it into the saltchuck with wheels spinning and spray flying and howling shouts of glee that would have warmed the hearts of a rampaging Kwakiutl.

Whenever we pass along that shoreline, I always half expect to see him splashing out to meet us!

Fishery Point is so blunted as to be hardly a point at all. It is fair. It was the site of early Indian and whiteman fish traps.

From Fishery Point to Point Hammond is another beach land that is washed by the swells from Boundary Pass. It used to be called **Severson's Bay**. It has lost its name on modern charts, however.

Jack Severson, incidentally, was one of the ex-quarry workers who stayed on the island and married and raised a family there.

Point Hammond was named after a quartermaster aboard Wilkes' ship, Henry Hammond. The point has a low knob and a submerged beam leading out to an off-shore islet.

The narrow bight southeast of Point Hammond has some submerged rocks and is not very inviting.

From the end of this bight to Mail Bay is not particularly remarkable. The off-

tached to. Despite the size of their pads, they lay only one to three eggs a year.

Another rude awakening about the critter: it is usually very lazy in food gathering. It prefers carrion—dead things that don't try to run away. They must not have very sensitive stomachs. They are not always scavengers, however. They will dive for fish and often make quite respectable catches. They were originally attracted to the San Juans because of the hordes of rabbits that roamed here. You used to see them hunting down at American Camp, a grassland. They would swoop down and without breaking the arc, pick up a full-grown bunny. Well, the rabbits got to be such a nuisance that some of the islanders im-

ported ferrets to keep the population down. The ferrets not only decimated the rabbits, they learned the rabbit's breeding habits: result, we are now over-run by ferrets! Ferrets are smarter than bunnies, they don't often get swooped up by eagles.

We've heard stories about eagles making off with baby lambs, too. The tales may be true, you hear them frequently.

Eagles eat their feathered neighbors, also. They snap up wounded ducks and geese.

But the national bird is not the only species of eagle we have around here. We have golden eagles, too. They are about the same size as their 'bald' cousins. They are even more predatory hunters of

shore waters are shoal and there are some rocks to be avoided.

There is a rather deep gunkhole that indents the shore just above the upper end of Mail Bay. It does not recommend itself as an anchorage.

And so, my hearty crew, we have circled the Churlish Isle without mishap, I trust. After a stop to perform an exorcism to rid the ship of any inimical influences, we can proceed on our merry way.

For the sake of tidiness only, let us backtrack a bit and note a few geographic features off the Waldron shores on Boundary Pass.

Skipjack Island is a wildlife preserve which will not tempt you unduly. There is a flashing white light atop a rock which the chart says is 55' above high tide. Notice there is a tiny islet about 200 yards off the pockmarked eastern shore of Skipjack. How come the name? Well, a skipjack is a fish that breaches from time to time—probably early explorers saw porpoises or killer whales playing there.

Bare Island is three-fourths of a mile east of Skipjack Island. As you will see from the chart, you do not want to make a beeline between them; there is an ugly reef about 700 yards west of Bare Island. It is just such a forlorn and invisible peril that can ruin a skipper's day; note its presence if you happen to be in the area.

Way out in the middle of nowhere is an area roughly bounded by Orcas on the east Waldron to the north, Spieden and Johns to the west and Jones Island to the south, there is a fairly significant amount of real estate—most of it wildlife refuge.

Flattop Island is the largest island in this group and its shape belies its name—at least at a quick glance. It doesn't look flat, but that may be because of the varying height of the trees. There are shoals around Flattop and now offers no anchorage,

warm-blooded prey, but they don't turn their beaks up at dead rabbits and sheep.

Goldens are not a talkative bunch, but they have a voice that is no more impressive than the balds. They make little catlike mewings, according to Audubon.

Okay, something is wheeling around overhead or perched on a beach snag; how do you know whether it is an immature or mature bald, or a golden?

For that information, we turn to our resident eagle buff, the former postmaster of Friday Harbor, Charlie Nash. He is one of the foremost amateur authorities on eagles. He knows where almost every nest is, he knows them also by territory. There is the Beaverton Valley eagle, which is a bald that roams the

fields just outside town on the Roche Harbor road. There is a Three Meadows eagle, an Eagle Crest eagle, etc.

As a matter of fact, most folks in the islands turn to Charlie whenever they want to get some information about the creatures. One afternoon Charlie got a call from an irate farmer who yelled, "Okay, Charlie, one of your danged eagles got my best rooster!" Charlie promised to speak to the culprit on the next opportunity.

So how do you tell balds from goldens, aside from the color? Well, says Mr. Nash, bald eagles soar with nearly level wings, goldens have a slight dihedral to their wings. (They tip up a bit.) Bald eagles have long heads and necks, about

although we do know of several small boats—rowing types—which have sought shelter on the beaches during roiling southerlies.

Gull Rock, slightly northwest of Flattop, is barren and populated by gulls and seals, as are White Rock and Danger Rock to the north of Flattop. We have cruised slowly and carefully around White Rock and have seen many seals sunning themselves. And as seals so often do, they will slip into the water and paddle out to look at us. These are wildlife refuges—don't go ashore, and please be gentle.

Jones Island

Jones Island State Marine Park has long been a favored spot with thousands of boaters in the San Juans. Although not as capacious as Sucia, this 188-acre island has much to offer and is a popular stop-over for boats heading to, and returning from, trips into British Columbia waters.

There are two excellent moorages for many boats, 20 campsites, water—unless it's a dry season—pit toilets and a dock in the northern cove. As many as 80,000 visitors arrive annually at the island, but with just a little maneuvering, you can manage to feel as though you're there all alone.

There are four mooring buoys in the northern bay, and there is space for at least a dozen other boats to anchor in depths from 15 to 40 feet. The bay is rimmed with rocky bluffs on two sides, but the head of the cove is typical of the San Juan Islands' gravelly beaches, which make it a good spot to pull up a dinghy or for the kids to romp.

as long as their tails. Golden eagles' heads and necks look much shorter than their tails. Golden eagles have feathers all the way down their legs to their claws.

Where are you likely to find eagles? All along the waters of the San Juan archipelago. They usually choose a dead tree—a snag—and perch in the very top where they can survey the scene below to look for careless fish.

On clear days when there is a bit of wind, they like to soar in search of food. After they take off, which involves a lot of energetic flapping of wings, they make large circles in the sky. Since they are aerodynamically well-engineered, they need only an occasional boat of their wings to coast for hundreds of feet.

Like all living things, eagles have moods. Sometimes you can sail right up to and even under the tree they are sitting on and they look you over curiously. Other times, they get spooked and change perches when you are a hundred yards away.

They all have one thing in common: they have a remarkable sense of sound. All you have to do is see one perched on a good clear sight, and pick up your camera and aim it, and they will hear you adjusting the focus and will disappear to another tree.

It is possible that every eagle thinks, "Oh ... not me! I take terrible pictures!"

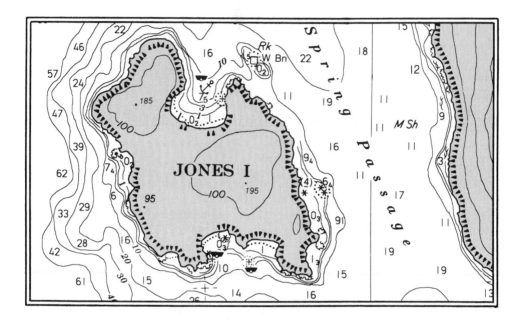

There is one danger on the bluff on the western side above the northern cove, where the trail crosses a sandy, eroding cliff. There the trails tends to disappear beneath your feet as the sand slips down the steep bank onto the tiny rocky beach below. The area is posted with danger signs, but some hikers insist on beating paths along the slippery sides of the bluff. Hardly a weekend goes by without boaters in the moorage below being summoned by pleas for help from some overly daring soul who has gotten into shifting sand and can't work back up to safety. Fortunately, there are always enough spare mooring lines available to equip a rescue crew, which can climb up the safe paths and snake lines down to the stranded person.

The south shore of the island has three buoys and a space for several more boats on the hook, with a rocky promontory bisecting the cove. The south shore is not a good place to spend much time if there is a southerly blowing up San Juan Channel. If you are on one of the three buoys, you are safe enough, although you may find yourself bouncing around a bit. If you have your own hook down and sufficient scope, you will roam around a lot and may spend a tense night.

The south shore of the island is the best area to spot the island's famous deer. There are a dozen or so of them on the island and they must know it is a wildlife preserve, for they are remarkably tame. Visitors come back with prized snapshots of their kids feeding fawns by hand. The deer are accomplished scroungers and panhandlers. They will hover around a camp, waiting to be noticed and fed. As a matter of fact, they can even become a bit of a nuisance. But they are unstintingly loved by most of the picnickers who often bring extra bread and apples along just for them.

The deer are most often in an old abandoned orchard above the southern shore of the island, usually at dusk, where they appropriate whatever fruit that appears and is reachable early in the growing season. If you look carefully, you can see the cleared site of an early homesteader's cabin near the orchard.

There are a lot of hiking trails on Jones; the favorite one, a well-worn path between the two coves. The forest is deep, but there is little underbrush, and an almost magical feeling pervades the tiny wilderness. Trails also skirt the shorelines on either side of the island and crisscross the hills which are as much as 200 feet high in places.

Jones has a fascinating array of tidal pools which show up among the rocks at low tide—particularly on the south shore of the island—where kids can explore with relative safety. Tiny fish, snails, crabs, barnacles, clams, urchins, starfish, and a host of other sea life can fascinate the kids. And while they could be termed 'hands-on' tidal pools, the kids can look and play but may not take home any of the live species because the San Juans are a vast wildlife preserve.

For divers, there are abalone, Dungeness crab and bottomfish swimming in the area. The reef off the northeastern tip is a favorite with divers. The chart shows plenty of water between the rock and Jones, but most boaters go out around it.

Jones Island, named for Captain Jacob Jones, a hero of the war of 1812, is also a favorite spot with campers who arrive by canoe or kayak. Jones is only about two miles from Deer Harbor on Orcas, a good spot for small boats to put in the water. Watch the currents and the weather and paddle on over.

Tidepools at Jones Island offer a wide variety of little sea critters for other little critters to explore, as Kwin and Gaea discovered.

Sentinel Island

This 15-acre island, just south of Spieden, is owned by the Nature Conservancy and unauthorized visitors are not permitted to land there because it is an eagle sanctuary. Even if they were allowed, there are no bays or inlets that are suitable for landings. Like its bigger neighbor, Spieden, it has a brief but colorful history.

In 1919, two lovable vagabonds, June and Farrar Burn, went to the land office in Seattle and asked about homesteading an island in the San Juans. There was only one left unclaimed, it was called 'Sentinel' for no reason that anyone could remember. It was cliff-sided all around, it had no drinking water, it had no beaches. It was 15 acres of rocks and trees and a few resident eagles. The Burns signed up for it.

They boarded a mail boat at Bellingham one morning in September and marveled at the almost uninhabited islands on the way into the San Juans. In her autobiography *Living High,* published in 1941, June wrote:

"That's Spieden," the captain said. "Ed Chevalier lives there. His wife's father homesteaded part of it and Ed has gradually gotten it all. Just on the other side of Spieden is the little island you are looking for.

"Across another channel, seagulls screaming. Around the immense hip of Spieden—and there was Sentinel Island, like a green gumdrop, fir trees lifting their beautiful crowns into the sky, sedum-covered bluffs sheering straight down into the rich, green-blue water."

The book doesn't give us a clue as to where they first landed their rowboat. It was probably on the rocks on the east-northeast side of the island. Once ashore, they had to haul themselves and their supplies up a steep ravine a distance of 100 feet.

They had some food, a tent they rented for $2 a month from the store at Roche Harbor, and Farrar had a part-time job working on the rock pile at the Roche Harbor lime kiln. He would row over from his camp across Spieden Channel at 7 every morning, bust rocks until noon and then row back home.

The job didn't last long, however, The other laborers complained about a man being able to work only part of a day. When Farrar saw the end coming, he providentially borrowed to the hilt from the company store. When he was let go, the company wrote off the debt.

The Burns were accomplished beachcombers and scroungers. The house they built on top of the island was one they 'beachcombed' from another island. It had been built some years before by fishermen who had abandoned it. Nobody seemed to lay claim to it, so the Burns dismantled it, towed it to Sentinel, hauled it up the cliff, and reassembled it. Beach wood was used to replace some of the old rotten siding. It was eight by ten with an earthen floor.

The Chevaliers showed them how to find edible plants. Ma Chevalier told June that camas was called 'Indian Potato'. June wrote, "She brought up a few tiny little slick onion-like bulbs, which when boiled, tasted precisely like solid air. Not a particle of taste and a slimy texture. I couldn't eat them."

Incidentally, if you decide to try camas for dinner, here's how a British Columbia handbook suggests cooking it. They may be baked, boiled or roasted. The Indians steamed them in leaves over campfire coals—a day and a night. The book says that

The Canadian training vessel 'Oriole' passes Spieden Island

"... when roasted, camas makes a delicious repast." Maybe Ma Chevalier wasn't fussy about taste. With modern technology, you might put them in a pressure cooker—or even a microwave!

The Burns also turned up their noses at sea urchins. June was taught to "crack the beautiful spines, pour out the slime, and there tight against the shell, in little yellow strips, is an egg-like, rich marrowy stuff which the Indian children eat raw but which we didn't like, even when cooked. It was too rich." Notice, she doesn't define 'rich'.

Thimbleberry shoots, boiled like asparagus or eaten raw were acceptable. The berries are similar to blackberries.

Miner's lettuce can be eaten raw in salads. When boiled, it tastes like spinach.

Nettles are edible when cooked, June says. She "sloshed them up and down in a pan of water with a wire potato masher and cooked them without being stung. They were a bit medicinal in flavor."

The B.C. handbook recommends boiling the young shoots as a substitute for spinach. For nettle tea, put five handfuls of young tips in a quart of water and boil for several hours. Early white men thought it was a cure for rheumatism.

Living High is certainly a book in the island tradition—it has very few dates in the text. It is reasonable to suppose the Burns were there the first time for only a year or so. They returned a few years later and lived there briefly before their son, North Burn, was born.

The Nature Conservancy bought the island from North Burn in 1979 in order to protect the eagles which nest there. Eagle experts claim that intrusion by visitors in

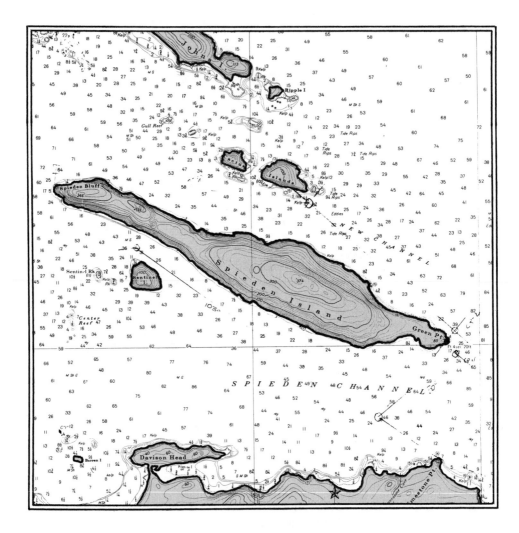

the area of their nests might cause them to abandon them. There are 'isolationist' eagles as well as people. If folks started climbing the hills to peek at them and take pictures, the theory is the national species of bird would decide, "This darned place is getting too overrun. We're going to move to some place where we can have some peace."

Now after all this fascinating historical bit on Sentinel Island, the least we can do is tell you something about going around it. That's easy. It's nice and deep, close to shore most of the way around this 'gumdrop', whose land mass rises about 100 feet with tall firs atop that. But be a little wary on the southeast corner and the northwest side where it gets about one fathom deep or so at mean low water. About 200 yards off the southwest side, there is a kelp-covered rock about four feet under the surface at low tide, and just beyond that is **Sentinel Rock,** a favorite spot for seals and sea lions to haul out and enjoy the sun and the scenery.

Southwest of Sentinel Rock about 3/8th of a mile is that well-known shipwright's friend, **Center Reef**. The buoy, however, is about 300 yards south of the reef itself, so give it wide berth or spend your vacation in the shipyard.

Spieden Island

It is pronounced 'speye-den', and that has bothered local English teachers for some time. It was named after another of those minor officers of Captain Wilkes' crew on the *U.S.S. Peacock*, an expedition ship of the 1840s. William Spieden, a purser, probably called himself 'speed-en'. History does not report whether William was pleased with his name being attached to what is considered an oddball island.

The strangeness of the place is due to its somewhat schizophrenic character. The southern half of the island is almost treeless and barren. When you come up San Juan Channel and see it in the distance, it looks like it has been somehow transported here from the South Pacific, like a barren, windswept atoll.

The northern side of the island is hilly and deeply forested in spots. A spine runs down the length of the land from the eastern tip to the high bluffs on the western end.

Spieden has history worth noting. The first white full-time resident was one of the English soldiers who had helped occupy the disputed San Juan Islands. After the territory was ceded to America, Robert Smith went to Vancouver Island and found himself a pretty little Indian bride named Lucy. With her and her mother, Smith moved to Spieden and built a small house in the trees in the western sector.

They had a daughter whom they named Mary—Mary Smith. They were not very imaginative in the choice of a name.

Soon after Mary was born, Smith died and was buried on the island. His wife, Lucy, the daughter and the grandmother continued to live in the old log cabin.

By 1894, Mary Smith, so the legend goes, developed into as beautiful a lass as her mother had been. She attracted the attention of a young man who worked as a cooper in the lime factory at Roche Harbor. He rowed past Spieden Island one day and had seen the half-breed girl braiding her long black locks.

The young man was Ed Chevalier—part of a large family that populated nearby Stuart Island. He had gone to the big island of San Juan a few years earlier to find his fortune. While fortune had escaped him, he had found the pretty young miss on Spieden. He was 20 years old and ready to settle down. He came to the strange island, won and married the girl and moved in with her and her mother and grandmother.

He soon discovered that the island had another resident, an old Russian sheepherder named Anton Cepas. For a while the two men co-existed on the island. After a few years, Cepas tired of sheep-raising and sold his flock and land to Ed Chevalier. Ed later became known as 'the King of Spieden Island'.

Ed and Mary, who became known as Ma and Pa to all, raised five children on the island. Chevaliers are well-known on San Juan, and the large family continues to grow with a new-generation baby boy born in the winter of 1984.

The island remained in the hands of the Chevalier family for half a century. In 1943, it was sold to an Antone Sulak, who began to develop the island. He built several buldings, including a boathouse at the eastern end of the island and a small sawmill nearby.

In 1970, the Spieden Development Co. bought the property from Sulak. The new owners, the Jonas Brothers, world-famous taxidermists in Seattle, hit upon an idea which they thought would be successful. They introduced a number of species of exotic animals to the island and offered it as a hunting preserve for trophy hunters at the same time renaming Spieden 'Safari Island'. They mounted a publicity campaign to attract hunters who could not afford to travel to distant wilds. The plan appealed to a few hunters, but it did draw the fire of thousands of environmentalists.

To the existing scattering of domestic sheep and blacktail deer, they added exotic quadrupeds: Barbary sheep, Corsican mouflon, Indian blackbuck, Indian axis deer, Japanese Sika deer, European fallow deer and Spanish goats.

Canadian-bound boaters for the next few years would cruise slowly along the grassy southern shore of the island and scan the landscape for strange grazing creatures. They seldom saw any 'great white hunters', however.

For a while, the safari fans stayed away in droves, but nevertheless the wildlife advocates set up a howl of protest. In all fairness, the animal lovers refused to take note of the poorly disseminated information that the rare beasts were not taken from natural, free-roaming herds. They had been bred in captivity for zoos and exhibits, and a greater percentage of them had been doomed to end up stuffed and on exhibit at museums anyhow.

The venture withered in 1973 and the operation closed down. That year the island was sold to a group of eight co-owners who are involved with Alaska Airlines. The island got its old name back, as you can see from the charts. It is now used as an R & R facility for Alaska Airlines employees, clients and friends. It is still all private land and is posted against tourists.

What about the foreign fauna? Well, it continued to live on, not harassed by hunters and mostly protected by game laws. As natural rates of reproduction continued in the benevolent climate, their numbers grew. A couple of years ago, it became clear to the owners that the grazing pressure on the pastures had reduced their numbers by malnutrition. Some of the more adventurous animals began to migrate to other nearby islands by swimming across the narrow channels. When they appeared on the properties owned by residents of other islands, they first seemed a novelty, but then they became something of a nuisance. It is rumored that a considerable number of the immigrants eventually ended up in stew pots.

The caretakers of Spieden came to realize that somethng needed to be done to save the remnants of the original herds from starvation. They appealed to warm-hearted folks on San Juan Island to fly over and help corral the excess animals so they could be caught and transferred to other islands where they would have a better chance for survival.

But it didn't quite happen that way. Jo went along on the round-up and she saw it firsthand.

Volunteers form a skirmish line on Spieden Island to round-up 300 exotic ungulates. Number caught: zero.

Spieden Round-Up

There must have been about 100 folks from grade schoolers to senior citizens that misty spring day. After a lunch of hot dogs, the whole group walked on down to the far western end of the island and then formed a human chain. Instructions were to hold hands, holler and yell, and supposedly all those renegade critters would get skitterish and head for the eastern end of the island and the corral, over two miles away.

As you can see by looking at the chart, or better still, at Spieden itself, it is a long narrow island, high centered, with steep forested bluffs on the north shore and treeless steep bluffs on the south shore. The leader decided that young men and women should work the rough north side, and older folks and kids would sweep the southern bluffs.

After the mile hike from the lodge to the west, everyone did an about-face, more or less joined hands and headed to the east. There was scrambling over logs, tripping over rocks and in gullies as the group pressed on—those barren southern bluffs are a lot rougher than they look from the water. A few timid sheep trotted docilely ahead. Everyone cheered. As the group of animals grew, so did rain-dampened spirits. Until suddenly the ram at the head of the flock decided enough was enough and turned back to the line, charging, with his faithful group in close pursuit. Hands were dropped and the sheep charged through the crowd. It was disappointing, but the round-up had only just begun.

Sad to say, it continued that way most of the day. As the wet and weary group moved east with a passel of sheep or deer, one would suddenly bolt and the rest would follow. The more than 300 animals on the overgrazed island were rebelling.

By late afternoon the round-up volunteers had reached the corral and they urged one lone deer behind the fence, lamenting the wasted afternoon. But the day was not quite over. That one deer, sensing something strange when 100 persons had finally captured him, raced to the water's edge, gave a mighty leap and dived in, obviously intent on swimming to San Juan Island. The currents off **Green Point** were more than he reckoned with, and the island's caretaker took off after the hapless animal in his outboard. He manhandled the deer over the side and into the boat and back to shore.

So much for the wild animal round-up on Spieden Island—it never worked out.

Cruise Around Spieden

Now if you want to cruise around Spieden Island, you should have no problems. Just remember the currents past the island are much stronger than shown in the Tidal Current book and you can be stalled for quite some time on either side of the island if they are against you. There are tremendous tide rips off Green Point at the eastern end of the island which you can usually see and should avoid if they start building.

The current book shows a secondary reference station at Limestone Point (San Juan Island) on Spieden Channel and predictions there are taken from those on San Juan Channel. Currents in San Juan Channel are shown as high as 5.1 knots, and the ratio at Limestone Point can be as high as 1.2 on an ebb. That means currents in Spieden Channel could get up to 6.2 knots. Can slow you down a bit, especially if you have a boat with a five-knot hull speed.

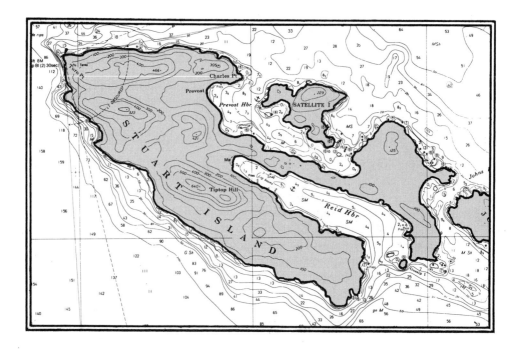

St. Speeder's Box

In Reid Harbor you will find a ghostly old boat at anchor near Smith Cove, a shallow bight with a long dock on the southern shore. It is about 70 feet long and very narrow of beam — 10 feet. It is called 'Speeder'.

During World War II it was used as a passenger ferry to Bainbridge. Prior to that, it was in the San Juans to make the runs between ports. It was supposedly the first gasoline engine boat in the islands.

Some time in the 50s it was taken out of service and moved to Reid Harbor where it has remained ever since, a virtual derelict.

In the winter of 1981, Father Ted Leche, vicar of the Episcopalian church in Friday Harbor, decided to use it for a chapel in which to hold services for the young people of Stuart Island. On a Sun-day, Father Leche would cruise up to Stuart in his boat, 'The Archangel'. When he arrived in Reid Harbor, the families and kids would row out to the old hulk. They would build a fire in the rusty old wood stove and get it warm enough for the services.

Father Ted in his down jacket would stand in the companionway that led to the wheelhouse. The children would come in, six or seven of them, and take their places on stools and the old benches. He celebrated communion on an old wooden crate.

He recalls with a smile that it was usually quite damp on board and musty smelling. But it did not affect the solemn-ity of the occasion. The tiny congregation affectionately dubbed it 'St. Speeder's'.

A couple years later, the services were moved to the home of one of the flock.

A private marina was built a couple of years ago on the southeast shore of Spieden, in the little bight inside Green Point. One of the reasons given in applying for a permit to construct the installation was for use as a refuge for boats in the event of storms or problems. So if you find yourself in trouble along there, feel welcome to duck in. It's plenty deep and while the floats were built for small boats, a boat up to 40 feet or so could take shelter if need be.

That is the only haven around the island. You can cruise close to shore—there are few rocks and they are well marked on the charts. Along the barren southern slopes you may notice grazing sheep, goats or deer, and there is a road from the marina warehouse along the island up to the lodge near the center. West of the lodge, the ridge is fairly level and there is a dirt air strip. Pilots who fly in there buzz the strip on a first approach to scare the grazing animals away. Then they come back for a second time to land.

Tall evergreens cover the rocky bluffs along the new channel side of the island down to the water. Watch for eagles—this is their kind of territory.

Stuart Island

Because of its proximity to San Juan Island, the marine parks on **Stuart Island** are a favorite stopping place for cruisers on their way to and from Canada and the San Juans. But in addition to location, Stuart Island is a fascinating place to visit.

From the entrance to Roche Harbor to the entrance to **Reid Harbor** on the southeastern end of Stuart it is just slightly over two miles across Spieden Channel. **Center Reef** and **Danger Shoal** about halfway across are well marked for good reason—they can cause serious hull damage.

There are often reefnet fishermen just before the entrance to Reid Harbor—keep clear of them. Also avoid the rocky shoals marked on the chart.

Gossip and Cemetery

Just at the entrance to Reid Harbor are **Gossip** and **Cemetery Islands**—two innocuous-looking little low rocks bypassed by most everyone on their way to and from the busy anchorage at Reid Harbor Marine Park. But this is what this cruising guide is all about—finding the lesser-known spots.

We anchored the *Sea Witch* just inside Reid Harbor in the bay north of the two islands, in about four fathoms, but well out of the steady procession of boat traffic.

We decided to explore Gossip Island first and were pleasantly surprised because there is far more to it than appears. It is volcanic rock with several small shell beaches suitable for landing a dinghy and we piled out and hiked around.

There are silvered snags and several small trees, lots of ground cover and few signs of human activity. The islands are both state-owned, undeveloped, and camping and fire-building are not allowed. They are, nonetheless, beautiful picnic or just-being-alone sites. The rocks sloping to the beach are covered at high tide, and at low tide are a mass of slippery seaweed, 'poppers' and barnacles.

The channel between Gossip and Cemetery is about 150 yards wide and filled with rocks just below the surface. We wouldn't want to go between the islands in a deep-draft boat. Cemetery is smaller. We found no signs of tombstones. There are no trees—just barren grasses and rocks. The shoreline is much the same as that of Gossip. These islands are ideal 'kid dumps'.

The passage between Gossip and Stuart is navigable with care.

Reid Harbor

Nearly one-mile-long Reid Harbor is wonderfully protected from all except persistent easterly storms. High bluffs surround it on three sides and the only beach is at the head of the bay where it is gently sloping sand and gravel, a good place to land dinghies, drop kids, dig clams at low tide and even swim in the summer.

State Parks has a dock and float, more than a dozen mooring buoys, and a couple of floats anchored out where dozens of boats can—and do—raft up. One of the wonderful advantages of Reid Harbor is that if all of the mooring buoys and floats are full, there is a lot more room for good anchoring. You can anchor in about four fathoms with sand and mud bottom anywhere in the whole harbor. You can go ashore only on State Park land where there are 44 acres to wander.

There are campsites, water, pit toilets, picnic tables and plenty of hiking trails: some high above the harbor on cliffs, others back in the woods—follow the signs.

To many of us who live in the San Juans and visit Reid Harbor regularly, the area has a special sentimental significance. We somehow feel that just at eventide, the spirits of Littlewolf and Gladys, the old woman of the sea, hover benignly in the mists.

Stuart Island's legendary Littlewolf fashions a copper bracelet

Littlewolf

As you enter Reid Harbor, you will see pilings, docks and homes on the right. There is a low area and a small bight with a launching ramp. This ramp is connected by a short road to the airport on Stuart. To the left of the ramp, you will see a small cabin, silvered with age. Next to it is a tall flagpole with a flag on which you will see the head of a wolf. Until May of 1984, this was the home of Littlewolf, who has become a legend in the islands.

Littlewolf's history is a melding of fact and fantasy. It is a wonderfully naive mixture of Romulus and Remus and Hansel and Gretel. But he told his story with such warmth and sincerity that visitors would willingly put aside their disbelief.

He was short, slight, and wiry. When he died May, 1984, at the Convalescent Center in Friday Harbor, his birth date was nebulously declared as "about 1908".

Unabashedly, he admitted that he had been a fisherman, a rum-runner and had even dabbled in smuggling. He learned rum-running in the years he worked for Al Capone in Chicago during the height of prohibition. Not all the booze he handled got delivered, however. His forays into Friday Harbor, even back in the days when it was a hard-drinker's town, were legendary. Many a time, the sheriff would have to escort Glen Chester (his white-man name) down to the dock, put him in his boat and shoo him out to sea. "And don't come back again!" the lawman would shout.

A few weeks later, the beloved hell-raiser would be back in town, swapping outrageous stories with his fishermen friends. In the course of the evening, a fracas would fulminate, the sheriff would be called, and Littlewolf would be ushered out of town. After all, you don't arrest a legend.

How did he get his name? When he was a small boy, he and his sister were rescued from the wilds by wolves, who took them in and nourished them. How

Prevost Harbor

A short walk of only a couple hundred yards from the Reid Harbor dock puts you in **Prevost Harbor**, an adjacent marine park (but they share the isthmus). Prevost, another 40 acres, has essentially the same facilities as Reid, but the surrounding waters are entirely different.

Prevost is entered from the north, between **Charles Point** on Stuart, and small **Satellite Island** which is owned by the YMCA.

As you enter the harbor, you can hold fairly close to Satellite Island until you reach the little rocky point. But stay clear of that point for there is a long, rocky shoal which heads southwest from it and then curls back into Satellite's little bay. Directly across on the Stuart shore is a lovely white farmhouse—but in front of that lurks another rocky shoal. Best bet when coming in to the harbor as you make the gentle turn to the left is to keep your depth sounder on and make sure the water doesn't drop below four fathoms at high tide. Once you're in between those shoals, you have pretty clear sailing all through the harbor and can anchor just about anywhere if you can't catch a buoy.

We suggest avoiding the tempting-looking opening at the east end of Satellite

did they happen to be alone in the wilderness? They had been taken there and abandoned by an evil babysitter. It is unlikely that Littlewolf had ever read Grimm's Fairy Tales, he was not the bookish sort. So, he told, with unassuming candor, of leaving a trail of bread crumbs on the path as he and his sister were being kidnapped.

The story continues: after an undetermined time as human cubs, the children were found by hunters, who returned them to civilization. They were placed in an orphanage where they lived until the sister was adopted and Littlewolf went AWOL and off into a life of adventure.

Sometimes the story includes a brief period in which the two children were picked up by a circus after their rescue. They were exhibited in cages as 'wolf children'.

It may even be, as he often said, he was world-famous—not for his stories, but for his creation, 'The Littlewolf Bracelet'. It is a circlet of heavy gauge copper wire. Its purpose: to ward off arthritis. He never kept count of his production, but he figured it was 'about three million'. His most illustrious client, he says, was former first lady, Betty Ford.

Does the bracelet work its medical charm? Hundreds of San Juan Islanders wear them and swear by them. There may be something magic about the fact that the material, #6 gauge solid copper wire, had been 'highgraded' from OPALCO, the maverick power company that serves the islands.

Another fact: the bracelets were free, to all. Nobody who presented himself or herself at the little cabin on Stuart Island was ever turned away or charged. A goodwill offering would be accepted, however. We always suggested bringing a staple he favored highly: McNaughton's —a fifth.

Island. We went through it once in a big boat but never again. It is a mass of shoals and rocks and every year large numbers of boats which attempt the pass wish they hadn't. It's great for small boat exploring, however.

If you enjoy walking, Stuart Island is definitely for you. There is nothing commercial on Stuart—you can't go buy an ice cream cone or sit in a bar. But you can visit some interesting places because the island is interlaced with state park hiking trails and dirt county roads.

Stuart Islanders may maintain a low profile, but they are justly proud of their new one-room schoolhouse in the woods about a half-mile walk from the head of Reid Harbor. The first school was a tiny log cabin not far from the present site. In 1902 a larger bulding was built. Youngsters rowed to school from Spieden and Johns Islands and from the eastern end of Stuart. Today's students still arrive in a school boat from the far end of Stuart.

In 1961, the Stuart teacher and his children, who were all students in the school, capsized in their boat while crossing stormy Spieden Channel and all but a baby were drowned. The school closed down and didn't reopen until 1977 when the student population on the island warranted local teaching instead of sending the children to San Juan Island.

The new school was completed in 1981 and since has won several architectural awards for its unusual design. The fan-shaped, one-room wood bulding has hardwood floors, two wood stoves for heating, a stage, library and all manner of modern conveniences not expected in the wilderness.

There is a full-time teacher, a half-time teacher, and aides who work with from 10 to 14 youngsters, who get an outstanding education.

All this is by way of suggesting a good hike is up the wide path at the head of Reid Harbor to the school.

Just beyond the school is the Stuart Island cemetery, a virtual 'Who's Who' of early islanders. Don't miss it.

More ambitious souls might want to take the two-mile hike from the school—it's not quite that far from Prevost Harbor—out to Turn Point Lighthouse on the northwestern tip of the island. While this point is neither the farthest north or the farthest west in the state, it is the farthest northwest. The walk is worth it.

The lighthouse at Turn Point on Stuart Island is on 69 acres of federal land, 62.4 of them leased to the State Parks on a revocable basis. The San Juan Island School District has been using the lighthouse as a teacher's home since 1983 on a lease from Uncle Sam. They must maintain the property and make no structural changes.

You can visit it and enjoy the spectacular view from the public grounds, regardless of who owns it.

There is a wonderful old caretaker's house (the light is automated so they need a caretaker, not a keeper) with a 300° view out over Haro Strait and Boundary Pass with the Canadian Gulf and Vancouver Islands beyond.

Just below the red-roofed white house, the grass slopes down to great rocky cliffs with a small building for the lighthouse's mechanical equipment and the modest little white tower which contains the workings of the light.

About 15 container ships pass the light daily, as do uncounted number of whales.

The lighthouse was built in 1893 and was equipped with a lens lantern and a steam-operated Daboll trumpet. Early lighthouse keepers had to deal occasionally with smugglers and shipwrecked vessels.

Tiptop Hike

For another hike on Stuart, turn left instead of going to the school, and you'll find yourselves on the way to **Tiptop**. Please understand, around here we call Tiptop a mountain, even though the chart calls it a hill. It is, after all, 640 feet high. We're inclined to call anything more than a couple hundred feet high a mountain—maybe it's because many of us miss seeing Mount Rainier.

Anyhow, Tiptop is owned by a group of generous folks who have said it's okay to hike up there with a minimum of restrictions. "Please use care," they say. "Don't build fires, don't throw rocks, and don't litter."

Now that you've had a chance to hike the island, see the light and school, swim in the harbor and maybe gather a few clams or set your crab traps, it's time to move on.

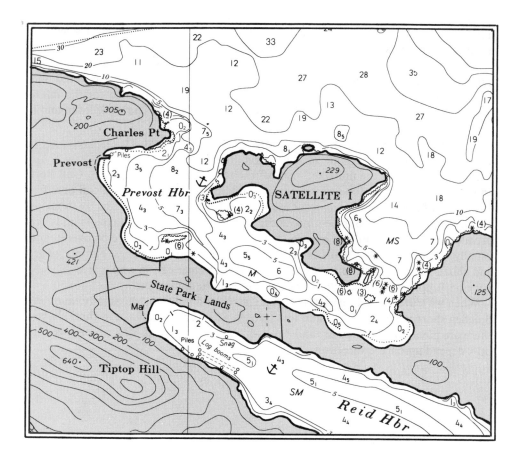

Around Stuart

The southwestern shore of Stuart is a sloping high bank, rocky all the way down to the water and offers no real shelter. There are several homes and indentations along this shore. There is supposedly good bottomfishing as the bottom rises sharply, but these bights do not provide good anchorages.

Pass Turn Point lighthouse avoiding kelp, and be aware of the tide rips that race past the point with amazing strength, often at more than three knots.

You are now heading basically east around the island and in just a little more than a mile is **Charles Point** with the entrance to Prevost Harbor. There is good bottomfishing off this entrance also where the water drops from 12 to 22 fathoms. Several of our cod jigs have taken up permanent residence there.

If you continue along the outside you will see Satellite Island and the rather large entrance bay between the eastern end of Satellite and Stuart. There is a meadow with several houses on this eastern end, rocky shores and a radio tower on the point which marks the opening for **Johns Pass** between Stuart and **Johns Island**.

Johns Pass

Johns Pass can be difficult in times of strong currents, with the flood running north and the ebb running south. The pass is also a short cut and sometimes leads to a haven for boaters during northeasterlies on **Boundary Pass**.

After you clear the pass there is a long reef which extends southeasterly about a half-mile from the southeastern tip of Stuart Island. The reef is kelp-covered and you can pass between the rocks in places, but it's not recommended for the faint-hearted. We discovered that when we line up with the western end of Spieden and a clearing on Johns Island, we are past the reefs.

Now that we've gone through Johns Pass, we can check out this less-traveled area. There are a number of private residences on Johns Island.

In an extension of the unnamed reef off the southeastern tip of Stuart, **Gull Reef and Cactus Islands** continue in the same southeasterly direction. You can pass between any of them if you are careful, but Cactus Islands are surrounded by shoals—watch your chart and your depth sounder. Both East and West Cactus Islands are privately-owned, so don't go ashore. There is a large rocky area, kelp-covered and usually visible, between Cactus Islands and **Ripple Island** off the east end of Johns, and shoals all around Ripple. We just tend to steer clear of the whole area. Shrubbery on Ripple Island—a wildlife refuge—resembles a crew cut.

When we travel **New Channel**, between Cactus and Spieden, we usually favor the Spieden shore which is deeper and less fraught with rocks. And as the chart shows, there are plenty of tide rips around here which tend to slow us down—or speed us up—depending on the direction.

Hotel De Haro, Roche Harbor
San Juan Island, Washington

SAN JUAN ISLAND

San Juan Cruise

We have saved, for the last chapter, *our island*—San Juan. Like all islanders, we consider the segment on which we live to be *ours*. As you may have begun to suspect, the phrase 'insular' really describes the fierce loyalty each group of islanders feel toward their own turf. Orcas is 'home' to Orcassians; Lopez is 'our island' to Lopezians; Shaw is the land of the Shavians; Waldronites and Stuartites are adamantly protective of their own rocks.

The San Juan Islanders—that is, the population of the whole county—are like a scattered family. They are very much identified by geography, there is even a sense of competition between them. But, like any family, when they consider the 'Off-Island' world, they forget their water boundaries and provide a unified front.

An interesting aside: when Queen Elizabeth visited Victoria recently, Jo, who as a reporter for the *Journal of the San Juans*, told Prince Phillip that she was from 'San Juan'. He politely inquired—"All the way from Puerto Rico?" How quickly they forget—even royalty!

Our cruise of San Juan Island will run clockwise, like most of the others. We will start with Cattle Point where our book began, sail up Haro Strait, through Mosquito Pass, eastward in Spieden Channel, down San Juan Channel, and end up at Cattle Pass again.

Let's start with **Cattle Point DNR Park**. You probably won't anchor and go ashore there, but you may decide to visit it by land. You can, incidentally, rent cars, mopeds, bikes, rowboats, outboards, and kayaks on the island.

The parking lot at Cattle Point Park is adjacent to an old concrete building which was an observation post and radio station during the Second World War. The structure has been converted into a picnic shelter. It houses several picnic tables and a big airtight wood stove.

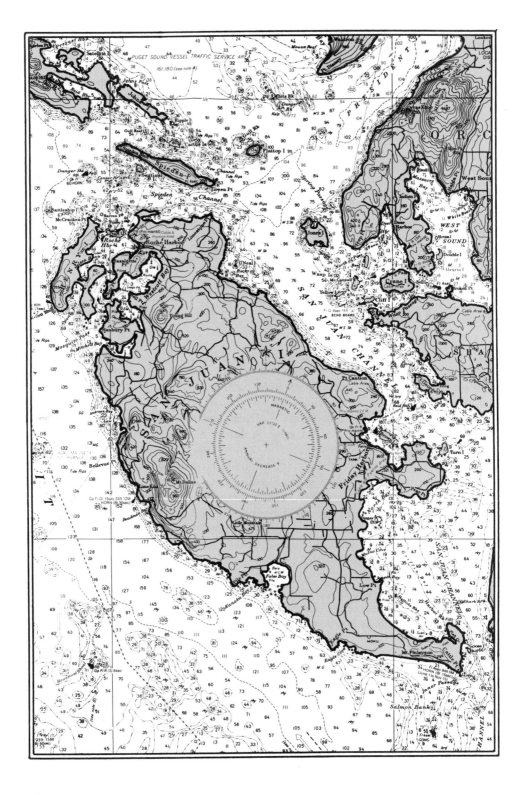

Otters on the dock in Friday Harbor

In front of the radio shack is a rocky promontory with a spectacular view of the eastern end of the Strait of Juan de Fuca. You can see much of the bottom of Lopez Island, including Iceberg Point. The view then sweeps eastward and south to include Smith Island, Admiralty Inlet, Port Townsend, then west to the broad reach of the Strait which aims at Japan, and the southern end of Vancouver Island.

There is a concrete compass rose built into the rocks with guideposts to the visible features in the distance.

If you stand on the rocky head, you may be able to see a family of river otters which live on the beach to the west and sun themselves on the rocks below.

This is a dramatic place from which to watch a storm in this end of the Strait. When there is a gale blowing, armies of whitecaps assault Iceberg Point and Long Island and fight against the constriction of Cattle Pass and **Goose Island**. The wind can take your breath away up there in a blow!

From this point, you can see the intricacies of the passage behind Goose Island that we discussed previously.

A path leads down to a beach below the radio shack which is a good place to beachcomb. At the southwestern end of this beach you will find an old water tower. It is several stories high and has some slit windows. If you clamber up the bank, you can look inside and see an old water tank of about 500 gallons capacity. There is a hole in the floor and a pipe ladder leading down to the lower level. There is no light down there and is not worth the inspection—only some rusty pipes that used to transport the water to the radio shack. Above the tower, you will find an old road that led down to it. Probably this was the way trucks brought water to supply the tank.

Several hundred feet from the tower are some old concrete footings that once supported the transmitting tower.

A short hike beyond the concrete footings will bring you to the Cattle Point lighthouse that stands out so brilliantly as you approach the pass from the sea. Like all modern lighthouses, it is automated, and the windows are boarded up. There is some graffiti on the walls of the lighthouse. 'Dawn H' and 'Tammy B' announced they were there—with a spray can. We would like to get Dawn H and Tammy B by the scruff of their necks and provide them with cans of paint thinner and rags!

Pig War Is A Bore

You'll find that San Juan folks get a glazed look about the eyeballs whenever someone mentions The Pig War. And no wonder. It's a story that has about as much pizzazz as the bit about The Father of Our Country hacking down the family cherry tree. It was no big deal.

The history of these rocks is studded with the stories of smugglers, highbinders, poets, drunks and dreamers. And what ends up being mentioned in tourist brochures? A tempest in a pig sty.

You won't find it in books on American history. It did not go down in the annals as a major rebuff to the British Crown.

If it weren't for Orcas Island writer David Richardson, we probably wouldn't even have known about the incident. I guess Dave hit on the story as a little grabber for his book on San Juan Island's history.

The tale, minus Chamber of Commerce puffery, goes like this:

In 1859 an old dirt-grubber named Lyman Cutlar did, with malice aforethought, convert one pig into shortribs. It had, on several occasions, invaded the Cutlar property and rooted up his rutabagas and he had had it with the interloper. The pig was owned by an Englishman who worked for the Hudson's Bay Company. Lyman was a Yank.

At that time there were two factions on San Juan Island. About 25 American families lived at the south end and a clutch of Britons lived up near Roche Harbor. It appears that in those days nobody was sure just which country owned the island. When the geographers had drawn the international line, they had come all over fuzzy and couldn't decide where it went between Vancouver Island and the U.S. mainland. Washington and London couldn't have cared less; it was obvious that this bunch of rocks would never amount to a hill of compost.

Up until this incident, the settlers contented themselves with yelling at each other such imprecations as 'Lousy Limey'! and 'Yankee Bum'! (That's the English 'bum' you understand ...) Such apostrophes seemed to satisfy their national prides. It might have gone on like that for decades had it not been for the peripatetic porker.

The incident tweaked the nose of the Imperial Lion and Redcoats appeared to cart Cutlar off to durance vile. The farmer met them with his flintlock cocked and offered to convert—with malice aforethought—some of the Britons, too.

The contingent to-the-rear marched and went back to their camp to get further instructions from Buckingham Palace. Lyman sent a note to the nearest U.S. Army outpost.

Captain George Pickett, bored with regimental life in Port Townsend, landed

The foghorn is in front of the lighthouse. We do not advise standing in front of it when it sounds—it can make your head ring.

One more feature of Cattle Point Park: there is an interpretative board with a description of the beach land and its resident anchorites and critters.

With good old chart #18434 for reference, we can begin our trip around San Juan Island, clockwise from Cattle Point.

You will notice that the water is quite shallow off the point, with depths ranging from one to three fathoms within 200 yards of the shore.

at Cattle Point with 66 good men and true.

The governor of the Crown Colony of British Columbia sent three warships.

Pickett called for more troops.

The governor sent two more warships.

A few weeks later, Pickett upped the ante to 461 troops and 14 cannons—most of which worked.

The British warships had 167 cannons and housed 2,140 troops. (Imagine how their bilges smelled!)

Well, the summer wore on. The Americans got bored out of their skulls by the lack of that one necessity soldiers hold so dear. The British suffered claustrophobia in the holds and their suply of grog ran low. It was time for high level decision-making.

An international tribunal was set up. The two sovereign powers called upon the good offices of Kaiser Wilhelm I of Germany. He tossed a pfennig—result: the San Juans became U.S. territory.

We've always wondered: who lost that toss?

Inner Passage

Inner Passage is the shoal area extending over the salmon banks to the buoy off-shore. Most pleasure boats will have no problem with the shoal-depth waters of this passage. It does not get shallower than about 10 feet even at MLLW—Mean Lower Low Water.

So—back to Inner Passage. It's safe to say it's fairly shallow. As a matter of fact, it is so shallow that the salmon tend to avoid it. They usually school on the fishing banks which are indicated by the green tint on the chart. This area is called **Salmon Banks** and the depths there are about 50 feet. During fishing season you will see a line of purse seiners or gillnetters all the way from the #3 Salmon Bank buoy up to **Kanaka Bay**.

The shoreline along Inner Passage is called **South Beach** by the San Juan Island folks. It's a great beach for combing and strolling. Island residents come there with their chain saws and cut cedar for their wood stoves. It's owned by the National Park Service and is part of **American Camp**. We'll tell you more about this and the other national park on San Juan Island later in this chapter.

Eagle Cove

Proceeding WNW along South Beach, the first indentation you come to is 600

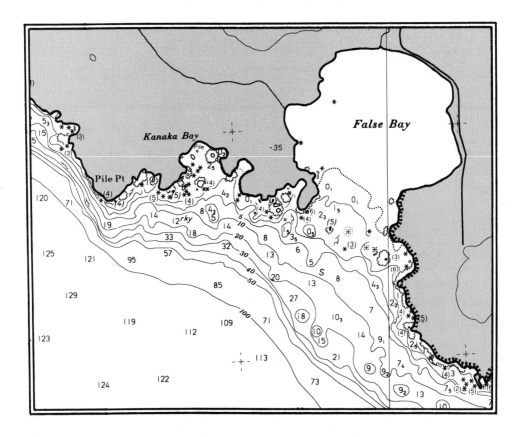

You're Safe Afloat

The truth is, yachts almost never sink in bad weather — not in the inland waters, although it's not unheard of. You may have a couple of hours of hell, though, if you get caught out in the Strait and everything goes wrong. Everybody from the skipper to the family poodle may be seasick. Every year the rawest novices get caught in blows off Smith Island. The helmsperson may do everything wrong. You may get lost, befuddled, dizzy, sick and wet, but you'll survive to tell the story (somewhat altered to protect the egos) of "the time when ..."

And in a real honest-to-God storm, an 80-footer from the Coast Guard station in Port Angeles or Port Townsend, Anacortes or Bellingham, will come steaming down to your position and get you to safety, if you need it.

Take that last phrase and look at it: "If you need it." If you call the Coast Guard with a 'mayday' they will ask a lot of questions that seem irrelevant, but they all have a bearing on your predicament. Besides, you really ought to know your registration numbers, the color of your hull, topsides and trim, the number of people on board, and have some fair notion of where you are.

The Coast Guard radio man on duty is required to ask certain questions about your situation. "Are you in immediate danger?" If you really think you are, say so. Describe what the danger is in no uncertain terms. Next, you will be asked if you will "accept commercial assistance". The Coast Guard has been told to back off from any towing which can be done by private enterprise. For years, they went dashing out to help some twit who had run out of gas or neglected to buy a proper chart or to take decent care of his boat. Cutbacks in the budget for the Coast Guard, like all other government services, demanded a reappraisal of the role they should play. Now, they will not roll unless they believe you are in real danger to life — not property — and you refuse to accept commercial assistance.

The criterion here ought to be, not, can you afford to ask for a tug — but can one get to you in time to protect you? Ask the Coast Guard how long a delay they would have in getting a tug on the scene. Then ask about their possible ETA. Now, you do not have to have the opinion of some grizzled old sea dog on whether your life is in danger. If you think it is — really is — say so. Don't pussyfoot around about it. The Coast Guard, like all other government bureaus, has to keep its derriere covered. Like everybody — they need to be needed.

As long as we're on the subject of help from the Coasties, we should mention that there is another great resource out there on the water with you — the other boaters. Many is the pleasure boater who rescued another pleasure boater. But be prepared, carry the necessary emergency items.

Know your boat, your crew and yourself so you can be prepared for the unexpected and be able to handle emergencies.

yards across and 300 yards deep and is covered at the east and west sides with long beds of kelp. There is good fishing just off this cove—it is a favorite place for sports fishermen as well as gillnetters. The shore is public and islanders frequently park in

Lime Kiln lighthouse on San Juan's west side

the lot above and walk the trail to enjoy the semi-privacy of this tiny cove. One day we found an upholstered chair on the beach. It didn't seem likely that anybody would have packed it in some hundred yards down the trail from the road. It must have fallen off the deck of some large yacht.

False Bay

False Bay, at high tide, looks like any nice, spacious bay. However, it goes totally dry at less than high water. Frequently someone misreads (or doesn't read) the chart and finds him/herself aground in the bay. False Bay is a U.W. Biological Station, so don't dig the clams.

Between Kanaka Bay and False Bay there is a little rocky inlet that is both picturesque and dangerous. It is filled with barnacle-covered rocks and reefs. There are plenty of kelp beds which warn you out of it. This is right around the corner from False Bay.

Kanaka Bay

Kanaka Bay is another small rock-filled inlet. This one was used for small boats and fish boats at one time. There are a number of pilings that have been set in the northern end of the bay. It looks like an ideal place for smugglers to dart in, offload their contraband and pop back out into Haro Strait.

There are a few small homes at the edge of Kanaka Bay. At one time a large development was envisioned there and an airplane landing strip was built at Kanaka Bay. There are modest homes on several of the subdivided lots at the edge of the strip. They have a spectacular view out over the Strait. Between the landing strip and the shoreline there are acres of rolling fields and low rock outcroppings. At **Pile Point** there is a surveyor's monument carrying a bench mark.

At this point, you can roll or fold good old #18434 and put it away, because we're sailing off it. There is another large scale chart of San Juan Island, #18425, which covers the northern end of the island. But for some unfathomable reason (and charts are supposed to have *fathomable* reasons, aren't they?) there is a chunk of the west shore of San Juan Island that is not covered in detail—the area around **Lime Kiln Light.** For this three miles or so, we will have to turn to the big overall chart of the islands, #18421.

While there are no moorages from Pile Point northwest along San Juan Island, there are a number of homes along the rocky bluffs. Deadman Bay is the next indentation of any size and was named, of course, because of a death. There are several versions, according to Bryce Wood, of whom actually was killed there. A couple of

Moclips

As you cruise past the Lime Kiln Lighthouse on the west side of San Juan Island, you can come in fairly close to shore and get a good look at it. If you look up into the glass rotunda of the tower, where the light is, don't be surprised if you see a person staring back at you. He or she is a 'whale watcher' from the Moclips Cetological Society. Let's break that imposing title down a bit. 'Moclips' is a town over on the Olympic Peninsula. 'Cetological' means they study 'cetaceans'. Does that clear it up for you? Oh, you do know what a 'cetacean' is? Well, look it up in the Encyclopedia Brittanica. You do have one on board, don't you? On the off chance that you neglected to on-load your Brittanica, I will elucidate: 'whales', they are ... also 'porpoises and dolphins'.

So—recapitulating, this is a gang who sit around and look for whales. It's a scientific discipline—like vulcanology—people who sit and look at volcanos.

It tells you one thing for sure—this is a good area to see killer whales. And that is always an exciting event.

The Lime Kiln lighthouse has been leased from Uncle Sam for the purpose of setting up a research team to study the migration and behavior of killer whales aka 'Orcas'.

While you and I might feel that one killer whale looks pretty much like another, apparently the researchers know the members of the three pods that ordinarily inhabit this area. We can imagine a whale watcher peering through binoculars at the fin of a frolicking orca and remarking to his companions, "Hm-m-m, J-10 looks a bit peaked this morning!"

Occasionally, killer whales are rounded up and the staff will install a small radio transmitter on his dorsal fin, (painlessly, I imagine—nobody would want to get in a free-for-all with a one-ton fish!) It would seem that the bugging of a selected denizen of the deep doesn't bother it much. It goes on about its daily life pretty undisturbed by the fact that they are tracking it on direction-finders.

At these observation stations, the M.C.S. also sinks waterproof microphones to pick up the continuous chatter of the passing specimens.

Considering the fact that they are being traced and eavesdropped on, they apparently don't take umbrage. You and I, friend, would become downright paranoid!

181

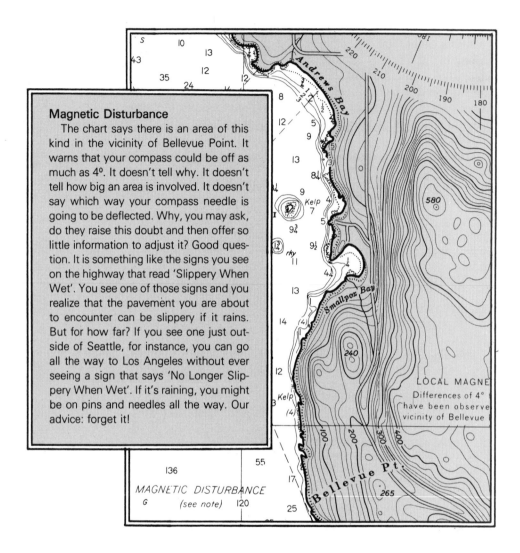

Magnetic Disturbance

The chart says there is an area of this kind in the vicinity of Bellevue Point. It warns that your compass could be off as much as 4°. It doesn't tell why. It doesn't tell how big an area is involved. It doesn't say which way your compass needle is going to be deflected. Why, you may ask, do they raise this doubt and then offer so little information to adjust it? Good question. It is something like the signs you see on the highway that read 'Slippery When Wet'. You see one of those signs and you realize that the pavement you are about to encounter can be slippery if it rains. But for how far? If you see one just outside of Seattle, for instance, you can go all the way to Los Angeles without ever seeing a sign that says 'No Longer Slippery When Wet'. If it's raining, you might be on pins and needles all the way. Our advice: forget it!

versions claims the first white man to have died on the island was buried there. Another version states an unnamed white man criticized a Chinese cook at the nearby Lime Kiln, and the cook killed him with a knife.

Just to the north and west of Deadman Bay is the light, commonly referred to as Lime Kiln Light. This solitary white lighthouse always signals that we are nearing the end of the rather long trip up the west side of the island and will soon find a haven. The indentation beyond the lighthouse contains the ruins of an old cookhouse at what was an active Lime Kiln enterprise around the turn of the century, Cowell's Lime Kiln. There even was a wharf built out from the cliffs. There is no shelter here although it is an interesting site. A local developer has tried unsuccessfully for years to get permits to build a residential community in the area.

At this point, you will want to unroll Chart #18433, which will serve you around the north end of San Juan Island—or you can refer to the San Juan Channel Chart—both are small-scale.

Bellevue Point

You can readily see that this feature is not a point at all. It isn't worth a darn as a navigation aid. There are no homes visible on this hillside. So why the name? Bryce Wood, the scholarly San Juan Islander who loves to research names, admits that he can shed little light on it. The point is on the northwest corner of the slopes of Mt. Dallas. At one time, San Juan Island was also known as Bellevue Island—the Hudson Bay Company chose that name for the whole island. If the British had been able to keep hegemony over the island after the Pig War the name probably would have been Bellevue Island.

There was a Bellevue Farm on San Juan Island, owned by the Hudson Bay Company, but it was not on Mt. Dallas.

The best guess is that early surveyors, not sure what the big island would be named, put a triangulation point on the bluffs at this area and called it, arbitrarily, 'Bellevue Point'.

So much for a designation on the chart that has no navigation value—the point that is not a point at all.

Smallpox Bay

Smallpox Bay is the location of **San Juan County Park**. There is a small cove with only marginally acceptable moorage for a couple of boats. There is a boat-launching ramp, however, and there are campsites for bikers, tenters and hikers, and picnic facilities on shore. During the height of the sports fishing season local fishermen haul their kicker boats there to fish the area between this bay and **Kellett Bluff**.

Islanders tell a melancholy story about the naming of this bay. It seems that in the 1860s, an unnamed boat anchored and two sick sailors were taken ashore and abandoned. They had smallpox. The Indians who lived in this pleasant little cove took pity on the men and tried to take care of them. The white men had some built-in immunity, so they survived. The Indians, who had never had to cope with this disease, were fully susceptible and the epidemic spread throughout the encampment. Many of them died. In desperation, the survivors burned their tents and belongings and migrated down the coast.

Just outside Smallpox Bay, you will find **Low Island**. Name sound familiar? Sure it does. There is another Low Island in Wasp Passage on the east side of San Juan Island. You would think the map makers would have the decency to at least call one of them West or East Low Island! Cartographers are obviously deficient in conscience!

The coast and geodetic people in 1894 summed up the mariner's view of this bay—"... it is merely an indentation and affords no shelter''.

Andrews Bay

It's probably not the sort of place you will want to explore or capture on film for posterity—but it does have some history. Back in the days when fish-traps were legal, it was one of the most productive areas for setting weirs. In one rig at the south end of **Andrews Bay**, the fishermen hauled in over 400,000 fish one year.

Shanties were built along the shore for the workers who attended the fish traps, but it is doubtful any trace of them remains.

It got its name in the 1890s when map makers, who had run fresh out of names of famous people and friends and relatives, started naming areas after the people who lived there. Somebody named Andrews must have lived at the cove. An elderly San Juan historian says that she remembers somebody named Andrews who had a log cabin on that beach; but land records do not show anyone by that name holding a title.

Like any other great American name, 'Andrews' has its black sheep on the local scene. An American 'liquor dealer' (probably you can read 'bootlegger' for that term) was booted off the island in 1917. It is not known where William Andrews, the bootee, lived on the island—but all of the coves and crannies on the west coast of San Juan Island were convenient delivery stops for rumrunners—and the fish-trap tenders would certainly have been good customers.

Another Andrews shows up as a signer of a petition in 1859—B.S. Andrews, 'citizen of San Juan'. There is no record of his owning land in the area, however.

Having thus presented you with too much information about this unimportant bight, we will proceed up the coast.

Smugglers Cove

Smugglers Cove may—or may not—have had a colorful past. All of the historical data we can find on this little dimple in the rugged coastline can be summed up in the recollection of one of San Juan Island's Grand Old Ladies. She says she remembers hearing that there was a cave in this cove where Indians would hide when the warlike Haidas came rampaging north. And we can't tell you whether the cave is still there—it's not the sort of place that invites gunkholing.

Could it have been a smugglers' drop? Certainly. It would seem that every little nick in the landscape on the west side of the island was used by the various genres of smugglers—wool, sheep, Chinese, opium, booze. A cynical historian suggests that the name got included on the chart at the urging of early real estate entrepreneurs because the lurid suggestion that it may have been the scene of skullduggery and derring-do would hype sales of lands to the romantics.

Incidentally, let us know if you ever find that cave!

Mitchell Bay

At last a refuge! **Mitchell Bay** is a place to duck into to get away from roaring sou'westers that howl up Haro Strait. And it offers some comforts and amenities! **Snug Harbor Marina** has transient moorage, fuel, propane, groceries, gear, ice and a few log cabins.

Mitchell Bay is divided into two bodies of water, the first just inside a reef. The rock at the end of the reef is above water at almost all tides and there is a prominent sign on it directing boats to stay to the north side of the reef. This section of Mitchell Bay is shallow—at low tides it can get down to only a few feet of water. Boats draw-

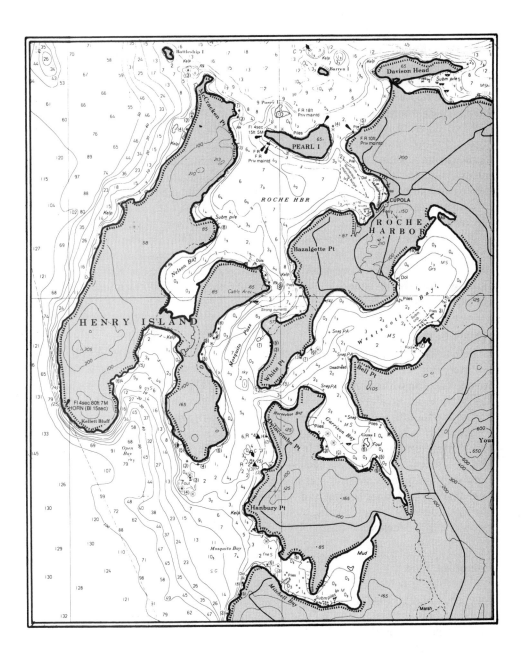

ing a fathom may find themselves mired in mud at extreme low tides, but there is seldom any wind in this area.

Having said that, it might be wise to mention that the protection against the weather is not absolute. In 1983, a freak wind of about 50 knots whistled in from the west and shook up the floats at Snug Harbor Marina and a couple of moored boats decided to go sailing without humans on board. Neighbors caught the runaways and secured them until the wind died down and the owners could tow them back to the marina. Not much damage was done, but it was an exciting night for the proprietors of the marina and waterfront residents of Mitchell Bay.

Mitchell Bay narrows at the eastern end and there is a slough beyond that is not of much use to transient boaters.

When entering Mitchell Bay, note that there is a small tombolo-island on the northern shore below **Hanbury Point**. Our lady pioneer says she remembers hearing there was an Indian burial ground on this unnamed islet. It is doubtful that any traces would remain, because you must remember, Indians did not *bury* their dead. (See the reminiscence of the Tulloch family in Eastsound in the Orcas chapter.)

Note also the rock on the northern side of Mitchell Bay as you enter. That rock is farther out in the bay than it appears on the chart. Give it plenty of room.

Oh, about the name. It appears that several Indian families who lived in the area took a fancy to the name Mitchell and used it as their 'white-man name'.

Leaving Mitchell Bay and continuing northward, you will see **Kellett Bluff** and **Open Bay** on **Henry Island**, the entrance to **Mosquito Pass** (which leads to **Roche Harbor**) and **Hanbury Point**.

Henry Island

Kellett Bluff is about as craggy and forbidding a bit of terra firma as you will encounter. But it is a favorite area for San Juan Islanders and long-time visitors who love to fish for salmon. Many of the derby-winning big lunkers have been caught off the bluff in an area from the rocky shallows off the south fork of **Henry Island**, across the mouth of Open Bay and around to the lighthouse.

Open Bay is a beautiful body of water and a nice place to visit but you wouldn't want to live on the hook there. It is, as the name implies, open to prevailing winds and is rather deep for anchorage except at the top. During the fishing season, you may find colorful reefnetter rigs in this bay.

If you happen to be fishing and in a small boat, you might want to go ashore at the lighthouse. It is public land, owned by the U.S. Lighthouse Authority. It might be interesting beachcombing.

Mosquito Pass

Returning now to the entrance to Mosquito Pass—this is a good time to learn to love your chart #18425. Notice the rocks and reefs and shoals off the southeast finger of Henry Island. You will do well to find the kelp-bed fringed area of Hanbury Point and hug it like a long-lost friend. Stay in rather close to shore and look for the red day beacon which bears the number '2'. The two-fathom shoal which lies southwest of the marker is covered with kelp and you should avoid it even though there are no hidden hazards underneath.

Look at the chart where the daybeacon is located: you will see that the marker is next to a rock. Since it is red and you are returning from a foreign port (so to speak) keep it to the right.

The black can number '3' warns you of a shoal that never quite dries—keep it to the left.

Pilings make convenient cormorant roosts.

Red daybeacon '4' is there just to keep you honest and away from another small shoal to the right.

Delacombe Point

Delacombe Point is not, as you can see, a point at all. It's a sort of rounded promontory just before **Horseshoe Bay**. Somewhere back in the late 19th Century someone decided it needed a name—or that Captain William Addis Delacombe, who commanded the Royal Marines at **English Camp**, would have his nose out of joint if he didn't have something named after him.

The passage between Delacombe Point and **White Point** does not have a name, which is unfortunate—it leads to two large bays and a world of sightseeing and anchorage.

Coming around Delacombe Point, which is a high, forested point, you see Horseshoe Bay. This is a pleasant cove which could take a couple of boats at anchor. The shoreline is a sandy beach and has a very nice little cabin. Rounding the north end of this cove, you will notice on chart #18425 there is a snag reported just off the head. The snag is there and you would do well to keep offshore a bit here.

The entrance to **Garrison Bay** narrows at this head, and the bay is a prime place for anchorage in front of English Camp. During the height of the tourist season, it can be as crowded as one of the marine parks. The depths are from 15 feet at the entrance (at minus tides, remember) to 10 feet just off Guss Island.

That faint line you see running parallel to the shore in Garrison Bay, is, of course, the 10-foot line. Notice there are two rocks just offshore in the area outside the marshlands on the southwestern shore—they are covered at all but minus tides.

Guss Island is about half an acre in area. It is open to visitors but signs ask you not to camp or clam there. There is a nice little beach on the west side to land your dinghy. The island is owned by the U.S. and is part of English Camp Historical Park. Incidentally, archeologists found a centuries-old Indian skull and some bone fragments on this island recently. Since the Indians of this area did not bury their dead, it is not a so-called 'Indian burial ground', and it is considered proper for archeologists to remove whatever old remains they find for study. The researchers asked us not to tell the public where the skull was found, because they do not want tourists poking around and upsetting the ecology. We doubt you will find where they dug up the relic, because it was in shallow strata and they carefully replaced the earth on the spot. Guss has about two dozen conifers.

So who was Guss and how did he get his name attached to this little island? Bryce Wood says the spot belonged to Augustus Hoffmeister—that accounts for the name.

'English Cemetery' at English Camp

Mean Lower Low Water

Chapter 20 of 'Piloting, Seamanship and Small Boat Handling', by Charles Chapman, is considered the Bible of the pleasure boater. The answer to almost any question can be found in its 600-odd pages. But sometimes the answers are not as rewarding as one might wish. On the matter of the Mean Lower Low Water, he says:

"On the Pacific Coast ... it is the average of the two low waters occurring each day."

Now that explanation may suffice for some people, but we are never sure what it means. It could mean, for instance, that the figure on the chart is the average of the two low tides on the particular day they happened to be surveying the spot. If they happened to be doing their soundings on, say — June 30th, 1983, they would find that the two lows were 5.6 and -0.1. Add them: you get 5.5. Divide them by 2 for an average and you get 2.75 feet. In other words, the water could be almost three feet shallower than the chart indicates.

You get your best definition of this term from the NOAA 'Tide Tables Book', back in the section called 'Glossary of Terms'. Here it's clearer:

MEAN LOWER LOW WATER (MLLW) — a Tidal datum. The arithmetic mean of the low water heights of a mixed tide observed over a 19-year Metonic Cycle ... Only the lower low water of each pair of low waters, or the only low water of a tidal day is included in the mean.

What that seems to say is: "This is as low as it usually gets." So if you go to all the trouble to calculate the depths from your clock and tide-table, you won't be off more than six inches or so — and you can easily live with that.

Why two s's in 'Guss'? Maybe that's the way they spelled that nickname back in 1868 when Hoffmeister kept "the suttlers (sic) store for the English Garrison". Or it may have been referred to as 'Gus's Place'. There are no remains of the store to be found, however. Certainly, the Indian who died on the island got there long before the storekeeper.

English Camp

Federal Park lands extend from nearly the end of the marshland in Garrison Bay across to the marshy area in Westcott Bay, where there is a series of pilings to mark the boundary. This area takes in all of **Bell Point** and **Bell Cove**. Bell Cove is not marked as such on the charts, incidentally, but it is the narrow bight just beyond the point.

The park extends north and east, inland, up to the top of **Mount Young**. We know the chart calls it 'Young Hill' but islanders call it 'Mount Young'. It is a favorite hiking spot for locals and tourists alike. There are some breathtaking views from the 680-foot high top of this little mountain. Take a camera with you if you decide to climb the trails to the highest point—it's a hike of about a mile and easy enough for the whole family.

There is a charming little cemetery en route called 'The English Cemetery'. There

English Camp's famous blockhouse

are seven marines buried there. They all died of natural causes—by the way—or else they drowned.

If you drop anchor in Garrison Bay and boat in to visit this Federal park, you may or may not be able to step out of your tender onto a dinghy dock. This all depends upon whether the Rotary Club of Victoria, B.C. has delivered its kindly-contributed 'new' float. If it isn't there, you may be interested in what happened to the old one.

Well, last year a 30-foot Bayliner tied up to the shoreboat dock, even though it was clearly labeled with a sign saying 'Dinghies only'. The crew spent the night on board. In the wee hours of the morning they departed. But they neglected to throw off the mooring lines and the Uncle Sam Dock went with them! Somewhere out in Garrison Bay they must have discovered the excess baggage, because they cast it adrift. It eventually floated up on the shore in Westcott Bay and was pounded to bits by the waves. The staff of the park muttered, "It takes all kinds ... even that kind!" Funds being scarce, they had to finish the season without a dock.

(We sort of hope the turkey who trashed the English Camp float reads this!)

The folks on Vancouver Island eventually got wind of the loss and gallantly volunteered to replace it.

By the time you get there, it will be in place.

So much for nitty-gritty about 'some' transient boaters!

Let's give you a word picture of what you will find on shore.

First of all, the blockhouse is right there on the beach. You will be able to duck inside the ground floor of that ancient structure, which has been lovingly rebuilt by the parks crews. The ceiling of the room is all fresh lumber—the original overhead disintegrated years ago, of course. Some of the old logs also decayed and had to be replaced. You may be able to detect which ones are modern. The corner braces are the old timbers, however. They must have been made of sterner stuff.

It is questionable whether you will get a chance to climb the stairway up to the second floor. You see, the four holes high in each wall acted as an invitation to the feathered critters over the last few years. They made their home in the Uncle Sam hostel. They were not a tidy lot, as you might imagine. The crew of the park fondly hopes to find some volunteers to go up and unmung the place. If they do, you will be able to go up and look out through the holes which will be covered by screens.

You will come to the conclusion that, no matter what you have heard, those ports were not made for riflemen. They are far too small. If you put an old flintlock through one of them and stood on your tiptoes, you would see very little of the landscape and the water. The rampaging Indians would be able to saunter up completely undetected! So much for exploring a minor legend.

The superintendent of the park has the theory that the building was a guardhouse. It was meant to house the men on guard. They probably slept there when on duty. The head ranger has another theory: the upstairs room might have been a brig. Every army unit has to have one, you know. No other one has ever been noted in the history of the place.

You will also see the whopping big maple tree. It is one of the largest in the world. You will also see another massive maple, even bigger than the famous one—but it is actually made up of several trees clumped together.

Weather

At this point, let's be candid about the good old NOAA weather service. Certainly they are the source from which all meteorological skinny comes. They do a great job of gathering information. But when it comes to disseminating it, they seem to leave a lot to be desired.

Take this all-too familiar situation: you are off Smith Island. The time is 11:30 a.m. You are listening to the weather channel. They are broadcasting the status report for Smith Island which was taken at 0800. At the time, the area was the proverbial mill-pond. But now you find your craft climbing six-foot swells and churning through spume-crested waves, rain beating into your face. The voice of the weather man drones on, however, about "Seas calm at Smith Island, wind two knots, visibility 10 miles . . . " etc.

Here's a tip: watch the TV newscasts at night. The friendly tube-weatherman may not be as authoritative as a minion of good old Uncle Sam, but he's a lot more likely to give you information you can use. Or if you're already underway, and chances are you don't have a television aboard, listen to radio stations which make regular reports on weather and sea conditions. Learn to read weather signs: clouds, the type they are and the way they're moving, and watch that barometer—if it's dropping, use caution, that can mean a storm moving in, and most of the storms tend to churn up from the south and southwest—especially in the Strait.

"Under the towering maple tree ..."

On the beach, you will find the remains of two old docks. One was just south of the blockhouse (guardhouse). All that is left of it is one old piling on the beach.

To the north of the block-cum-guardhouse you will find nine pilings —another footing for a dock which has long ago disappeared.

If you look along the shore you will see millions of clam and oyster shells. As a matter of fact, when crews dug into the clearing, they found that the whole area has a thick underlayment of shells. It seems probable that Indians had thousands of shellfish dinners and didn't clear up the area afterwards. This is called a midden. You will find a number of places where the topsoil has eroded away and you will see the strata of shells. It is probable that the British marines found the area and shooed off the peaceful redmen.

There are three reconstructed buildings in their original locations: a commissary, near the beach; a tiny building that served as a hospital; and a barracks building. This latter structure houses an interesting exhibit of the day-to-day life of the soldiers who were stationed there during the Pig War era.

The formal garden is laid out exactly as the original one was, although there isn't a great profusion of flowers. It doesn't take much imagination to see the officers sitting with their ladies on benches and taking tea. It's probably a good guess that the grunts of the day were not invited in—except, of course, to plant and weed!

One advantage the common soldiers had over the braid was the fact that their bunkhouse was right at hand. The officers had their quarters on promontories up the hill to the south.

We are told that not a lot of visitors trudge up the hill to have a look-see. If you do hike up, you will find earthen steps with the original stones still in place.

It's a short hike up to where the subalterns lived. The building is not still standing, of course, but there are some old daguerrotypes of it. It was, to say the least, not very posh.

The good old Captain had more of a hike to his domain—all uphill. Probably the only exercise the old boy ever got!

In a clearing on a rise is the site of the Captain's quarters. There is a monument there—placed by the Park Service—dedicated to the Kaiser of Germany who decided that the turf belonged to the Yanks. Now, you know, the British would never have put up such a memento!

If you look carefully, you will see that the site is all terraced. You can imagine who did all the work involved in putting in fieldstone bulkheads and carrying soil! The stones are still there. Traces of the sweat of honest toil of the dogfaces who built the place have long since washed away.

Continue along the trail, away from the water, and you will see a remarkable sight. There is an ancient tree that has been laced by a gargantuan creeping vine some time in the past. It is not your usual 'strangler' vine. Undoubtedly, somebody planted and tended it back in the mid-19th Century. It's dead now, but it is still very tough wood. If you get good light, take a snapshot of it. If you happen to know what kind of a plant it was, tell the ranger. He's always wondered.

Another path you might like to stroll is the one that leads along the shore out to Bell Point Cove. There are a couple of picnic tables, in case you brown-bag it. One note: there is no drinking water on the premises. But then, who drinks water anyway?

The Bell Point hike is a favorite for families. The trail winds through evergreen and Madrona trees, just above the shell-covered beach. Look for two Madrona trees with horizontal gashes in them just above eye level on the right side of the trail. To the left is a tumble-down fence. We surmise this fence at one time may have been supported by the trees.

The trail, about a half-mile long out to Bell Point, goes from Garrison Bay to Westcott Bay and ends on the beach. Pack a lunch and enjoy the peace and quiet of Bell Point when you arrive.

One more item of interest—there is an impressive old two-story mini-mansion just off the campground and back in among the trees. It was built by Jim Crook, one of the Yankee ineritors of the land, in 1889.

Since it was not part of the original English Camp, it has not been restored for the exhibit. It is on the roster of historical buildings, so it cannot be removed. If you get down into Friday Harbor and go to the Historical Museum, you will find some of the very ingenious machines Mr. Crook invented to do the subsistence work of an old settler.

There is an interesting bit of masonry in the front yard of this old house. It was once part of a sawmill which burned down decades ago.

For those of you who have a penchant for toiling up steep paths and gaining the lofty and panoramic viewpoints—there is the trek to the top of Mount Young. The trail passes the English Cemetery with its historic headstones. From the top of this little mountain, you can look out over much of Mosquito Pass and its connecting bays, out to Vancouver Island across Haro Strait. Considering the number of shots taken by scenic photographers, it would justify Eastman Kodak to install a funicular railway.

One of the guides, who logs impressions in this tome, made some inquiries before his ascent. He discovered that there are no Sherpas available. It is rumored that there once was a squad of Tibetan baggage-carriers who used to assist the climbers. In recent years, howver, they joined a Teamsters' Local (according to one story) and priced themselves out of work by demanding a 'cost of lifting' wage increase.

If you arrive at English Camp during the tourist season, you may be able to sit in on a demonstration of life in the old days in the camp. Park employees, dressed like the British soldiers of that period, enact a little playlet to give visitors a taste of regimental life in the old days. The English dialects occasionally leave something to be desired for authenticity, but the whole performance is done with such gusto that audiences are delighted.

Westcott Bay

Entering **Westcott Bay** around Bell Point, you will notice that it is made up of two bodies of water and a narrowed waist. The preferred anchorage area is the southwesterly body of water: the depths are ideal and the bottom is good for ground tackle.

The northern body is rather shallow but has some interesting features to see.

Westcott Bay Sea Farms produces gourmet oysters and clams for northwest gourmet restaurants.

You will notice an acre or so of brightly colored floats just off the pier on the eastern shore. This is an aquaculture enterprise called 'Westcott Bay Sea Farms'. It is the most successful venture of its kind in the San Juan Islands. The farm produces oysters and clams and mussels for a number of fine restaurants in the Seattle area. One of the remarkable facts about this body of water is that it is almost ideal for bivalve culture. The salinity and temperatures are just right. For some unexplained reason, the red tide almost always passes by this area. The workers at the farm rigidly monitor the harvests to be absolutely certain they are free of contamination—and they seldom have to hold back the shellfish. The buoys around the pens are marked with signs asking boaters to stay away from the lantern nets.

You will notice on the chart the area is marked 'submerged crib'—a designation used for something submerged intentionally.

On the western shore of this water, you will find the remains of an old quarry—it is labeled 'ruins' on the chart. It is not very dramatic, however. You can see where the limestone has been hewn away from the cliff. There are a number of 20-foot trees in the quarry, so it has not been used for decades. You can also see where there was once a kiln on a point of land. A road comes down to the waterfront over a build-up of 'tailings' from the kiln. There are also old skid logs on the bank. The chart notes pilings offshore in this area. We avoided the spot, so we cannot report whether they are still there. But when in doubt, avoid the close-in waters just to be safe.

There is a beach on the shore opposite Bell Point, also used for oyster culture.

Deadly Sin Number 1

Do not worship the bowline above all other knots! In particular, do not insist that your little woman make a fetish of it. Above all, be patient with creative knot-tying. Let me explain more fully.

To be sure, the bowline is a jim dandy knot for a lot of circumstances, but it is not a knot for all seasons. Charles F. Chapman be hanged, the bowline has some almost fatal weaknesses. I will get to a discussion of them after I first establish some facts about the knot.

One of the chief virtues of the knot is that it is easy to teach to beginners, thanks to the little litany about the rabbit. I have been making bowlines for more than a quarter century and I still quietly whisper to myself the magic formula involving the tree.

I know as a matter of research that the scurvy crew of the 'Pirate Blackbeard' in the 18th Century used the same doggerel. The swashbuckling captain would overtake and capture a merchant vessel. When the hapless victims were herded on board, he would order his scrofulous band to tie them hand and foot. Daggers in teeth, black eye patches covering empty sockets, scars decorating their stubbled faces, they would approach the cringing gentlemen and cowering crinolined damsels with hempen ropes in hand. As they tied their captives they would recite in unison:

"And now de rabbit comes up of de hole and goes around de tree dis way?"

Now to the fatal flow of the bowline. It is a peachy knot to whip up when you are standing on the deck of a boat with a group of admiring ladies watching you illustrate it. But the catch is this: it has to have a freestanding loop in the business-end of the line. Not at all hard to hold between your pinkies when there is nothing tugging at the line. But when that line is secured to a bitt on a 20-ton boat tossing in five-foot waves and the little lady mate is standing on a pitching float trying to tie it off to a mooring rail, it just doesn't work. It would take someone with the muscle of a Godzilla to hold the nice little rabbit-hole loop while you lead the bitter end under the rail and back up through it.

If the lady deckhand, at a time like this, makes several nice overhand knots, similar to tatting, it is no time to stand on the foredeck and shout demands for a bowline. You are likely to hear a rebuttal like this:

"Look, Ahab. I am here safely on the dock and you and your precious boat are about to be blown onto the breakwater. If you give me any more of your smart alecky remarks about my imaginative knot-tying, I will untie the line and let you explain to the insurance adjuster why you had to swim ashore!"

I have known Conrad-quoting skippers who could wax eloquent about how much more preferable is a carrick bend with a double becket to a studding-sail halyard bend. I also happen to know these seagoing purists at Christmas time, when tying packages to mail off to distant relatives, will shout frantically for their ladies to hurry in and put their index pinkie on the overhand knot in string.

As you leave Westcott Bay, notice the rock that uncovers at six feet. It would be wise to stay in the four-fathom contour around the point.

Off **White Point** you will find a red marker number '6'. It may not be on your

Pole Island—keep to the east of it!

chart. It marks the eastern shore of the channel where there is a shoal designated 'rky'—'rocky'.

Once again in Mosquito Pass you will see a beach on the eastern shore of Henry Island. The water is shallow and rocky off that beach. Currents in Mosquito Pass are likely to be very swift during wide tide ranges. At the end of the beach, you will see a tombolo with a shoal leading out like a finger pointed south. At the end of that shoal is a rock called 'Brant's Bump'. It uncovers at seven feet and our friend, who named the spot, once deposited his boat on it for one complete tide change. He claims it as his private property and forbids you to tresspass on it—be warned or suffer horse laughs and 'I told-you-so's' from Mr. B.

At this point, you are looking at **Pole Island**. At almost all tides it would appear that you could go on either side of it. If your draft is shallow and you are very lucky, you might make it through the passage on the west side. If not—you can join the ranks of dozens of skippers each year who get nailed on it. The folks who live on the beaches along this passage have a grandstand seat to watch unwary boaters who scoff at charts. Seldom a week goes by that some yahoo in a fast cruiser doesn't go sledding into the area and end up fanny over teakettle on the deck. Pole Island belongs to the U.S. Government. It is a bird rookery, but there isn't much to stare at while you're waiting for a salvage boat. Like Pole Pass, it gets its name from Indian poles and nets designed to trap unwary birds, back before the white man populated the area.

But don't be in too big a hurry to pass through the eight-fathom channel to the east of Pole Island. There is something worth seeing in the little hook just past the cable area. It is another of the old lime kilns, out of use for many years. This one is not so smoke-stained as most of them, but it is still interesting to see.

The passage around the Pole Island widens out at Bazalgette Point. Around to the left, you will see a false bay named **Nelson Bay**. Only the very center of this body of water is deep enough to moor in—and on a short anchor rode.

At the entrance to this bay is an extensive moorage as this is an outstation of the Seattle Yacht Club. Only members of that club, or those clubs with reciprocal privileges, can use the facilities.

This is a very attractive spot with a beautiful meadow and several tall alders. The clubhouse and caretaker's quarters are just to the south of the marina. It is an impressive old three-story house.

You are now through Mosquito Pass.

Bazalgette Point gets its name from the first commander of the British marines in the area. Poor old Captain George Bazalgette suffered, as most men with exotic names do, with a welter of misspellings of his name in the old records. He was AKA Bazalgettil, Bazalgetti, Bazalgene and even Bagatelle. Somewhere up in the British Admiralty section of heaven, the old boy must be very relieved to know that the map makers have finally learned how to spell his name.

There is a small unnamed bay on the western side, around the finger from Nelson Bay. This is dubbed by local sailors as 'Booze Bay'. Americans returning from British Columbia used to anchor there to drink up their remaining liquor before heading into the Customs dock at the Roche Harbor Marina. It is still a decent moorage for a few boats at anchor.

Roche Harbor

You are now in historical **Roche Harbor**. The entrances to this body are Mosquito Pass and **West Pearl Island Passage** and **East Pearl Island Passage**.

The entire eastern shore of Roche Harbor is dominated by the complex of the Roche Harbor Resort. The bay in front of the resort has 52 mooring buoys which belong to the marina. A sign indicates that the fee is $10 for overnight tie-ups. Skippers who do not want to pay the fee can drop their anchors in the area to the west and avoid paying, of course. The depths are ideal for anchorage.

Roche Harbor is now, and has been for decades, a company-owned community. There are some luxurious condos on the southern shores. The marina is almost world-famous and no trip to the San Juans is complete without a visit to its many attractions.

Pearl Island is a very choice residential area. There is a community dock at the west tip that has privately-maintained flashing red lights on its extremity. When entering from the north at night, be alert to the fact that these are not navigational markers and do not try to keep them to your right returning home.

The entrance marker to Roche Harbor is on the western tip of Pearl Island—it is flashing white.

The preferred channel for entering and leaving Roche Harbor is the passage west of Pearl Island. It is quite possible to use the passage east of the island, however, if your boat is not too deep of draft and the tide is in; the water gets to a low of about seven feet at minus tide. The only hazard you encounter is a couple of rocks off the north end of Pearl Island. One of the rocks had a six-foot pipe driven into it last time we went by—it will probably still be there.

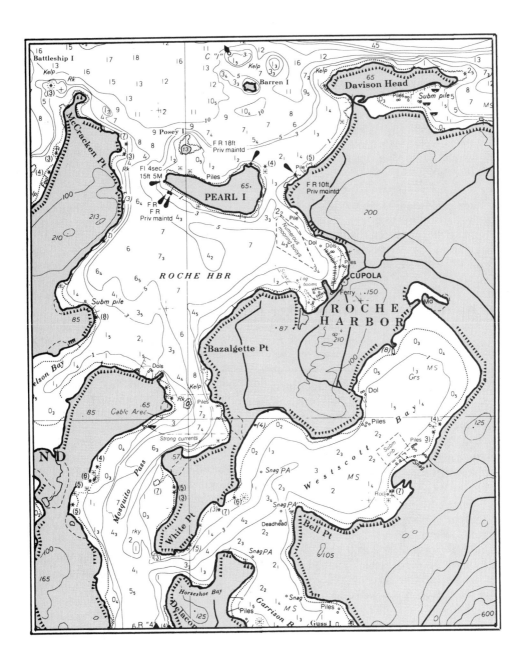

Notice that if you are using the west passage, you should avoid the shallow water that covers a sandspit leading out to Posey Island.

Posey Island

Posey Island was not named after a flower. While roses do not grow there, old-timers of the area say they used to be able to walk out the sandspit to the island and

Roche Harbor Resort

Frankly, it's hard to resist the temptation to crib some of the halcyon phrases found in the colorful brochure that the resort passes out. Phrases like 'steeped in tradition', 'a page out of history', 'elegant and old-world' seem to be fairly close to the mark.

A visit to the San Juans would not be really complete without at least a quick visit to this establishment. You can savor the charm of the place without spending a penny if you wish. You can shoot up a roll of film very easily without exhausting the picture possibilities.

We suggest at least a stroll of the grounds and a peek into the various buildings. Using a free guide map, you can fill several hours quite pleasantly on a summer afternoon, just sightseeing.

Historian Dave Richardson sketches the history of the place. He says that John S. McMillin, in 1884, was president of a lime-producing company in Tacoma. He was asked by the company to scout out rumors that there was a working set of kilns and a good supply of stone in the Roche Harbor area of San Juan Island.

He found the reports to be true and formed the Tacoma and Roche Harbor Lime Company in which he bought stock. The whole San Juan Island works cost $40,000. John had $1,800 invested in it.

Within seven years, the ex-Indiana lawyer built the place up to become the most valuable limeworks in the Pacific Northwest.

But the mining and smelting operation had a colorful history even before McMillin saw it.

The first quarrying and reduction of lime was done by two men, N.C. Bailey and Augustus Hibbard in 1860. The partners had a falling out about a prized resource—a pretty young Indian woman.

The upshot was that Bailey wasted Mr. Hibbard and took over the lady and the lime. The military authorities took umbrage at Mr. Bailey's behavior and chucked him in the pokey and closed down the kiln.

In 1879, Robert and Richard Scurr, in partnership with a Mr. Ross, reopened and fired up the limeworks. These were the fellows from whom Mr. McMillin bought the whole shebang.

John McMillin realized that the tourist value of the flourishing area would be enhanced by building a posh new hotel. He built the ornate mansion which stands now—the Hotel de Haro.

Since Roche Harbor was a 'company town', the old satrap provided a church for the family and the faithful employees. In 1892, he had a chapel built and a circuit-riding Methodist minister officiated there. During the week, the building served as a schoolhouse for the children of the employees.

When new owners moved into the Roche Harbor complex, they were devout Catholics, so they renovated the chapel which was named 'Our Lady of Good Voyage Church'. It is beautifully appointed. It is a jewel. It is also the only privately-owned Catholic church in the United States.

Old John S. had strong instincts toward the mystic. He created a very elaborate mausoleum of marble, limestone and granite. It is reminiscent of an old Greek temple—without a dome. In the stone terrace within the Doric columns, you will find six stone seats and a limestone table. The stone chairs are practical as well as symbolic. They represent a table set for the deceased members of the family to gather in their spiritual returns to earth. They also serve as containers for the ashes of the parents

Historic Roche Harbor Resort

and family. You will notice that there are six seats, but there is space for seven. Legend has it that one of his sons didn't toe the line and the old boy banished him from the afterlife reunions.

Dave Richardson, who can be relied upon to document the truth no matter how much it wars on romance, says that the story is not true — that it was planned that way. On the other hand, Dave wasn't around during those days — so you can nurture the legend if you wish. We've strolled up to visit the spot many times. We think it's beautiful and charming and somewhat hokey. We crack jokes about the ghosts of the McMillin family sitting down to dinner. What would be on the menu? Graveyard stew? Divinity fudge?

Other interesting places to visit includes the old cemetery, the 'company house', the Log Cabin built by the Scurr Brothers and 'The Doctor's House'.

The McMillin spread was sold to Reuben Tarte of Seattle in 1956. It is now operated by Neil Tarte and his family. We think he has done a good job of renovating the historical features of the area without sacrificing any of the charm and continuity.

Before we drift away from a word picture of Roche Harbor Resort, we should mention one further item that you will probably remember if you have visited the place. That is, the 'Flag Salute'.

It's a colorful — and possibly campy — ceremony performed at dusk during the peak of the visitor season. The procedure begins with a medley of patriotic songs and the national anthems of Canada, Britain and, of course, the U.S. A platoon of the high school-age employees of the resort, all dressed alike in white shirts and slacks, march out to the flag mast at the end of the Customs dock and lower the Canadian and American flags.

The performance is almost as famous as the resort itself. Even the most jaded and world-weary travelers admit to reactions ranging from warmly bemused to a swelling of patriotic spirit.

Posey Island's primitive Sanikan

pick Easter lilies. On the little one-acre state park you will find a campsite, a fire pit and a picnic table. There is also a typical outdoor toilet. On the western side of the island, you will find an old, no longer used outhouse. It's not particularly inviting in its present condition. The interesting thing about it is that it is built out *over the water*. This arrangement made no problem of disposal of the waste—the sea did it. Imagine the kind of Environmental Impact Statement you would have to fill out to replace it with another saltwater flushing privy! The island is great for kayakers, canoeists and rowboaters. There is room for a group of campers on the southern end of the island. One of the things you could study from a hike around the island is the remarkable shape of **Battleship Island**.

Battleship Island

This island is the most aptly-named geographic feature in the whole San Juan Chain. From a distance out in **Haro Strait** or up **Spieden Channel**, it looks for all the world like a real battleship. Once you are close to it, you begin to see the little bluffs that look like superstructure and trees that look like masts. In the morning and evening light, the illusion is dramatic.

As a matter of fact, there is a story about this island in San Juan history. In 1904, President Theodore Roosevelt paid a visit to the Roche Harbor area. He had previously ordered monuments to be placed at American and English camps to memorialize the two national forces that contended for the island. He ordered the *Wyoming* to be present for the ceremony. He also expected a British battleship to come for the event.

Commander V.L. Cottman was in his cabin on the morning the *Wyoming* headed for the entrance to Roche Harbor. He was called by a crewman and told "Battleship ahead, Sir." The commander replied, "Have the saluting crews go to their stations to fire a salute." He was sure that it was his British counterpart arriving in port. With the men at their cannons waiting for the order to fire a salute, the *Wyoming* neared the apparition. Then, and only then, did someone realize it was only an island. He canceled the order. He later told a historian, "If I had given the order to fire that salute I could never live it down for the rest of my days in the Navy, saluting an island for a battleship!"

In the late 20s, a fire destroyed two of the trees that had given the illusion of masts and spars. But the remaining outline still is clear enough to surprise visitors to the area.

Before continuing with our cruise around San Juan Island, we should, for the sake of comprehensiveness, note that the western shore of Henry Island is unremarkable. The only house visible from the water is one at the top of a hill halfway up the shoreline, near the legend 'kelp' on the chart.

If you decide to fish along this shoreline, take note of the very dangerous reef about a half-mile south of **McCracken Point**. Note also that passage between Mc-Cracken Point and Battleship Island is safest if you stay close to the battleship. There are shoals and reefs coming out in the passage.

Davison Head

From the entrance to Roche Harbor going toward **Davison Head**, be on the lookout for black can buoy #1. If you pass over it your fathometer will flip from 10 fathoms to seven feet at low tides, so give the can a respectable berth.

Battleship Island's profile

Davison Head is an area with some impressive beachfront homes.

Davison Head Cove, between Davison Head and San Juan Island, is a favorite short-term anchorage. Only the outer third of it is suitable.

Limestone Point

The north shore of San Juan Island has more waterfront estates, from Davison Head to **Limestone Point**. The view they have of Spieden and Sentinel Islands is priceless and the fishing is also spectacular.

There is one resort at Lonesome Cove which is not really much of a cove, but has some picturesque beaches and rocks.

There is moorage at the resort only if you stay in one of their cabins. They also have small fishing boats to rent if you decide to go there by land.

Limestone Point is a white rocky headland. The old quarries that provided the stone for building materials for Seattle and other west coast cities is still visible. At one time, there were commercial buildings at the quarry, but they have disappeared.

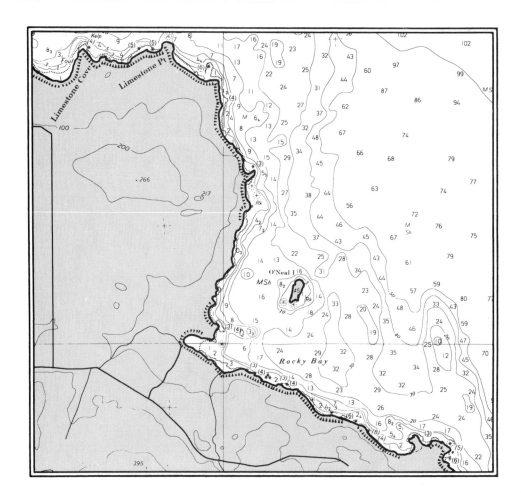

Avoid the bow thumper

Turning south into San Juan Channel, we proceed to a relatively new park, **Reuben Tarte Park**. It was donated to the county by the owners of Roche Harbor Resort. It is a tiny bight on the channel and does not offer anchorage. One of the chief advantages of this park is that most tourists do not know of its existence. It is a fine place for landbound visitors to come and picnic. The view from the rocky point of the park is quite compelling. You will recognize the park from the water by the steep road that leads down to it and a green sign tacked on a tree at the bottom of the road.

Rocky Bay is a large triangular body of water that extends from Tarte Park down to the small hook that is called **Mineral Point,** although this name is not on the charts—in fact, there is no name on the chart at all.

Meet the Topper Buoys

When you're securely tied to one of the State Marine Parks mooring buoys, did you ever wonder just how safe you are? Well, here's the straight skinny on those contrivances—from the State Parks and Recreation Commission, which is responsible for them. (Incidentally, they're called 'Topper' Buoys—the commercial name of the manufacturer.) If you will study the accompanying diagram, you will see they are pretty reliable.

Starting with the ground tackle, the main anchor is a one-ton block of concrete. After it is in place for a while, it usually hunkers down into the sand or mud and the result is it takes more than a ton of lift to get it free.

The fastenings at the block end of the rig are all three-quarter-inch galvanized material, which should lift about ten tons with no trouble. The six-plus feet of one-inch ship's anchor chain means that the material in the links is one inch in diameter. If it's beefy enough to hold a freighter in a storm, it's probably going to take good care of you. The reason for the chain is two-fold: one, it adds a lot of weight to the tackle: two, it will not chafe as rope does if it lies in sand or shale.

At the end of the chain is what is called a 'bouncer'. This is a quarter-ton chunk of concrete. In high winds, a heavy, moored ship will lift it off the sea floor from time to time. It acts like a spring to keep tension on the line at these times. From the bouncer to near the surface, the tackle is one-inch nylon line—the kind tugboats use. The last ten feet below the float is made up of chain—this time three-eighths-inch chain. This is so the line will hang straight down from the buoy—reducing the chance that you will run into it with your prop.

Two other little additions to this tackle: a buoy that helps to keep the nylon line off the bottom most of the time, and a pendant of three-eighths-inch chain to keep the line hanging straight down.

To recap the lengths—there is enough chain at the buoy end to reach to within ten feet of the bottom at extreme high tides. Add to that a minimum of 30 feet of one-inch nylon line. At barest minimums, that would give the tackle a 3:1 scope.

Some other information you might find helpful:

The Park Rangers have been instructed to limit the number of boats that may raft up to each mooring buoy, as follows:

Boats up to 24 feet — 4 maximum to a buoy

25-36 feet — 3
36-45 feet — 2
45+ feet — 1

And here's a bit of trivia for you: each buoy system costs the state $521 for materials.

This might also be a good place to bring up another matter involved in riding on ground tackle like the marine parks buoys—the strain on the mooring lines.

Sometimes, when wind and current catch your boat, you may find the line (which is usually doubled) stretched somewhat taut. You might be inclined to get nervous about its holding power. The breaking-strength of the line you are using has been calculated by the manufacturer and you can make a mental note of it the next time you visit a chandlery and read the statistics.

But how much strain is there on the

line? It is probably calculable by a marine architect and a weather observer working together with their computers. But there is a quick and dirty way of estimating the force. Just pull in on the line, moving your boat forward.

We have been out on the hook in winds of up to 50 knots and have checked to see how well the anchor is holding. We have found that in almost gale-force winds we can heave in on the anchor line on the 'Sea Witch'—she weighs about six tons—and actually move the bow of the boat against the wind. How much force are we developing? Well, probably

not more than 50 to 100 pounds of pull. In any case, it is much less taut than when we put the engine in reverse to set the hook.

So we have come to the conclusion that, unless your line is frayed or deteriorated or fastened over a sharp surface, it is capable of holding you safe against almost any conceivable wind in the inland waters.

And, if you get nervous, you can always bend a second line through the mooring ring and secure it to the bitt on board. That should keep you safe and sound. So, relax.

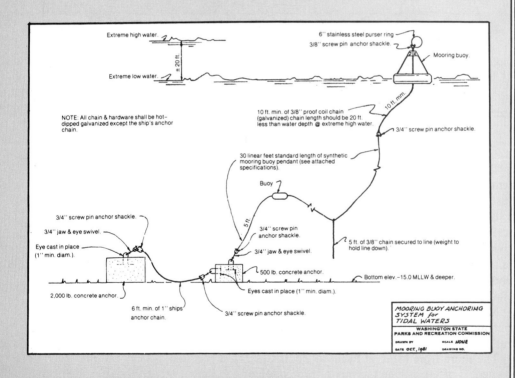

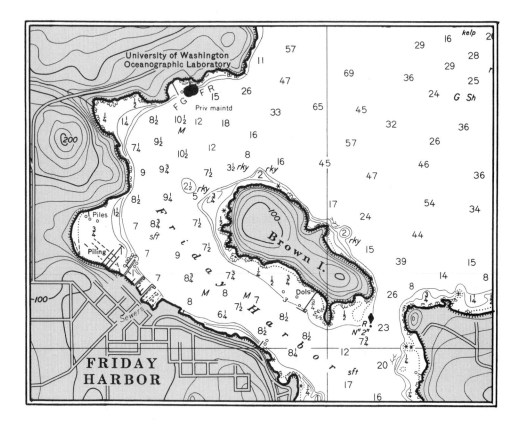

There is a small cove and marshland at the apex of the triangle. It could afford temporary anchorage for one or two boats to ride out a sou'wester. Notice the reef just off the entrance to the cove.

O'Neal Island in Rocky Bay was once owned by a man named Neal. Old records state that the island once was the site of a quarry, but there is no evidence of such activity visible from the water. The records also say that it was used for a sheep range at times, but it seems unlikely as there is no fresh water on the tiny island. The south end of this island is flanked by reefs and rocks. There is one house visible on the island.

Mineral Point has a cluster of fine homes along the waterfront both inside and outside the small bay. Shelter from a storm could be found here, but the area is rather small.

The shore from **Mineral Point** to Point Caution is forested, rocky, and privately owned. It offers little in the way of protection or good moorage, although is slightly less rough in a southerly than farther out in San Juan Channel.

Much of the land south and west of **Point Caution** is owned by the University of Washington Oceanographical Labs. Local residents see researchers along the beaches quite frequently during the summer. The land is posted but does not forbid trespassing.

From Point Caution to the entrance to Friday Harbor is one of the favorite sports fishing grounds in San Juan Channel. During the season, small boats make long trolling runs along the shore, across the opening to the harbor and over to the east shore of **Brown Island**.

The designation on the chart for the **University of Washington Oceanographic Laboratory** indicates a short dock. This is called 'The Cantilever' although it is not a proper description. You will see a small storage shed and a large transparent glass tank on the shore. Water for experiments at the Labs is pumped at the 'Cantilever'.

The main complex of the Lab installation is further inside the channel. There is a series of docks and floats that are used by university personnel. This is called 'The Labs Docks'. It is posted, and vessels not on university business are prohibited from tying up to it. (During the height of the tourist season there are always hundreds of boats trying to find moorage.) The scientists who come there to study the marine life of the area need the space for research and research vessels. There is often a collection of scientific tools and instruments on the dock and there is no adequate policing of the area to prevent pilferage or disruption of experiments.

If you want to visit the Labs, you will have to come in to Friday Harbor Marina, tie up and get land transportation to the compound. It's an easy walk of about one and a half miles from town.

Before discussing Friday Harbor and its marina, we should look at **Brown Island**.

Brown Island

And that *is* the name: **Brown Island**! To be sure, you will hear Chamber of Commerce and realtor types call it 'Friday Island'. It's even listed that way in the phone book. So—repeat after us: 'Brown Island'.

It was named after John G. Brown. In 1841 he was a 'Mathematical Instrument Maker' (whatever that is) aboard the *Vincennes,* one of the exploration ships under the command of Lt. Wilkes.

In 1858, some turkey aboard the *H.M.S. Plumper,* an English ship, put in the log that they were anchored inside 'Robert's' Island, probably a friend or crewmate of the duty officer. Some higher-up noticed the attempt at renaming the spot and struck a line through the spurious entry and penciled in 'Brown Island'.

An interesting historical note of recent origin: a decade or so back, the island was offered by the owners to the town of Friday Harbor for a price of $25,000. The town fathers turned the offer down. There was no ready water supply on the island and nobody in their right minds would ever build on it, they decided.

Today $25,000 would probably buy you a peapatch-sized lot in the interior of the island.

The island is about 80 acres in size and the lots are all of one acre. They get their water by pipes from the town of Friday Harbor. There is one mile of road down the middle of the island, but only one car and a fire truck—communally-owned. The rest of the residents drive golf carts. They have a volunteer fire department—and almost everybody on the island belongs to it. They have fire drills on Saturday mornings, so don't look for smoke if you hear the sirens. There is a community dock, since everybody has to boat back and forth to San Juan Island. There is a swimming pool and tennis courts for the residents.

'The Labs' In Friday Harbor

In the year 1903, two UW scientists found a nearly ideal spot for marine research — San Juan Island. It was ideal because it provided nearby sea depths ranging from 200 fathoms to shallow beaches. A brochure says, "The region is remarkably rich in marine flora and fauna. The diversity of species and abundance of individuals of both plants and animals were important considerations." The sea beds offer almost all possible factors, ranging from solid rock to mud. The waters are free of industrial pollution. In other words, the biologists found a natural laboratory just waiting for the researchers.

The original pair of marine biologists were H.R. Foster and Trevor Kincaid. The latter name may seem familiar — he was the father of Nor'westing publisher, Tom Kincaid.

The U.W. profs set up shop in the Friday Harbor fish cannery until 1910 when they found a four-acre plot just south of town. Scientists began to arrive in force and the small installation soon was outgrown.

In 1921, President Warren G. Harding took note of the work being done there and awarded a veritable bonanza to the UW — 484 acres that were a surplus military preserve at the edge of the town of Friday Harbor. Construction of the new laboratories was begun in 1923 and the biologists moved into them the following year.

In 1962, the National Science Foundation granted funds to build a sophisticated new complex. A library was established which now holds over 8,000 volumes of standard references and research journals. There are rooms for specialized photography, microtechniques, radio-isotopes, and a couple of electron microscopes.

The center provides two programs, one for training advanced students, the second for independent research. Not all of the study deals with life forms, there is on-going investigation of chemical and physical oceanography and even something termed 'oceanographic meteorology'.

The roster of scientists who have

worked at the Labs reads like a Who's Who of the world of biology.

A savant from Nuremberg, West Germany, looked at "... the development of 'Brachiopoda', a comparative study of inarticulata and articulata."

A respected voyeur looked at "... the mating behavior of gastropods."

A doctor from Kyoto (Japan) University wanted to know about 'cytoplasmic control of cells in echinoderm eggs'.

Dr. Schmid from the University of Basel, Switzerland, studied something described in two sentences that have only two words familiar to laymen: 'of' and 'and'.

A man from Aberdeen, Scotland was interested in the 'buccal mass' of a species of octupus. (We translated that one—he looked in their mouths.)

The rest of the scientists came from practically every major university in the United States. And this is just the list of researchers in the year 1983!

How does all of this interest you as boaters? Glad you asked. During the summer, you can walk or hitchhike a mile out to the Labs on Wednesdays or Saturdays between 2 and 4 p.m. and rubberneck. Many of the buildings are off limits to the curious because, according to the director, some of them are involved in experiments using radioactive materials. And in others, the men in the white coats are lost in study and don't take kindly to being asked, "Hey, whatcha doin', mister?"

Incidentally, remember the tip in the cruising section that deals with Friday Harbor—there is no mooring or even tying up at the docks at the Labs.

You may not be interested in peering at specimens in the public display at the institution, but you cannot escape their influence: all of San Juan County has been declared by the state to be a Marine Biological and Game Preserve.

Not to worry, though. That doesn't mean you can't fish or dig clams—if you obey the rules.

Meet "Cyanea Capillata" — BUT DON'T SHAKE HANDS

Those pretty little, almost transparent jellyfish you see in the summer are called aequorea aequorea, don't ask why they have a name that stutters. After all, there are humans named Simone Simone. It's okay for kids to pick them up and study them — they don't bite. As far as we know, they are not edible, these jellyfish, so don't spread them on bread.

During the sunny weather they come to the top to recharge their batteries — they are solar-powered. Up in Desolation Sound, they get so thick in the warm water that they almost turn the bays into gelatin. You will see scientists from the University of Washington Labs walking around the docks in Friday Harbor catching them in small dip-nets. Everybody in port asks, "Whaddeya do with them?" They get sort of tired explaining, so we will act as public relations for the biologists. The jellyfish are collected and a tiny bit of enzyme is extracted from each one. It's called aequorin. It lights up in the presence of a chemical that is exuded by muscle tissue when it moves. Somehow the scientists use this jellyfish extract to detect slight muscle movement. We are told that some very valuable medical knowledge has been advanced by this test, but we didn't understand it. Go ask the guys in the white coats in one of the public tours of the Labs in Friday Harbor.

But what we wanted to tell you about really was good old hateful Cyanea Capillata. It's a jellyfish that gets to be the size of a washtub. It is not as translucent as the pretty little ones we mentioned. It gets an ominous yellowish brown color. It looks mean. It is. You can get a helluva rash if you pick one up or swim into one and it stings you. We think it's a domestic cousin of the dreaded Portuguese Man-of-War which supposedly kills people.

We cuss them and hit them with oars.

One of the delightful legends about Brown Island is that, during prohibition the speakeasies in Friday Harbor kept their booze hidden somewhere on the island. Twice a day, bartenders would row over and pick up supplies.

Anchorages In Friday Harbor

The 300-yard channel between Brown Island and the San Juan Island shoreline is about 60 feet in depth. Some skippers who eschew the comforts of the marina will anchor in the area, mostly near the ferry dock. The holding quality of the bottom is good, but considerable scope is required, because the current can be a bear.

If you ride on the hook in Friday Harbor, you will get tossed around by the incoming and departing ferryboats. During the summer, the last one comes in long after midnight and shakes up sleeping crews.

Some anchorage can be found just north of the marina in a bay near the labs if you are careful to allow for the swinging of the permanent residents' buoys. A second caution: set the hook well. There is a flourishing bed of sea lettuce and the foliage tends to pile up around the flukes of a newly dropped anchor, preventing its digging in. So, drop the anchor, let out at least a scope of three, put 'er in reverse and hit the throttle.

Another warning: the depth drops to about four feet in most places at minus tides and you can get mired.

The reason we are offering such elaborate warning is that our boats, the *Roanoake* and the *Sea Witch* are often moored in this area during the summer when the transient rates at the dock make it impossible for us to afford it on a liveaboard basis. Every year we rescue a dozen or so errant boats whose anchors are skidding. We spend a lot of time out on our decks with boat hooks fending off vessels whose skippers have dinghied into town.

In other words, if you want to come visiting, don't send your boat over by itself!

Beaverton Bay

Beaverton Bay is the cove between Friday Harbor and the Labs. It gets its name from a sometimes stream that originates near the center of the island and flows through Beaverton Valley. This appellation is not mentioned on the charts, incidentally.

This is a pleasant place because there are no homes on the shore and you can feel a little 'away from it all'. The shore lands are all owned by the University of Washington. They are posted as belonging to the U but there is no 'Keep Out' implied. But don't camp or build fires.

Enjoying the town docks

The bottom in Beaverton Bay is invitingly deep—six to 10 feet at low tides. But, like the north end of the marina, the bottom is not good holding ground and the sea lettuce is a detriment. Here again, it is wise to put a lot of strain on your anchor line before you can be confident of its holding. The ferryboat wake stirs things up here also.

Port Of Friday Harbor

Friday Harbor Marina used to be called 'Robinson Crusoe Marina'. We've wondered who coined that name! It has just recently doubled itself like an amoeba. In 1983 it accommodated as many as 300 boats at one time during peak periods—many of them rafted out.

The newly expanded marina opened in May, 1984, and can now accommodate nearly 600 boats, about 130 of them transient vessels. There is a new seaplane and Customs float at the most northerly floating breakwater, and a narrow dogleg entrance between two breakwaters into the harbor itself. During the summer season you can clear Customs at the end of the breakwater, and there will be a harbormaster to direct you to a transient slip. The new facility includes power and water to the floats, and there are also eight new showers in the port building, bringing the number to a total of 14.

A new shoreside park will also delight the incoming boaters, with lawns and a fountain, picnic tables and flowers. Friday Harbor has grown up.

Beneath the marina office are public bathrooms and a Porta-Potty dump. Out on the breakwater there is a coin-operated holding tank pumpout facility. As you know, if you have holding tanks, there are precious few of those in Puget Sound waters.

Immediately to the east of the port docks are two commercial fuel docks at adjacent marinas. The Union 76 dock sells propane as well as gas and diesel, and there is a repair service at the dock. San Juan Marina is a full-service marina with a complete ship's store, engine repair, boat sales and fuel.

The Town Of Friday Harbor

When you are tied up at the marina, you are only a couple of blocks from the main shopping center of the San Juan Islands. The town of Friday Harbor has all of the amenities you could ask for. There are two grocery stores about half a block apart. There is a discount serve-yourself type market a quarter-mile or so up the main street, out near the airport.

The in-town grocery stores offer down-to-the-dock delivery service so you can comfortably stock up. And it's free. They also have a big mountain of cardboard boxes that are free. How long has it been since you've seen that at a grocery store?

There are two hardware stores. Both of them have complete lines of boating/camping gear and a good selection of frequently-used parts and repair kits.

There are two boat repair facilities on the waterfront and a traveling repair truck that handles primarily heavy equipment and diesel engines.

A number of scuba divers have their posters displayed in case you need to get your glasses or binoculars off the harbor bottom.

Port of Friday Harbor

There are, of course, a good dozen restaurants close to the waterfront, three bars, and several taverns. There is a charming small-town movie house that gets surprisingly up-to-date flicks. There is one drug store. It is noteworthy that the owner lists his home phone number in case you need help after business hours.

There are the usual boutiques, antiques, gift shops, and book stores, and a Sprouse-Reitz store and a bustling 'dry goods' store. There are shopping arcades both next to and across from the ferry landing.

Oh—the liquor store—we almost forgot! It's up Spring Street—that's the main east-west street at the point where it makes a fork with Argyle Street. The angle of the fork has a shopping mall. The Booze Bazaar is next door to the Sprouse-Reitz store. Another necessity: two laundromats. One is in the back of the San Juan Hotel on Spring and the other is beneath a restaurant with a somewhat checkered history—it may or may not be open. It's next to the ferry loading lines.

There's a Sears catalog store, naturally—and a lady barber and a jewelry store and a travel agency.

And, if you look carefully, you might just spot a real estate office somewhere—usually within arm's reach of where you are standing!

For you voluptuaries, there are hot tubs for inside skinnydipping in the basement of the town's hostel, the Elite Hotel.

For those of you who have last-minute business necessities, there are two secretarial services.

Down on the waterfront, you will find a parking strip upland of the marina office. At the north end of the parking, you will find a marine electronics shop and a famous sailmaker's establishment.

By the time you are clutching this tome in your hot little hands, there will be a number of new shops and arcades along the waterfront. As we write this, shops and stands and buildings are springing up in dizzying profusion—just as rapidly others are folding up.

The constant is change in a small, tourist-oriented town, as you know. We would love to tell you about some of our favorite places. But we have no assurance they will be there when you come to visit.

There are some enduring things, though. The Electric Company and Herb's Tavern are pretty sure to be here—they are the two axes of our society. They might change hands, but they wouldn't change names.

Chances are, the 'Driftwood' will still be here. It is called 'The Drive In', although you can't drive in. It is another hub of our world. If we didn't go up there and have coffee at least one morning a week, we would never know who is with whom now and all the other vital scuttlebutt.

If you want to pretend you're an islander, go up there about 10 a.m. and pour yourself a cup of coffee, then take the pot around and see if anybody needs a warm-up. Everybody in the place will whisper, "When did he move here?"

While we're on the subject, let's talk about San Juan Island folks. They are, of course, all pretty much friendly to each other—unless they're mad at each other—which can happen. None of them admits he likes tourists, but you have to understand the meaning of that term. A 'tourist' is a newcomer you haven't met. Almost anybody will talk to anybody else. If you come into town and go back down to your boat without at least having someone smile at you or nod "Hello," you'd better look into a mirror.

There are two places where you can start a conversation—if you want one—in front of the vegetable counter at King's Market and near the meat counter at Whitey's. People sort of congregate there.

Other incidental intelligence about Friday Harbor. At 7 p.m. each Monday, the fire siren lets out a deafening wail. They're testing it—and also rallying all of our volunteer firemen to a weekly meeting.

There's a fascinating museum on Front Street. It is the 'Whale Museum'.

Most of the information in this book about Killer Whales and the Whale Watching outposts has been gleaned from the pamphlets and the exhibits at the museum. Like most other specialized museums, you can stroll through the rooms and get a quick education on most of the Pacific mammals. Or you can spend time at each exhibit and learn just about everything there is to be known on the subject. The Whale Museum is open daily in the summer, 10 a.m. to 5:30 p.m., and the admission fee is nominal.

There are several community festivals on San Juan Island. The 'Jazz' is a festival of Dixieland music that takes place each July. Up to a dozen great traditional bands from all over the west come to town to purvey two-beat music. The harbor fills with boats, the streets are packed with two-stepping people. The music often is wafted down to the marina and the boats at anchor—it's an exciting time.

The County Fair is a real, no-nonsense county fair. It's one of the few times when the whole county—all of the islands—get together to celebrate and compete in the dozens of crafts and activities. It is always the third weekend in August and you can't help but have a wonderful time. The fairgrounds are just a half-mile walk from the waterfront.

You may have read that the islands have a very high proportion of PhDs and ex-business magnates. It's true. One of the most charming things that happens here is

Stoplights

When you go ashore in the islands and wander the big towns of Friday Harbor, Eastsound or Lopez Village, you will be happy to notice the lack of stoplights. There aren't any in the San Juans.

There are a couple of red flashing lights which signal a stop for traffic whenever there is a fire alarm. The one in Friday Harbor is at First and Spring Streets, but it doesn't contribute much to safety because the moment the big fire siren in town goes off, following by the deafening wail of the fire engine—just a short block away—everything comes to a stop.

The signal in Eastsound on Orcas Island has a spotty history. It was privately donated and there are no funds for its maintenance and repair. Fortunately, the same thing happens in Eastsound when the sirens go off: the traffic stops just fine, stoplight or no.

during the County Fair when some retired bank president or brokers stays up nights nourishing his prize cauliflower or begonia, hand-carries it tenderly into the fair building, scrambles for a choice display position, suffers agonies waiting for the judging, and walks off proudly displaying a blue ribbon and $2.50 in cash, which he usually donates to charity.

One event that arouses a lot of spirited competition is the 'Sheep-to-Shawl' Race. Teams from the islands shear sheep, wash and card wool, spin yarn and weave a shawl. It's not just a race. Woe betide any weaver who misses a warp or woof! Judges inspect the sheep after their haircuts and teams are marked down for every little nick or cut on their shorn hides.

On the Fourth of July, we have the usual parade and fireworks. Three years ago, the honor guard all dressed meticulously in perfect uniforms and white gloves, marched down Spring Street, arms at right-shoulder, the flag billowing free. At the bottom of the hill, they neglected to turn wide enough around the big spreading tree at the tiny circle and the flag got hooked into a low branch and had to be disengaged by somebody standing on someone else's shoulders.

There are fireworks displays down in the harbor. The sound of the explosions echoes from the hills, the elaborate flashes make a light-show in the water, and there is usually some inebriated turkey down at the marina who fires a rocket or a flare and people in nearby boats end up trying to stamp it out. The deputies keep a sharp

Jensen Shipyard - a busy place

eye on the proceedings. If they catch unauthorized displays, the offender gets hustled up the dock to the town lockup.

To get back to necesary services to be found in town. San Juan Airlines flies into the airport which is just out of the downtown area. A flying service from Seattle maintains a fairly regular service of float planes to and from the city during summer months.

We have a good selection of doctors and dentists, there are a couple of veterinarians and chiropractors. Our medic unit is one of the best anywhere, we think. We can get people evacuated by air to the big hospitals on the mainland in about the same time it takes an ambulance in the big city to make the run from a suburb to a hospital.

What we don't have—not one psychiatrist.

Before we resume our clockwise trip around San Juan Island, we should look at some of the other features of the harbor.

South End, Friday Harbor

From the water you will notice lots of moorages—most of them private. Just south of the ferry landing is the Cannery Village moorage; beyond that are KDT Marina and Capron's Landing.

In the south end of the harbor, you will find **Shipyard Cove**. It used to be a marine repair facility, but now is all private condominium moorage.

The big yard in this end of the harbor is the almost legendary **Jensen's Shipyard**.

Albert Jensen and Sons Shipyard started out in the early 1900s in downtown Friday Harbor and later moved to its present location. The yard was famous for the boats it built back in those early days—passenger and freight steamers, workboats, fishboats and now and again a classic yacht. Many of the old boats are still plying Northwest waters.

But for the past decade or two, with the advent of cheap fiberglass construction, the boat building has slowed down and the tenor of the yard has changed to repair. A new Jensen boat is built every year or so, but nowhere near as many as in days past.

It is the most complete repair facility in the San Juans. There is a railway that will accommodate boats up to 80 feet in length. There is also a crane with lifting straps to pick up smaller boats to be sidetracked in the yard. There is a shipwright's shop with heavy power tools for shaping timbers and building bulls. There is also a machine shop and engine repair service.

The place is admittedly not one of your fancy boatyards, parts of it are probably considered ramshackle. But Nourdine Jensen, the owner, loves it just the way it is. We who live in the islands also feel a tender attachment to it. If it ever got painted and spruced up, we would feel it had lost its wonderful character and we would wail about the insidious march of modernity that threatens some of our favorite island institutions.

Up behind the shipyard you will see a mountain being carved down to what will eventually be a mole hole: the gravel pit. The whole hill is made up of high-yield gravel. Bargeloads of gravel get hauled out from the loading dock just across the peninsula from the shipyard. Most of it heads to British Columbia. Somebody once quipped that the English may have lost the island in the 1800s but they are buying it back now—ton by ton!

On the waterfront beyond the shipyard there are a couple of palatial estates and extensive docks with large world-cruising yachts moored to them.

Leaving Friday Harbor by the passage east of Brown Island, note the shoal that

Turn Island State Marine Park—just a stone's throw from Friday Harbor.

reaches out from the island. There is a daybeacon to mark it. In one place, you may see a Clorox bottle on a pole driven into some of the outlying rocks to act as a warning.

As you round the point heading out into San Juan Channel, you will come across a good example of a shoal looking small on the chart, but actually extending north quite a ways from San Juan Island. It's not named this on the chart, but the reef that is limited by the green beacon is called **Minnesota Reef**. When the tide is out, this reef looks like a giant set of false teeth 'lowers'. As a matter of fact, give this short shoreline a wide berth; there are also a few bad rocks outside of Minnesota Reef Marker.

As you pass the reef, you will see Turn Island in the distance. This is a little jewel.

Turn Island

Turn Island is another State Marine Park, 35 acres in area. There are three buoys in the harbor on the west side of the island and they are usually taken by early afternoon in the cruising season. Here's a tip: do not anchor in this spot for an overnight stay. The holding ground is not good and the currents that swirl around the island can be very speedy.

There are two beaches, with campsites and firepits and privies. The southern beach, away from the mooring buoys, is very attractive, but there is no moorage. It's a favorite spot for boaters who arrive by kayak, canoe or rowboat, since it is all

Theodore Cannery, Friday Harbor

Tombolo

The Shoreline Master Plan for San Juan County has a complex definition of the word 'tombolo'. It goes several steps beyond the good old dictionary definition: "A sand or gravel bar connecting an island with the mainland." The master plan explains that "the causeway-like ... spit ... connects an offshore rock or island with the main shore." They "develop from bars (submarine beams, i.e. 'narrow shelves') that build up as a result of sedimentation in the ... zone between the wave barrier (rock or island) and an active driftway." (The dictionary does not define 'driftway'.)

We have included these complex descriptions to point out the imponderables that confront some poor soul who owns one of these embattled areas.

Because not only does the tide and wave action threaten these partially-connected islands, the land use planning rules severely restrict what the land owners can do to protect his property.

Such tombolos have been designated as 'natural' or 'conservancy'. There are stringent rules that prohibit construction of breakwaters, bulkheads and jetties to cope with current and wave action. Utility umbilicals, such as electric, phone and water cables that are buried in these spits are frequently threatened by changes in sedimentation.

Landholders have tried petitioning or fighting the planning department, but they have had little success.

It must be mighty frustrating to own a little island, one that may have been in your family for generations, and be told that you cannot protect your beach or yard.

The justification for these regulations is that the building of a breakwater on one section of beach land transfers the energy of the waves to the neighboring beach, sometimes heightening it.

They point to the erosion of beaches in Miami and on the Washington coast. The loss of sand caused the high tides to threaten the structures that had been built too close to the water. When a breakwater was built to protect the remaining high ground, it forced the adjoining property owners to erect them. Somewhere along the beach the waves would find an unprotected area and attack it in force. In short time, it would dig a shallow channel inland, and then flood back along the residences, creating a marshland in their backyards.

Such explanations might make sense in the long run to those concerned about the environment, but they do not remove the bitter taste of the pill that the tombolo owners have to swallow.

tideflat area. The tiny islet is called 'Indian Island' by local folks, but we don't recommend that the chartmakers pick up the terminology—there must be a dozen little islands in the San Juans that are called 'Indian Island' by the local residents. A sandspit connects this islet with the main part of the island, but if you walk out there at low water, be prepared to stay overnight if the tide comes in.

There is a little hook on the southern end of Turn Island. It's a neat place to hike to and spread out a picnic blanket.

On shore, you will find a path that skirts the waterfront all the way around the island. On the eastern and northern shores of the island, the path is high and rocky and there are almost no beaches to visit or paths down to the water. At the southeast end of the island you will have a beautiful view down San Juan Channel—clear down to Cattle Pass.

The middle of the island is heavily forested. There is a 100-foot high hill in the northeasterly quarter of the island. There are a few sketchy cross-island trails, but we've never seen anything particularly noteworthy off the main trails.

One of the things that may strike you as you hike the paths is the appearance of massive shoulders of rock jutting out of the ground in places. On the low hill above the mooring area you will find some giant rounded rocks that look strangely out of place—as if they had been projected onto the island by a huge catapult. They are smooth, as though they had been tumbled some distance to wear off their edges. This must be the result of glacial movement millenia ago.

Turn Rock, Reef Point

If you want to cruise around Turn Island, there is no particular problem. Note

to Upright Head and then take the ferry to Anacortes."

It took me a few moments to adjust to the scope of the thing. I could imagine the ferry pulling into a terminal at Roche Harbor, disgorging a flood of semis, campers, motorhomes and cars. I could see them snaking down Roche Harbor road, through Friday Harbor, out Argyle and Cattle Pass Road, bottlenecking at the toll bridge while the toll takers separated the U.S. and Canadian currency, answering questions, giving directions, registering beefs.

Once over the Cattle Pass Bridge they would thunder down the roads through the quiet little valleys of Lopez Island, air-horns sounding, Jakes-brakes squawking, tailgating each other trying to be first in line at Upright Head. I could see it: all-night service stations, Golden Arches, Chicken Colonels, Denny's with acres of pink formica, maybe even a VIP's. Sam interrupted my daymare.

"They even had a plan to build bridges to Shaw and Orcas."

"That might not be a bad idea. It'd be neat to be able to drive over to Orcas and back," I offered weakly.

"Naw, we'd lose the sense of community if we did that," he said matter-of-factly. I didn't quite understand that, but I let it go.

"Folks around here weren't for the idea, eh?"

"Some were, some thought it would be good for business and tourism."

"You were against it, eh?"

"Yeah," he nodded ... "But I bought Goose Island, just in case. Sold it later to the Nature Conservancy." We shook hands and I left with my story. I was glad that there weren't any Golden Arches and Finger Lickers.

I must confess, however, that sometimes I wish there was just one little old Seven-Eleven somewhere around. But then, I'm still a new immigrant.

that the deep water is in the middle of the passage. You will see the ugly reefs off **Reef Point**, south of Turn Island, that extend northerly. They are almost always visible. It is perfectly possible to go between Turn Island and **Turn Rock** with its flashing light. The water is deep and you may encounter strong currents in the area. Most clued-in skippers who leave Friday Harbor headed for Cattle Pass take this shortcut. There is a considerable field of kelp that surrounds the rock, and most of it covers shoal water. Stay fairly well away from the rock. Fishing is good out there if you are so inclined.

Before we head down the channel, we would like to direct your attention to **Reef Point Islet**. This is a classic tombolo. It is connected to the mainland by a spit that dries at minus tides. It's owned by a friend of ours. There is a melancholy story connected with that piece of real estate. It has been declared 'natural' by the county. That means that the owner cannot make any changes in the shoreline. The wind that comes howling up San Juan Channel from the Strait sends waves crashing up onto the shore on the south side of his islet. Little by little, they are carving away some of the choicest land. He is prevented by law from installing any riprap or bulkheads. He feels sure that within a generation or two, his island will be reduced to a fraction of its present size. He loves the land dearly and is terribly frustrated at the injunction against protecting it. He has fought the battle all the way to the Supreme Court, but has failed to dent the stony decision of Big Brother.

The wave action has created some very threatening rocks and reefs off Reef Point. Be sure to stay out in the 24-fathom curve as you leave Turn Island. If you stay close to shore from Reef Island down to **Pear Point**, you will have to steer wide to avoid **Danger Rock**. You can see it at almost any tide but at low water you will be able to see little breaking waves that curl up around the rocks that flank it. Notice also the reef that extends out from the shore just south of Danger Rock.

North Bay

There are some fine homes in this area around **Pear Point**. This whole peninsula, the headland that is girdled by the south end of Friday Harbor and the north reach of **North Bay**, is called **Madrona Peninsula**, but that name is not on the charts. Once you see the area, you will know why it got that name.

At the bight in the north end of North Bay you will see the Friday Harbor Sand and Gravel installation. There is a large loading dock for filling barges with the material. Note the rock just offshore, in case you decide to come in closer for a look at the gravel works.

Jackson Beach

The beach just beyond the Gravel Company is called **Jackson Beach**. For many years, this privately-owned beach was open to the public. Just a year ago, the owner became discouraged because it was the site of many beer-busts and beachwood fires. He fenced it off and put up no trespassing signs. We used to gather firewood from that beach.

Little Island, at the end of Jackson Beach, isn't—an island, that is. It may have been at one time, but there is now a road that leads along the beach. This is now the location of the J.J. Theodore fish cannery.

There is a remarkably large tide pool that all but surrounds the cannery.

Argyle

Argyle was a town at one time. It had a big dock and steamers from Seattle and Port Townsend used to stop there to offload supplies toward the end of the century. Legend has it that a Scot, by the name of McDonald, was the first white man to build in that area. He named it after his home county, Argyll, in Scotland.

In 1873, a post office was established there and was called 'San Juan'. The name Argyle was reapplied to the community in 1886, probably because the local folks still referred to it by the name given the area by the old Scot.

The rocks that uncover at one foot are just west of **Dinner Island** near the shore and used to be called **Argyle Shoal**. They were a navigation peril that inbound steamers were careful to avoid.

Dinner Island

Dinner Island may have been named by a previous owner who swapped it to a

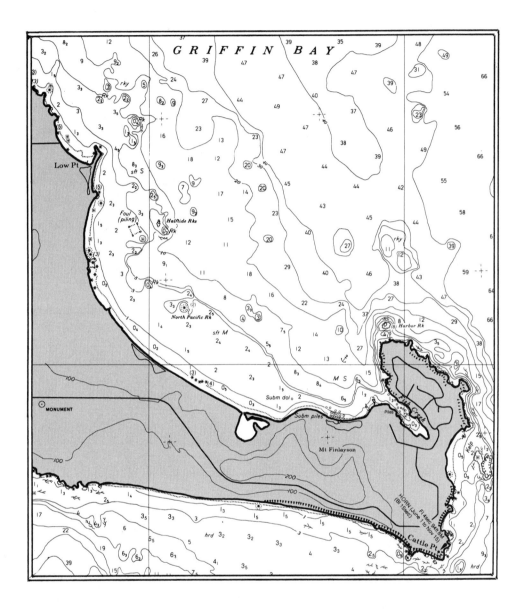

restaurant owner in Friday Harbor for a square meal. It's a little jewel.

The waters around Dinner Island are a boater's nightmare. The local sailing club frequently uses the island as a turning point for its races. It adds to the challenges because skippers try to cut inside each other's course and still avoid the hangups.

One Sunday afternoon we got the *Sea Witch* up on one of the reefs. It was one of the three rocks you will see on that chart in a string of three off the southern tip of the island, marked with (6) (4) (3). I think we ran afoul of (3). We tried to back off the rock by putting the engine in reverse, but the little propeller, powered by a

22-horse Palmer inboard engine, couldn't budge it. The tide was falling; we were in danger of sitting out a full tide—stuck like a fly on flypaper—in clear sight of friends who live on Argyle Beach who would hoot at us. We finally managed to get her free by backwinding the jib and all hanging over the starboard coaming. We had a good excuse for losing that race.

Practically everybody, it seems, has made the acquaintance of the various rocks around Dinner Island. People have their own names for the various grabbers: 'Snack', 'Tidbit', 'Lunch' and 'Bite' Rocks, for examples. There are other names but we can't print them in a family book.

You will see an anchor symbol on the chart in North Bay. It is a good place to drop the hook in calm weather. In a blow, you might get some lee from Dinner Island, but it would be rough. Waves forming in the channel north of Cattle Pass march out like an invading army to stir up the whole of **Griffin Bay**.

Merrifield Cove, Mulno Cove and **Jensen Bay** are all named for the people who own the adjoining uplands. There are some beautiful beaches in these areas, and some are owned by the DNR and therefore are open to the public—providing you stay on the beach.

If you anchor offshore and dinghy in for some beachcombing, you should check to be certain that the tidelands are public property.

Griffin Bay

All of Griffin Bay's shores from just south of **Low Point** to the entire north shore are private, but there are a couple of delightful public areas in the southern third.

The newest state park in the San Juans is the DNR park south of Low Point. This ten-acre site, accessible by water only, was just finished in the spring of 1984. Southeast of that is the federal land of the National Park Service—San Juan Island National Historical Park—otherwise known as American Camp.

Beach at Griffin Bay DNR Park

Jaekel's Lagoon at American Camp—that's Mount Baker in the background.

You'll need chart 18434 to help find the DNR park. It is about 600 yards south of **Low Point**, immediately inshore of **Halftide Rocks**. 'Foul piling' is marked on the chart between the rocks and the beach as well as a couple of other rocks and kelp, but once inside that you have two fathoms of soft bottom in which to anchor offshore. Keep a bow watch and have your depth sounder on all the way in.

You'll be able to spot the typical DNR park sign on the shore, along with some trees and a long narrow field upland of the park. There low bank waterfront on a lovely gravelly beach is good for beachcombing and playing. Just remember there is private property on either side of that 300-foot strip of park shore, and while the natives are friendly, they don't approve of trespassers and there are fences on either side of the park.

There are two picnic sites above the beach, but the campsites are at the far end of the 1,000-foot-long park as are the toilets, group picnic sites and a hand-pumped well. It could be quite a trek if you're heavily laden. The park features solar toilets and the new right-angle grates on the outdoor fireplaces.

The park is a great place for the kids to run off steam, and the beach is lovely for walking, sitting, swimming, beachcombing, paddling about or just doing nothing. Mount Baker peeks over Lopez Island and all of San Juan Channel is there to be enjoyed. Sunrises are spectacular at Griffin Bay Park.

American Camp

Several hundred yards south of the Griffin Bay campground, the big American

Camp Park begins—it starts just about due west of **North Pacific Rock**. That rock is the last of the major underwater impediments in this area. There are a few more rocky spots, but they are right along the shore.

You can't camp overnight here at American Camp, but this is a wonderful spot to anchor, row ashore and spend lots of time. Wear good walking shoes as there is a lot to see.

At the most northern part of this area is a picnic ground and beach with a privy. Next are three lagoons, all shown on the chart, but none of them show names. The most northern is **First Lagoon** and a trail takes off from there to **Jaekel's Lagoon** and follows on down to **Third Lagoon**.

Almost all of both sides of this peninsula is public, except for about the last half-mile or so which is a private residential area called **Cape San Juan**.

Starting with First Lagoon, hike to Jaekel's Lagoon following along the old roadbed. It is a quiet walk beneath tall Douglas firs which shelter many birds including eagles and other raptors, and some deer.

Continue on to Third Lagoon, or head up to **Mount Finalyson**, a 290-foot hill covered with scrub and grasses. An easy walk and when you reach to the top you can see east to Mount Baker, southeast to Mount Rainier, south to the Olympic mountains across the Strait of Juan de Fuca, and west to Vancouver Island.

Or from your anchorage walk to the main island road, Cattle Point Road, cross it and walk across the peninsula on Pickett's Lane which leads you to South Beach, the longest public beach on San Juan Island. There are a multitude of shore birds: terns, gulls, plovers, greater and lesser yellowlegs and bald eagles. If you're lucky you may see a pod of whales. During low tides you can find tidal pools farther west. There is a privy and there are several picnic tables at South Beach. It's a fantastic area for beachcombing because heavy surf from the Strait washes all manner of treasures ashore.

Back up the hill you will find the Park Headquarters and several other buildings to the west of Pickett's Lane. The Redoubt, an earthernwork barrier built to protect the soldiers, overlooks the entire area. Farther along are former officer's quarters and laundress' quarters and the Bellevue Farms site. A self-guiding Interpretive Trail points out most of the sites of interest.

From mid-June through Labor Day weekend park employees dress in period costumes and demonstrate aspects of the life of the American soldiers who occupied the site from 1859 to 1872. They also schedule special tide pool walks and other programs. There are announcements of these activities listed on park bulletin boards.

The Park Service brochure on the historical parks urges safety and stresses that visitors "exercise caution and common sense at all time. Look out for insecure footing on the primitive trails and watch for overhanging branches and downed limbs". The brochure advises that swimming isn't a good idea because of the cold water and strong currents, and that tree-climbing is dangerous and harmful for the trees.

After you've finished exploring all the beauties of American Camp, you can continue east and take a quick look at **Fish Creek**. This area, which almost bisects the southeastern end of San Juan Island, is not a creek at all, as you can see on the chart, but a long, narrow bay. In the summer during fishing season, there is usually a large fish-buying barge and all manner of gillnetters and purse seiners anchored in the sheltered waters. Fish Creek itself is filled with docks and private boats belonging to the residents of Cape San Juan, the prime residential area on the southern end of the island.

You can cruise between **Harbor Rock** and the island if you wish. Fishing boats usually cut a swath through the kelp between the rock and the island.

Incidentally, this area all along the American Camp shore offers excellent protection from southerlies—we know—we've anchored there on occasion when crossing the Strait didn't seem particularly enticing.

And now you're back in San Juan Channel and our cruise has ended.

INDEX OF GEOGRAPHIC FEATURES

GENERAL INDEX

BIBLIOGRAPHY

Fieldbook Of Pacific Northwest Sea Creatures, Dan H. MacLachlan and Jack Ayres, 1979, Naturegraph Publishers, Happy Camp, CA.

Guide To Edible Plants Of British Columbia, A.F. Szcawinski and G.A. Hardy, 1972, B.C. Provincial Museum, Victoria, B.C.

James Francis Tullock Diary, 1875-1910, Gordon Keith, 1978, Binford & Mort, Portland, OR.

Magic Islands, David Richardson, 1973, Orcas Publishing Co., Orcas, WA.

Oh, Shaw! And Other Islands, Jo Ann Morse, 1978, Longhouse Printcrafters, Friday Harbor, WA.

One Hundred Days In The San Juans, June Burn, 1946, Longhouse Printcrafters, Friday Harbor, WA.

Pig War Islands, David Richardson, 1971, Orcas Publishing Co., Orcas WA.

San Juan Islands, Afoot And Afloat, Marge Mueller, 1979, Mountaineers, Seattle, WA.

San Juan Island Place Names, Bryce Wood, 1980, University Microfilms, Int., Ann Arbor, MI.

San Juan Saga, Emelia L. Bave, 1976, private printing.

San Juan Story, Carter Morgan, 1966, San Juan Industries, Friday Harbor, WA.

Seashore Life On Puget Sound, Eugene N. Kozloff, 1973, U W Press, Seattle, WA.

They Named It Deer Harbor, Edith McLachlan, 1972, Concrete Herald Publishing Co.

Voices From The Islands, Gorden Keith, 1982, Binford & Mort, Portland, OR.

What's What In The San Juans, Beatrice Cook, undated, pub unknown.

Who The Hell Was San Juan?, Doug Cardle, 1982, Coastal Press, Lopez, WA.